PALGRAVE MACMILLAN STUDIES IN BANKING AND FINANCIAL INSTITUTIONS
Series Editor: **Professor Philip Molyneux**

The Palgrave Macmillan Studies in Banking and Financial Institutions are international in orientation and include studies of banking within particular countries or regions, and studies of particular themes such as Corporate Banking, Risk Management, Mergers and Acquisitions, etc. The books focus on research and practice, and they include up-to-date and innovative studies on contemporary topics in banking that will have global impact and influence.

Titles include:

Yener Altunbaş, Blaise Gadanecz and Alper Kara
SYNDICATED LOANS
A Hybrid of Relationship Lending and Publicly Traded Debt

Yener Altunbaş, Alper Kara and Öslem Olgu
TURKISH BANKING
Banking under Political Instability and Chronic High Inflation

Elena Beccalli
IT AND EUROPEAN BANK PERFORMANCE

Paola Bongini, Stefano Chiarlone and Giovanni Ferri (*editors*)
EMERGING BANKING SYSTEMS

Vittorio Boscia, Alessandro Carretta and Paola Schwizer (*editors*)
COOPERATIVE BANKING
Innovations and Developments

COOPERATIVE BANKING IN EUROPE
Case Studies

Allessandro Carretta, Franco Fiordelisi and Gianluca Mattarocci (*editors*)
NEW DRIVERS OF PERFORMANCE IN A CHANGING FINANCIAL WORLD

Dimitris N. Chorafas
CAPITALISM WITHOUT CAPITAL

Dimitris N. Chorafas
FINANCIAL BOOM AND GLOOM
The Credit and Banking Crisis of 2007–2009 and Beyond

Violaine Cousin
BANKING IN CHINA

Peter Falush and Robert L. Carter
THE BRITISH INSURANCE INDUSTRY SINCE 1900
The Era of Transformation

Franco Fiordelisi and Philip Molyneux
SHAREHOLDER VALUE IN BANKING

Hans Genberg and Cho-Hoi Hui
THE BANKING CENTRE IN HONG KONG
Competition, Efficiency, Performance and Risk

Carlo Gola and Alessandro Roselli
THE UK BANKING SYSTEM AND ITS REGULATORY AND SUPERVISORY FRAMEWORK

The full list of titles available is on the website:
www.palgrave.com/finance/sbfi.asp
Palgrave Macmillan Studies in Banking and Financial Institutions
Series Standing Order ISBN 978-1-4039-4872-4

You can receive future titles in this series as they are published by placing a
standing order. Please contact your bookseller or, in case of difficulty, write to us
at the address below with your name and address, the title of the series and the
ISBN quoted above.

Customer Services Department, Macmillan Distribution Ltd, Houndmills,
Basingstoke, Hampshire RG21 6XS, England

Cooperative Banking in Europe

Case Studies

Edited by

Vittorio Boscia
Alessandro Carretta
and
Paola Schwizer

First published 2010 by
PALGRAVE MACMILLAN

Palgrave Macmillan in the UK is an imprint of Macmillan Publishers
Limited, registered in England, company number 785998, of Houndmills,
Basingstoke, Hampshire RG21 6XS.

Palgrave Macmillan in the US is a division of St Martin's Press LLC,
175 Fifth Avenue, New York, NY 10010.

Palgrave Macmillan is the global academic imprint of the above companies
and has companies and representatives throughout the world.

Palgrave® and Macmillan® are registered trademarks in the United States,
the United Kingdom, Europe and other countries

ISBN 978–0–230–57677–3

This book is printed on paper suitable for recycling and made from fully
managed and sustained forest sources. Logging, pulping and manufacturing
processes are expected to conform to the environmental regulations of
the country of origin.

A catalogue record for this book is available from the British Library.

A catalog record for this book is available from the Library of Congress.

10 9 8 7 6 5 4 3 2 1
19 18 17 16 15 14 13 12 11 10

Printed and bound in Great Britain by
CPI Antony Rowe, Chippenham and Eastbourne

Contents

Part II The Cooperative Banking in the New EU Countries

List of Boxes

List of Figures

List of Tables

About the Editors

Vittorio Boscia (MA; PhD) is Professor in Banking at University of Salento (Lecce, Italy), Faculty of Economics "Antonio de Viti de Marco." He holds a B.Sc. (Economics) degree from the University of Bari (Italy), and an MA and PhD from the University of Wales, Bangor (UK). He is also member of the PhD in Banking and Finance academic board at the University of Rome "Tor Vergata." He is Visiting Researcher at the School for Business and Regional Development, University of Wales, Bangor (UK). He is the author of a number of articles on several topics: structure and efficiency of banking systems, small and cooperative banks, regulation. At present, he is researching in the area of Corporate Banking, Project Financing and Public Finance.

E-mail: v.boscia@economia.unile.it

Alessandro Carretta is Professor in Financial Markets and Institutions and Director of the PhD Program in Banking and Finance at the University of Rome "Tor Vergata." He has been teaching banking and finance for more than 25 years, formerly at the Universities of Urbino, Lecce, and Milan Bocconi. His main research interest relates to banking management, focussing on banking groups and diversification; regulation and control; corporate governance, culture and organizational change in banks. He has widely published in this area more than 100 books and articles in academic journals. He is member of committees and boards of several journals, research bodies and financial institutions.

E-mail: carretta@uniroma2.it

Paola Schwizer is Professor of Banking at the University of Parma and Professor at the SDA Business School, Bocconi University, Milan. She is the author of several publications in the fields of banking strategies and organization, corporate governance and internal control systems of financial institutions, regulation and competition in the financial system, corporate banking and financial services for SME, and value creation in banks and other financial institutions.

E-mail: paola.schwizer@unipr.it

Notes on the Contributors

Massimo Biasin is Professor of Financial Intermediaries at the University of Macerata, Faculty of Economics, where he teaches banking and real estate markets and investments. He holds a PhD in Business Administration from the University of Venice. His research interests and publications focus on real estate investments and include the international comparison of financial systems and banking markets. He was visiting for research purposes at the University of Florida.

E-mail: massimo.biasin@unimc.it

Candida Bussoli is Lecturer in Banking at "LUM Jean Monnet" University in Casamassima (Bari, Italy), Faculty of Economics, where she teaches economics of the securities market. She holds a Master's in Tax Law and Corporate Tax Accounting at "LUISS Guido Carli" University in Rome and a PhD in Economics of Corporations and Financial Intermediaries from "G. D'Annunzio" University in Chieti. Her research interests include financial systems' regulation, financial innovation and consolidation, trade credit.

E-mail: bussoli@lum.it

Matteo Cotugno is a Post Doctoral Fellow in Banking and Finance at the University of Bologna, Department of Management. He holds a PhD in Banking and Finance at the University of Rome "Tor Vergata." His research interests and publications include corporate and investment banking, financial accounting, performance management and measurement in banking.

E-mail: m.cotugno@unibo.it

Roberto Di Salvo is an economist and has an MPhil in Bankng and Finance. He is the Deputy General Manager at Federcasse–Credito Cooperativo. He supervises several offices dealing with economic research, financial regulation analysis and implementation, international relations and strategic projects. He is also the editor of the Quarterly Journal *Cooperazione di Credito* and usually writes papers and essays on banking and cooperative issues.

E-mail: rdisalvo@federcasse.bcc.it

Juan Sergio Lopez is Chief Economist of the Research Department of the Italian Federation of Cooperative Banks. He previously worked for the World Bank and holds an MPhil from the Social Policy Research Unit of the University of Sussex. He has published articles on banking and credit markets.

E-mail: JLopez@federcasse.bcc.it

Pietro Marchetti is Lecturer in Banking and Finance at the University of Salento (Lecce, Italy), where he teaches banking management. His research interests and publication include corporate governance, project finance and mezzanine finance.

E-mail: p.marchetti@economia.unile.it

Arianna Sabetta has a PhD in Banking and Finance from the University of Rome "Tor Vergata" and the University of Salento (Lecce). Her research interests include finance for small and medium-sized enterprises (SMEs), guarantees and mutual guarantee systems in Europe and in Italy in particular. At present she works at the Financial and Fund raising Bureau of the University of Salento (Italy).

E-mail: arianna.sabetta@unile.it

Igino Schraffl is Professor of Public Choice at the Faculty of law of the Lumsa University in Rome and Palermo.

E-mail: ischraffl@tin.it

Valeria Stefanelli is Lecturer in Banking and Finance at the Telematic University of Human Science "Niccolò Cusano" of Rome. She was a Visiting Fellow in Banking at the University of Wales, Bangor (UK) and she holds a PhD in Banking and Finance at University of Rome "Tor Vergata". Her research interests and publications include corporate governance and internal control systems in financial intermediaries, merger and acquisitions, bank management and organization.

E-mail: valeria.stefanelli@unisu.it

Preface

European banking systems are affected by two concomitant kinds of trends. The international trends – such as globalization, innovations, deregulation, size, shareholders value, and so forth – have dramatically changed the structure, conduct and performance of financial and banking operators around the world. More specifically, European banking systems are influenced by other events, such as the completion of the Single Market Programme, with the extension to other Eastern countries; the European Monetary Union; the regulatory developments, like structural deregulation and the concomitant supervisory re-regulation, the privatisation process, and so forth.

All kinds of financial operators have been challenged by these changes. As result, especially in the European banking markets, the level of competition has generally enhanced, influencing the quality and the price of financial services, and squeezing banks' performance. Also **cooperative banks** are involved in these changes. In particular, cooperative banks might be threatened since their traditional model is based on specific features (that is, mutuality, locality, ethics, solidarity, social cohesion, and so forth) which might be inconsistent with the new environment.

The interest of policy-makers, academics, operators and practitioners is actually directed on the likely future of cooperative banks and whether it is possible to identify – among the European cooperative banking countries – a "best" model which starting from common roots has evolved better than others to face properly the new competitive scenario. The cooperative banking sector is a "system" among the major players in the European financial system, which encompasses 4,500 cooperative banks, with 60,000 branches or outlet and 720,000 staff members; 140 million customers served and, in the retail banking sector, an average market share of about 20 per cent.

The aim of this book is to highlight the main differences among the cooperative banking systems around the Europe, dealing with a wide and comprehensive "country case-study" analysis. It is virtually divided in **two parts**. The first part deals with the historical European countries; the second section deals with the group of newly European countries.

The completion of this book is the result of the contributions and assistance of many people. First, we wish to express our gratitude to

Phil Molyneux, Professor at the University of Wales (UK), who incited us to start this study. The book has been written with the contribution of several authors. To them goes our gratitude. Finally, a special thank goes to Lisa von Fircks (Palgrave Macmillan) for her kind and professional support and comprehension during the period of production of this study.

1
Introduction

Vittorio Boscia, Alessandro Carretta and Paola Schwizer

During the past few decades, there has been an intense process of political, social and economical integration within the European Union countries. With the exception of the completion of the Single Market Programme, the European banking system has been influenced, due to the extension to other Eastern countries, by specific events such as the European Monetary Union with the new policies in public debt, the privatization process, the structural deregulation and the concomitant supervisory re-regulation, and so forth (see Gardener 1995; Economic Research Europe 1997). Besides these events, the European banking system is also influenced by international-worldwide trends; that is, globalization, innovations, deregulation, disintermediation, dimension, shareholders value, and so forth (see Schmidt 2000; European Central Bank 1999, 2004, 2005; Rybczynski 1988; Pavel and McElravey 1990; White 1998).

Overall, these trends have dramatically and rapidly changed the structure, conduct and performance of the European financial and banking system. In such a new competitive landscape, where deregulation has opened the controlled restricted and protected national frameworks, the European banking systems would be, theoretically at least, integrated and opened to free competition. Indeed, among the major expected effects in the market, there is a relevant increase in the level of competition. Consequently, this implies for consumers an increase in the quality of services and a reduction of the cost of financial services; and for banks a widening of activity in terms of volume and risks, the reduction of profit margins and the consequent pursuit of efficiency.

The European integration has started gradually from the wholesale banking market, already globalized, to retail banking which still remains segmented. It represents, in many respects, the "last great barrier" towards the full integration of European banking for the presence of some specific obstacles; that is, incompatible national laws, consumer protection rules and tax treatment specifically in the areas of mortgages, consumer credit and cross-border retail payments (see Shirreff 2007). Moreover, this market is characterized by entry barriers which prevent free competition. These barriers range from investments in branch network and technologies to human capital and the time necessary to set up lasting relationships with customers (see Vives 1991).

But this sort of oligopoly will be gradually eroded under the pressure of a more qualified demand and of the strong competition of other operators. Thus, many banks, with various dimension and institutional forms, might lose their power and share in local markets (see Gardener *et al.* 1996; Schmidt 2000). In conclusion, all these structural and competitive changes highlight a new challenging environment where only efficient banks and managers would survive.

Obviously, cooperative banks are also involved in these changes. Their business model might be inconsistent with the new environment because it is based on concepts such as mutuality, locality, ethics, solidarity, and social cohesion, and on the promotion of economic interest and value creation of their members-customers-employees. Actually, the present scenario would threaten the traditional competitive advantages of cooperative banks. New competitors, more sophisticated customers, new regulation, and so forth would request new and specific responses in terms of strategies, resources and competencies (see EACB 2004a, 2004b).

In this field, many arguments draw the interest of policy-makers, academics, operators and practitioners, such as the main question on the likely future of cooperative banking. Indeed, they have traditionally played a fundamental role in the development of economy, at micro and macro level. Even the European integration is founded on cooperative banks for their role in supporting and financing "diversity" within the single European market (see Pleister 2006). Moreover, they motivate competitiveness since they are overall among the major players in the European financial system. For example, the European Association of Co-operative Banks (EACB) represents the interest of 4500 cooperative banks, with 60,000 bank branches or outlet and 720,000 staff members; 140 million customers served and, in the retail banking sector, an average market share of about 20 per cent (EACB 2007). Recently, the European Union has emphasized the importance of cooperation, promoting several initiatives to support the sector.[1]

This book deals with the cooperative banking in Europe; it aims to investigate the main features of the evolution of the cooperative banking model within European countries in order to assess whether it is possible to treat the European cooperative banking as a unified system and whether it is possible to identify "best" cooperative model around Europe.

The book is structured in two parts, which rely on a wide and comprehensive "country case-study" analysis. The first section deals with the historical European Union countries: Portugal, Spain, France, United Kingdom, Netherlands, Germany, Italy, and Finland. The second section deals with the other newly admitted European Union member countries, grouped into two homogeneous clusters: the first comprises the countries that remained under the influence of Soviet Union until the end of the 1980s (Czech Republic, Estonia, Latvia, Lithuania, Hungary, Poland, Slovakia, Slovenia, and Bulgaria and Romania); the second one comprises those under the Anglo-American influence (Malta and Cyprus).

Each "country case study" is analyzed following a quite homogenous scheme. First, an introductive part summarizes the structure, legislation, performance and trends in the financial and banking industry of that specific country. Then, the domestic cooperative banking system is analyzed from its origins to the present. Finally, in some countries, forms of aggregation (i.e. networks or groups) developed at central level by cooperative associations are analyzed. Other analyses regard specific features of cooperative banking in the country, such as activity, governance, culture, and so forth. In some cases, the "country case-study" is supplemented by a "bank-firm case-study" as an example of the cooperative banking model.

Note

1. See, for example, the statute of the "European Co-operative Society" (Council Regulation (EC) N. 1435/2003; Council Directive 2003/72/EC); the European Commission communication on the "promotion of co-op societies in Europe" (COM (2004) 18), and the Micro-credit programme (http://europa.eu.int/comm/enterprise/entrepreneurship/financing/microcredit.ht).

References

European Association of Co-operative Banks – EACB (2004a) *Co-operative Banks in Europe: values and practices to promote development.*
European Association of Co-operative Banks – EACB (2004b) *Vision of European Co-operative Banks: "Committed to an Integrated Market."*

European Central Bank – ECB (1999) *Possible effects of EMU on the EU banking systems in the medium to long term*, February.

European Central Bank – ECB (2004) *Report on EU banking structure*, November.

European Central Bank – ECB (2005) *EU banking sector stability*, October.

Economic Research Europe, Ltd. (1997) *The Single Market Review: Impact on Credit Institutions and Banking*. London: Kogan Page.

Gardener, E.P.M. (1995) "Banking strategies in the European Union: financial services firms after the Cecchini Report," *Institute of European Finance*, University of Wales, Research Paper, 95/7.

Gardener, E.P.M., Howcroft, B and Williams J. (1996) "The new retail banking revolution," *The Service Industries Journal*, 19 (2), 83–100.

Pavel, C., and McElravey N.J. (1990) "Globalization in the financial services industry," *Federal Bank of Chicago, Economic Perspective*, May/June: 3–18.

Pleister, C. (2006) European Association of Co-operative Banks (EACB), http://www.coopseurope.coop, accessed 5 August 2008.

Rybczynski, T. M. (1988) "Financial Systems and Industrial Re-structuring," *National Westminster Bank Review*, November, 1–11.

Schmidt, R. H. (2000) "The Future of Banking in Europe," *Financial Markets and Portfolio Management*, Vol. 15, No. 1, pp. 429–449, 2001.

Shirreff, D. (2007) "European retail banking: Will there ever be a single market?," Centre for European reform, Policy brief, London, http://www.cer.org.uk/pdf/policybrief_retail_banking_dec07.pdf

Vives, X. (1991) "Regulatory reform in European banking," *European Economic Review*, 35: 505–15.

White, W.R. (1998) "The coming transformation of continental European banking?," *Bank of International Settlements*, Working Papers, No. 54, Basle, 1–37.

Part I
Cooperative Banking in Western EU Countries

2
The Cooperative Banking System in Portugal: The Case of Credito Agricola Mutuo Group

Valeria Stefanelli

2.1 Introduction

The purpose of this paper is to show the characteristic structure of the cooperative credit system in the Portuguese Parliamentary Republic. The Portuguese cooperative movement, almost exclusively identifiable with the Credito Agricola Mutuo Group, presents particularly deep historical roots, since its importance for the economy of the country has been recognized at a constitutional level. For this reason the national legislator has gradually redefined the structure of cooperative credit providing a three-level model which characterizes some European cooperative systems and has allowed it to survive and develop even in particularly unfavourable economic conditions as it is the case with Portugal. The following sections survey the main characteristics of the context in which the cooperative movement hinges before analysing in detail its institutional, organizational and managerial characteristics.

2.2 The role of the credit system in the Portuguese economy

Compared with the EU, the Portuguese economy seems to be more and more penalized by the loss of competitiveness and productivity it has accumulated in the last years (OECD 2005; Blanchard 2006). The European institutions and the economic operators agree the braking of the economic dynamism is due to specific reasons within the country. In particular, they single out a series of key factors that show how the reforms started and the efforts made, even if appreciable, seem to be still insufficient: poor productivity, because of the slowing down of the technological innovation; disequilibrium of the public finances, made worse by the growing deficit towards foreign countries; the still inadequate level of modernization of the State and Public Administrations; limited efficiency of the educational system (Banco de Portugal 2005; ICE 2005; Fondazione Rosselli 2005).

If we observe the data concerning 2005, we see how the Portuguese economy is characterized by a really unfavourable economic trend, which is influenced by the international economic state. The increase of the price of oil, the decrease of the foreign demand due to the reduction of the European market activity, and the increased international competition particularly in traditional productions are the three main external factors that have made the trend of the Lusitanian economy worse in the last year. The rate of the real growing of the Portuguese gross national product is 0.3% in opposition to 0.5% provided by the Stability and Growing Agreement and it remains among the lower ones in the European zone (Banco de Portugal 2005).

The Portuguese economic structure of production is mainly hinged on the tertiary, which in 2003 represented on the whole 71% of the gross national product. In the same year, in fact, the agricultural sector showed an undoubtedly inferior weight, which was about 4% of the gross national product. The agriculture sector is characterized by a not homogeneous land-structure: little dimensions piece of ground in the north, big extension properties in the south, some of which managed by cooperatives. In spite of the Government incentives and the contributions from the EU for the modernization of the economic structures and technology, the Portuguese agriculture continues to suffer from low returns. The cost is so high that makes the Portuguese products less competitive than those of those of neighbouring Spain.

On the contrary, the industrial sector, which represents about 17% of the gross national product, is facing a continuous restructuring process with regards to the techniques of production, the quality of the products and the distributive organization. The aim is to improve the competitiveness of products "Made in Portugal." The Portuguese industrial activity is mainly based on intermediate technologies; that is, textile hand-made products, footwear, wood and cork processing, pottery and alimentary products. It has recently started a diversification of the production so as to increase the weight of the electronic and metal mechanical sectors that employ nowadays about 15% of employees. In the same sectors the foreign investments have a predominant role and are mainly addressed to the exportation.

If we analyse these sectors in detail, the higher weight regarding the gross national product is given to the public sector, which involves the medical, administrative, and educational services – with about 23%. The building and alimentary sectors are at the decidedly inferior level of 7%. The weight of the financial sector is at the same lever as the two previous ones (see Figure 2.1).

However, the calculus between the different sectors in 2005 compared with 2003 shows a remarkable growth of the tertiary to the damage of the other economic sectors. In particular, the comparison points out an increase of the weight of the financial sector to 11.2% of the gross national product, together with a growth of the electronic sector, which has risen to 5.4% of the gross national product (see Figure 2.2).

The fact that the financial system has assumed a role of support of the economy of the country is a particularly unfavourable economic trend: the amount of the domestic loans shows that the credit intermediaries granted in 2004 is 1.7 times big as the gross national product in contrast to the stock market capitalization that is 0.7 times the gross national product (IMF and World Federation of Stock Exchanges in ECB 2005).

The national financial system has developed financing projects particularly for the depressed areas and has granted specific types of credit for the realization of several industrial projects of interest for the country. More specifically, the main regimes of facilities existing in Portugal to encourage the investments provide analytical programmes that support projects of reinforcement and modernization of the little and middle firms (SIPIE), incentive systems for touristic initiatives (SIFIT), for the modernization of

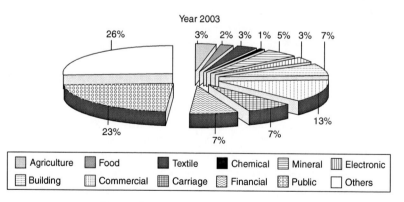

Figure 2.1 Weight of the different economic sectors of the country as percentage on the gross national product
Source: data from Banco de Portugal.

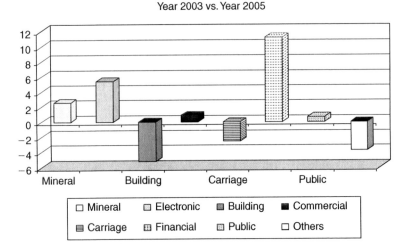

Figure 2.2   Weight of the different economic sectors of the country as percentage on the gross national product
Source: data from Banco de Portugal.

the textile industry (RETEX), for the saving of energy and the improvement of the quality of the products at a regional level (SIR) (ICE 2005). The number of loans the banks gave to firms in 2004 is 84,079 million Euro, which is 16% higher than the loans given in 2001 (ECB 2005).

Within the financial sector it is possible to single out a plurality of different credit intermediaries, according to article 3 of the Framework of Credit Institutions and Financial Intermediaries,[1] among banks (*bancos*), savings banks (*caixas economicas*), central mutual agricultural credit banks (*caixas central de credito agricola mutuo*), credit financial institutions, financial leasing companies, factoring companies, credit purchase financing companies, electronic money institutions, and mutual guarantee companies. In 2005 the structure of the financial system was characterized by a high number of credit intermediaries, subdivided among 61 banks and 121 cooperative banks; the financial intermediaries sector was numerically small in comparison with the previous one and was populated by three investment banks, four leasing companies, three factoring companies (see Figure 2.3). If we consider the structural characteristics of the Portuguese financial system and the aims of this paper, the following analysis refers to the widest segment – that is, the properly called credit sector: commercial banks and credit cooperatives.

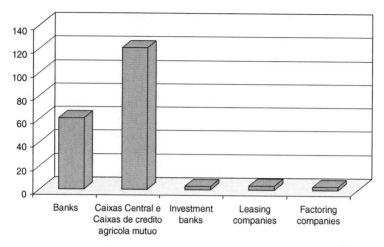

Figure 2.3   The main financial intermediaries in Portugal (2005)
Source: data from Banco de Portugal.

2.2.1 The commercial banks

The entry of Portugal in the EU has marked the beginning of a deep liberalization process of the national banking system with the privatization of most institutes. The State is still the owner of a bank (Caixa Geral de Deposito) and of an insurance company.

From a structural point of view, in the last years the Portuguese banking system has been characterized, like other European systems, by a progressive reduction of the number of institutions. Whereas in 2001 there were 212 banks in the Portuguese market, by 2004 they were reduced to 197. During this period, the main banks started a general strategy of restructuring the network of their branches in order to improve the efficiency level of the system. While in 2001 there were 5,534 branches in the country, they were reduced to 3% in the following three years (see Figure 2.4).

As a consequence of the several operations of mergers and acquisitions (M&A's) mainly carried out within the European borders and addressed to the Spanish market during 2001 and 2004 (see Figure 2.5), the level of concentration of the sector, expressed in terms of market quota of the first five national banks, has risen from 59.8% to 66.9% in 2004, placing itself much over the annual average of the 12 European Countries (52.9%) and of the 25 European Countries (59%).

Although the economic trend is unfavourable for the country, the bank system shows a particular solidity and a variable profit state

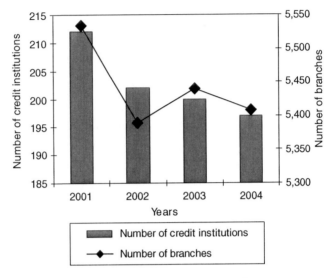

Figure 2.4   Credit institutions and branches in Portugal
Source: ECB (2005).

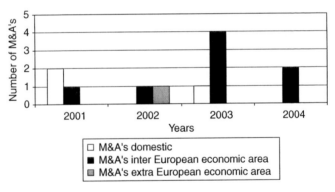

Figure 2.5   M&A's in Portugal banking sector
Source: ECB (2005).

but in a limited manner. If we consider the associated patrimonial data (see Figure 2.6), the period 1998–2004 shows an annual average growth of the active total of the Portuguese bank system of about 6.6% from a balanced resort to the running into debt, which has kept the leverage level of the system steady (15.7 in 1998 and 15.5 in

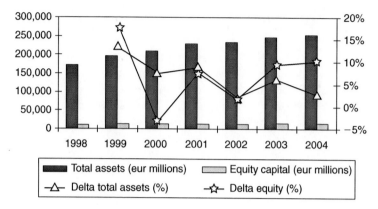

Figure 2.6 Trend of the active total and of the equity of the Portuguese bank system
Source: Banco de Portugal.

2004). Similarly, there is an annual average increase of Portugal's own means of about 7%.

In regards to the system of associated economic account, bank profitability has remained solid, as the declining contribution of net interest income has been partially offset by other sources of income (such as fees and commissions) and cost-cutting (Banco de Portugal 2005). The analysis of the profitability of the Portuguese bank system is developed according to the methodological note reported in Box 2.1.

On the basis of the articulation contained in the methodological note, Table 2.1 points out a variable trend of the ROE, that has increased till 2002 and has decreased in the following years: minimum value 11.55% in 2002; maximum value 14.85% in 2000 (see Table 2.1a). The gross profitability of equity (OpR/E) put in evidence a higher variability of the results and not always a full coincidence with what has been recorded in regards to the net profitability of the country's own means (the minimum value was 10.77% in 1999, while the maximum one was 17.08% in 2001).

This points out an important incidence of the extra-characteristic management, as for example the extraordinary and tributary ones. In particular, it rises the almost constant presence of extraordinary components of income with the exception of 2004, when the balance became negative. The results put in evidence a clear reduction trend of the tributary pression.

Box 2.1 Methodological note

The analysis of the profitability of one's own means (ROE, Net Result on Equity) can be carried out through the connected interaction of the results relevant to different managerial areas. As the below reported formula points out, it is expressed as the product between the gross profitability of one's own means (OE, Net Result on Equity), to be considered as the profitability of one's own means deriving from the operative/characteristic management of the bank (excluding the possible evaluations of the extraordinary and fiscal components), as profitability deriving from the extraordinary management (Gross Result/Operational Result), and, finally, as profitability deriving from the tributary management (Net Result on Gross Result).

The gross profitability of one's own means is in its turn decomposable in the following formula:

$$ROE = \frac{NeR}{E} = \frac{OpR}{E} \times \frac{GrR}{OpR} \times \frac{NeR}{GrR}$$

where:
OpR = Operational Result
GrR = Gross Result
NeR = Net Result
E = Equity

$$\frac{OpR}{E} = \frac{IM}{E} \times \frac{IntM}{IM} \times \frac{OpR}{IntM}$$

where:
IM = Interest margin
IntM = Intermediation margin

The above proposed decomposition singles out the contribution to the profitability that other areas offer in the operative management of the intermediary, that is the profitability deriving from the management of the Interest Margin (Interest Margin on Equity) and that deriving from the management of the proceeds from services (Intermediation Margin on Interest Margin) reduced of the influence of the operative and managing costs the intermediary has beard (Operational Result on Intermediation Margin).

It is possible to formulate the following considerations in regards to the characteristic management of the Portuguese banks (see Table 2.1b):

- The profitability deriving from the management of the Interest Margin is in strong reduction as it went from 40.76% in 1998 to 30.61% in 2004.

Table 2.1 Decomposition of the associated bank ROE

a.

Years	ROE	OpR/E	GrR/OpR	NeR/GrR
1998	13.60%	14.84%	118.70%	0.77
1999	13.62%	10.77%	154.50%	0.82
2000	14.85%	13.57%	132.50%	0.83
2001	14.51%	17.08%	101.10%	0.84
2002	11.55%	12.85%	108.00%	0.83
2003	13.10%	14.27%	107.30%	0.86
2004	12.04%	13.80%	99.20%	0.88

b.

Years	IM/E	IntM/M	OpR/IntM
1998	40.76%	1.56	0.23
1999	36.18%	1.54	0.19
2000	35.86%	1.59	0.24
2001	38.45%	1.52	0.29
2002	37.58%	1.54	0.22
2003	33.56%	1.67	0.26
2004	30.61%	1.72	0.26

Source: Banco de Portugal.

- A recovery of the profit margins because of the increase of the proceeds from services was reduced from 1.46 in 1998 to 1.72 in 2004.
- A progressive recovery of efficiency by means of the reduction of the operative and managing costs from 0.23 in 1998 to 0.26 in 2004 aimed to make up for the reduced interest margin.

2.2.2 The cooperative credit banks

Portuguese Agricultural Credit Cooperatives play a significant role in the national banking system. They are the second largest national banking network with a stand-alone brand, with 400,000 members, almost 600 branches and over 1.5 million customers (Credito Agricola Mutuo Group 2004).

The importance of the cooperative credit in Portugal has been also recognized by the national legislator: the Portuguese constitution, like in other European countries (as for example, Italy), considers the cooperative movement the "third sector," qualifying it as an important factor of support for the economic development of the country. By virtue of this recognition, the institutional and organizational evolution of the Portuguese cooperative credit system seems to be the result of the changes of the national rules rather than of settlements endogenous to the movement itself.

The origins of the Portuguese cooperative credit system date back to 1900 and developed thanks to two main segments which are autonomous and independent from one another: the credit cooperative (savings banks or economic banks) and the Caixas de Crédito Agricola Mutuo (CCAM). While the credit cooperative segment, which is linked to mutual aid associations or cooperative stores, became of limited importance in the long run, CCAM have gradually developed and distributed all over the national territory and can be identified without any doubt with the present Portuguese cooperative system.

The historical origins of CCAM date back to the Santas casas da misericordia, which were first constituted in 1498, and to the Celeiros comuns (common basements), which were first formed in 1576. At the end of nineteenth century, the Celeiros didn't exist any more and the *Santas casas da misericordia* were in part transformed into *Bancos rurais* (rural banks) (see Box 2.2). The evolution of the rules the Portuguese

Box 2.2   The origin of Credito Agricola Mutuo

The roots of the Credito Agricola Mutuo can be traced back to the "Santas Casas da Misericordia" (poorhouses), which were founded in 1498 on the initiative of Queen Leonora, wife of Manuel I, and to the "Celeiros Comuns" (community warehouses), the first of which was established by King Sebastiao in Evora in 1576. In the course of 300 years, 53 community warehouses were established on the initiative of the kings, local governments, parishes and by private individuals. They were administered by a senior government servant, a clergyman or the mayor as representatives of the King, the clergy or the aristocracy respectively.

These community warehouses also acted as credit institutions for the support of farmers in those years when the harvest was poor. Seeds were made available and a minimal interest paid back in kind at a later stage, as in the case of a loan. Mention must be made of the fact that it was only at a much later time that similar institutions developed in Scotland (1649), and more than 200 years later in Germany (1765). In 1852, administrative council consisting of the mayor, the parish priest, the magistrate and two citizens elected from a short list of five took over the management; elections took place in January of each year.

The importance of the community warehouse declined in proportion to the increase in interest rates. They were reformed in 1862 and payment in kind was gradually replaced by monetary payment, thus granting these institutions the same status as real credit institutions. Their management was now in the hands of local government. The poorhouses also contributed to credit farmers. The one in Lisbon was the first to introduce this practice in 1778; others followed its example. This initiative induced Andrade Corvo to introduce legislation (1866) allowing poorhouses and fraternities to use their funds, either under their name or that of the society, to set up provincial or district banks or poorhouses banks); the "Lei Basilar" followed in 1867, as the first Portuguese Act dedicated to cooperatives, and in fact the second of its kind.

The Minister Brito Camacho was the real founder of agricultural credit in Portugal in 1991, by decree of March 1st which laid down in detailed the form and functioning of the Caixas. The first mutual society for agricultural credit (Caixa de Credito Agricola Mutuo) founded on the basis of the Act issued by Brito Camacho was established in Elavs in 1911.

Source: Cardoso (1999).

legislator, which were set in 1975, has reinforced the cooperative movement in the economic context of the country in the long run. Not only has itdetermined the organizational structure but also it has grantedwide margins of managerial autonomy to each caixa at the same time.

At the end of 1990s the national rules have introduced different institutions that form the present Portuguese cooperative model, which has developed on the following three levels: local, represented by the associated banks which manage the essential services in the customers' favour (partners and not partners) as it happens in the case of agricultural loans; regional, represented by seven "unions" in defence of different agricultural areas (Credinorte, Credicoop, Unicaba, Ferecc, Unicama, Credicentro, Regivouga), which are not headed by any regional bank; national, represented by the *Federacao nacional das caixas de credito agricola mutuo* (FENACAM), which, by belonging to the intersectorial confederation (CONFRAGRI), constitutes a sectorial association together with the commercial and winegrowers associations.

The regulation reform presents the following features: the institutional recognition by FENACAM, with representative and operative functions; the presence of a Caixa central, whose purpose is to finance the associated banks' credit activity through the cash inventory of each excesses of liquidity and the distribution of the capital according to the needs of investing them; the constitution of a Guarantee Fund, shared by the Caixa, CCAM and the Banco de Portugal in order to ensure the solvency of the system.

The national level of the cooperative credit system is, therefore, identified with FENACAM, which is currently constituted by 132 cooperative banks and 592 banking outlets (see Table 2.2). The Federation forms part of the credit branch of the cooperative sector (article 4 of the Cooperative Code) and its end purposes are to promote and improve Mutual Agricultural Credit, economic, social and collective interests of agricultural banks and its associates.

The organizational structure of FENACAM is subdivided into the three following units:

- The General Assembly, which has the decision power and consists of all the associated banks, give their vote on the basis of the majority by each bank (a vote for each bank).
- The Direction, which has the strategic and administrative power, consists of five associated banks elected by the General Assembly every three years.
- The Fiscal Council, which has the power of financial management and fiscal assistance, consists of three associated banks elected by the Assembly every three years, as it happens in the case of the Direction.

Together with tasks of institutional delegation, FENACAM carries out the following functions (Credito Agricola Group 2004): to promote the development of its associates by all means at its disposal; to stimulate the creation of new Agricultural Banks and to reactivate those which

Table 2.2   Key statistics of FENACAM

Key Statistics	Coop. Banks	Banking Outlets	Members	Clients	Staff	Total Assets (euro millions)	Deposits (euro millions)
FENACAM	132	592	300,000	1,600,000	3,670	7,501	6,477

Source: ICE, European Association of Cooperative Banks (2005).

are in a precarious position or which have been dissolved; to take steps to ensure compliance with the principles and with the specific nature of the cooperative system of mutual agricultural credit; to promote technical and training support to agricultural banks in joint coordination with regional unions; to promote, undertake and coordinate activities of common interest to its associates, thereby activating their spirit of cooperation, and striving for their constant technical improvement; to organize and maintain the operation of an auditing service for agricultural banks, under the terms of the legislation in force; and finally to sign collective work agreements in representation of agricultural banks and the respective unions, their associates, and of the Central Bank.

Unlike FENACAM, Caixa central is both an organ of regulation and control of CCAM and of all the organizations of the cooperative sector. Recently, Caixa central placed more emphasis on its role, since it has been identified almost as the financial top of the cooperative system. The legislative reforms promoted thanks to the entry of the Community instructions about credit and carried out at the beginning of 1990 have given birth to the *Sistema integrato do credito agricola mutuo* (SICAM), which is a network model supported by Caixa central together with each CCAM.

Taking into consideration the particular organization of the cooperative credit movement, which is based on a constellation of autonomous local banks that do not have any element of vertical and horizontal integration (Schraff 1999), the Portuguese legislator has considered it opportune to define a group hinged just on SICAM. According to the national rules, SICAM has some particular facilities. For example, SICAM can present consolidated accounts following requirements of solvency and liquidity and the delegation to Caixa central of specific activities of inspection and control, which are otherwise developed by the Banco de Portugal.

From the organizational point of view, SICAM is at the top of the Credito Agricola Mutuo Group, which is a real group with an articulated structure and the ability to develop other functions together with the traditional credit ones, because of its participation in other societies (see Figure 2.7).

In the long run, the advantages of localism have seemed to be no more sufficient to grant the economy of the management of the cooperative group. Therefore, together with pure credit intermediation services, SICAM offers its customers the following services: personal and financial intermediation, insurance, advice, and studies of feasibility and financing of specific initiatives of agricultural development.

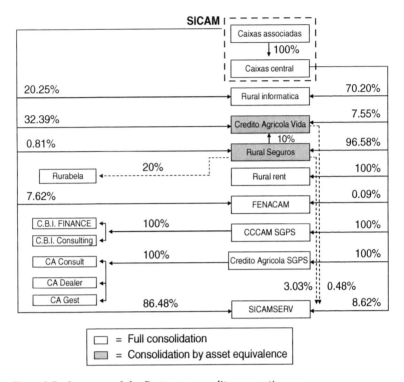

Figure 2.7   Structure of the Portuguese credit cooperative group
Source: Credito Agricola Mutuo Group website (accessed 28 January 2004).

Over the last decade the structural problems faced by CCAM have made it increasingly difficult to attract equity capital and have obliged many to undertake economic and financial restructuring. The most visible aspect of this process was an intensive wave of mergers: between 1993 and 2002, 64 mergers involving 143 CCAM took place (almost 70% of these in 1993 alone), with some banks being involved in more than one merger (Rebelo e Cabo 2003). Subsequent horizontal fusions have reduced the number of CCAM to 121 (Banco de Portugal 2005).

Taking into consideration how limited the historical series of data is, the cooperative movement's revenue and patrimonial aspects played an important role in the analysis of the cooperative movement's profitability (see Table 2.3).

With reference to 2003 and 2004, the analysis of profitability of the Portuguese cooperative movement's own means points to a reduction of

Table 2.3 Decomposition of CCAM's associated ROE

a.

Years	ROE	OpR/E	GrR/OpR	NeR/GrR
2003	14.98%	20.23%	92.10%	0.580
2004	13.80%	16.64%	100.72%	0.82

b.

Years	IM/E	IntM/IM	OpR/IntM
2003	53.76%	1.25	0.30
2004	48.36%	1.26	0.27

Source: Credito Agricola Mutuo Group (2004).

ROE from 14.98% to 13.80%. These figures are higher to other recordings of the Portuguese banking during 2003 (13.1%) and 2004 (12.04%) (see Table 2.3a). At the beginning, this variation was attributable to a decrease of the gross profit of Portugal's own means (OpR/E) rather than to variations of the extraordinary and tributary components. In fact, the incidence of the extraordinary VOICES was positive in 2004 in contrast to the negative incidence recorded in 2003. Also the incidence of the tributary management (NeR/GrR) decreased from 0.80 in 2003 to 0.82 in 2004.

The level of gross profitability of Portugal's own means is superior to what the Portuguese banking system has recorded. There is also an incidence of the tributary management superior in the BBC in comparison with the banking system. From the decomposition of the characteristic management, it is possible to formulate the following considerations (see Table 2.3b):

- The contribution produced by the interest margin management (IM/E) decreased in 2003 in comparison with 2004, as it was reduced from 53.76 to 48.36% and established at a clearly superior level in comparison with the banking system (30.61%) in 2004.
- The contribution to the profitability offered by the services area (IntM/IM) seems to be slightly on the increase (1.26% in 2004), but it is still inferior to the level the banking system recorded in the same year (1.72%).
- The reduction of the operative costs has allowed to recover efficiency (OpRIntM) for the sector, which falls into line with the condition of the traditional banking system.

The slightly decreasing trend of ROE can also derive from the reduction of the leverage of the sector (TA/E), that passed from 14.6 in 2003 and 13.3 in 2004, a level anyhow inferior to that of the banking system (15.5 in 2004). This data confirms the policies the cooperative system has usually adopted as to the reserve funds of the annual profit, and it grants a level of capital adequacy that is usually the highest in the traditional banking system.

Note

1. This is the main regulation in the banking field in Decree-Law no. 298/92 of 31 December, amended by Decree-Laws no. 246/95 of 14 September, no. 232/96 of 5 December, no. 222/99 of 22 June, no. 250/2000 of 13 October, no. 285/2001 of 3 November, no. 319/2002 of 28 December and No. 252/2003 of 17 October.

References

Banco de Portugal (2004) *Annual Report*, Lisboa.
Banco de Portugal (2006) *Bank Lending Survey*, April, Lisboa.
Blanchard O. (2006) Adjustment within the euro. The difficult case of Portugal (*available at http://www.bportugal.pt/events/conferences/IIIDEP/4.pdf accessed 28 January 2006*).
Cardoso J. C. (President of FENACAM) (1999) The background of the Portuguese Credito Agricola Mutuo and the role of FENACAM in defending the Cooperative System and the Rural Environment.
Fondazione Rosselli (2005) *Rapporto Innovazione di Sistema. Analisi comparata del potenziale innovativo dei principali Paesi industrializzati.* Sintesi dei risultati., Edibank, Milano.
International Monetary Fund (2005) *Country Report: Portugal*, no. 05/375, October, Washington.
Istituto per il Commercio Estero (ICE) (2005) *Rapporto sul Portogallo.* European Association of Cooperative Banks (2005), Activities Report, Roma.
OECD (2005), "Economic Outlook Database (December)," in O. Blanchard (2006) *Adjustment within the euro. The difficult case of Portugal (available at http://www. bportugal.pt/events/conferences/IIIDEP/4.pdf accessed 28 January 2006).*
Rebelo J., Cabo, P. (2003) *Why do Agricultural Credit Cooperatives Merge? The Portuguese Experience*, working paper ICA.
Rebelo J., Cabo P. (2005), *Governance control mechanisms in Portuguese agricultural credit cooperatives*, working paper.
Schraffl I. (1999) "Dalle riviste estere, Osservatorio Estero, Modelli di integrazione dei sistemi bancari cooperativi. I casi di Radobank, del Crédit Mutuel e del Crédito Agrícola Mútuo," *Cooperazione di Credito*, no. 166, pp. 303–331.

3
The Cooperative Banking System in Spain[1]

Valeria Stefanelli

3.1 Introduction

Since the 1980s Spain has started an intense process of political and structural reforms, to support either the phase of democratic transition or the entry to the European Union. The effects of such process have been positively shown in the course of the last years, in which the Spanish economy has been characterized by a substantial phase of expansion of the economic cycle, as a result of the strong increment of the internal demand in terms of consumptions and national investments (Camera di Commercio e Industria Italiana per la Spagna 1998; Banca di Spagna 2003 and 2004).

In confirmation of a favourable national economic trend, Spain currently sets itself between the main European Countries, with a differential of positive economic growth regarding the continent's average (3.1% in 2004 against an average European growth of 1.7% in the same year) in a context of low inflation and increase of the occupation rate (Banca di Spagna 2004; Ministero degli Affari Esteri 2006).

A determining contribution in the economic development of the country is generated by the Spanish cooperative system, which is the subject of the analysis of this article. In fact, in the Spanish financial panorama, the entrepreneurial model of cooperative bank, rooted for a long time in the Spanish territory, has been able to conjugate in a balanced way the mutualistic principle with the entrepreneurial typical principles of the business activity assuming a competitive position in the sector and obtaining, on various fronts, higher results to the traditional banking intermediaries.

This chapter can be subdivided in two parts. The first part illustrates the general arrangement of the Spanish financial system by mainly elaborating on the characteristics of the banking segment and the institutional and management profile of its main actors: banks, savings and loan companies and credit cooperatives. The second part of the chapter focuses on three models of banking intermediation and develops an analysis on their achieved performances over the last couple of years; and it draws attention, where possible, to the eventual strong and weak points in the practicality of the single models.

3.2 The general arrangement of the financial system in Spain

Until the mid 1980s, the Spanish financial system contemplated a wide variety of institutions whose subdivisions were based on the public or private nature of the property (Forestieri, Onado 1989). Up until today, it substantially develops along three main segments of market on which the activity of supervision and national control of the Ministry of the Economy through the Bank of Spain are explained (see Figure 3.1).

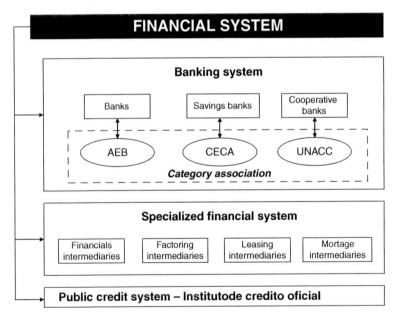

Figure 3.1   Arrangement of the financial system in Spain
Source: UNACC information (2000).

The first segment is represented from the banking market itself. It is populated of banks (*bancos*), mutual saving banks (*cajas de ahorros*) and credit cooperatives (*cooperativas de credito o bancos cooperativa*); and constitutes the carrying structure of the Spanish financial system. In 2001, banks, mutual saving banks and credit cooperatives represented approximately 77% of the financial system; throughout 2004, as a result of the general process of banking consolidation, the division under investigation has been reduced to 6%. However, it covers 95% of the requested financings altogether from the private segment and approximately 98% of the requested financings from the public segment (Banca di Spagna 2004).

Each typology of credit intermediary heads to an own national association. It is nominated to carry out functions of representation on a national and international level, and in some cases, also specific support activities of the management and the efficiency of single affiliates. In the case of banks, the Asociación Espanola de Banca Privada (AEB), established in 1977, is identified like a trade association; in the case of mutual saving banks, only as recently as 2000 has the Confederacion Espanola de Cajas de Ahorros (CECA) been instituted; finally, in the case of the credit cooperatives, the category association is the Union Nacionale de Cooperativas de Credit (UNACC) established in 1969.[2]

The sector of the cooperative credit in Spain contributes in determining measure to the development of particular segments of the social economy of the country. In fact, from 2000 on, the credit cooperatives, in conjunction with mutual saving banks, have assumed a gradually increasing weight inside the sector, reducing consequently the spaces of local growth of the banking competitors and gathering altogether, in 2004, approximately 46% of the active total of the sector (see Table 3.1). In 2004 there were 132 banks belonging to the division of cooperative credit, subdivided between 46 mutual saving

Table 3.1 Relative weight of various institutions in the credit sector compared to the active total (data in %)

Intermediaries	2000	2001	2002	2003	2004
Credit Co-operatives	3.7	3.9	4.1	4.1	4.2
Savings Banks	38.5	39.5	41.3	41.5	42.2
Bank	57.8	56.6	54.6	54.4	53.6
Total	100.0	100.0	100.0	100.0	100.0

Source: UNACC data (2004).

banks and 85 credit cooperatives (Banca di Spagna 2004; UNACC 2004; CECA 2004).

The mutual saving banks and the cooperative banks pursue the same purposes through a model of business, which is substantially; it is mainly based on the localism and the development of an entrepreneurial activity to the service of the customers' retail. However, their difference resides various elements of differentiation that derive from the legal form, the government bodies, the property, and the organizational arrangement of the system.

The second segment of the Spanish financial system financial is constituted from the specialized financial intermediaries (society of leasing, society of factoring, society of concession of mortgage credits). In 2001, such division represented 23% of the banking sector, constituted by 84 intermediaries, subsequently reduced to 79 throughout 2004 (Banca di Spagna 2004).

The third and last segment on which the Spanish financial system is based is represented by the sector of public credit *(Entitades de Credito Oficial)*. This segment has been gradually reduced throughout the years as a result of the process of privatization that has characterized the Portuguese banking system alongside other European countries (for example, Italy and Portugal).

3.3 The banking system in Spain

3.3.1 The banks

At the beginning of the 1960s, the public banking system was constituted by 5 credit institutions under the control of the Instituto de Credito Oficial (ICO). Each credit institution has its own operative area directed to the concession of financing in support of the main national economic sectors. In particular, the institutes belonging to the division of public credit were the following ones (see UNACC 2001; Forestieri and Onado 1989):

- the Banco de Credito Agricolo directed to the distribution of financings to the primary sectors (agriculture and farming);
- the Banco de Credito Local directed to the concession of financings to the agencies and the local administrations;
- the Banco de Credito Industrial particularly active in supporting financially the process of industrial restructuration of the country: modernization of industrial and mining installations and development of the fishing activity;

- the Banco Hipotecario de Espana specialized in the concession of financings guaranteed from mortgage;
- the Banco Exterior de Espana engaged in the credit financing to the export in conjunction with the private banks and the mutual saving banks.

From the 1990s onwards, the process of liberation of the Spanish banking market and the political attempt to eliminate every privilege in the public financing circuits reduced the efficiency of single institutes. It turned them into participating societies from ICO, bound to offer financings to the same rates of the financial market. In the Spanish financial panorama, the banking segment represents therefore the main component.

The scenario of the financial market is widely favourable; it is characterized by a reduced curve of the long period interest rates in the euro, which marked the good performance of financial markets, reduced unpredictability, and widened the margins of liquidity. It is significant to note, however, that the traditional banking sector faces some difficulties in the area of traditional credit activity: in order to compensate the reduction of interest margins the banks have increased their own "appetite to risk," assuming riskier credit positions and recurring to financial solutions (financial derivates and hedge funds) from the particularly complex and sophisticated management. This has been reflected on the profitability margins, which have determined a Roe greater than 14% in comparison to the European segment (Banca di Spagna 2004).

As it will be argued, during the last few years the positive tendency of the performance of commercial banks in Spain, like in all Europe and North America, has continued (BRI 2005). The profitability is improved, even though at a more moderate rhythm. Family financing has continued to represent a stable source of interests and commissions. On the contrary, the credit to the enterprises has endured a light bending because of further efforts completed from the companies in order to rebalance their budgets and absorb the excess of returning investments to the age of the technological bubble (Banca di Spagna 2004).

An important factor of the profitability improvement has been the reduction of operative costs. The favourable credit climate has been translated in a decrease of the allowances, while the rationalization of the cost structures, the strategic flexibility and the technological innovation have generated efficiency gain. On a European level, many banks have announced plans in order to further reduce staff by means of externalization and fusion of operating lines.

On a national scale, the Spanish banking system has started a slow merger and acquisitions process. It aim is the consolidation of its own position in the international market and the recovery of the margins of profitability and the spaces of efficiency.

In fact, the number of the present banks in the Spanish market has been reduced from 153 in 1998 to 137 in 2004 (see Table 3.2). The number of branches has decreased from 17,569 in 1998 to 14,199 in 2004 with a reduction of 19%. Consequently, the decline of the dependent from 135,164 in 1998 to 118,833 in 2004 is recorded making a diminution of 19%. On the contrary, the ATM number has grown to 27%, increasing from 15.042 in 1998 to 19.051 in 2004. The number of banking concentrations recorded from 2001 to this day is equal to 14, of which only five completed inside the European borders (see Figure 3.2).

Dynamics of input/output of the market of the banks put in evidence the percentage of foreign banks in the Spanish territory has grown from 50% in 1998 to 61% in 2004. Therefore, in addition to the front of aggregations made in the sector, the degree of concentration of the sector in terms of market share held by the main five banking groups is decreased from 44.6% in 1998 to 41.9% in 2004 (ECB 2005).[3]

However, if one compares the champion of concentrations of greater dimensions made by the main European banking systems against European targets (see Figure 3.3), the Spanish banks have made the greater single number of concentrations in 2003, presenting a historical series nearly scarce in the previous years. Remaining banking systems are instead presented as being mainly dynamic.

Table 3.2   Number of banks, employees, counter machines and ATM

Years	Banks	Employees	Branches	ATM
1998	153	135,164	17,569	15,042
1999	147	131,460	16,963	16,193
2000	143	127,582	15,873	18,470
2001	146	118,833	14,818	17,590
2002	144	114,040	14,128	18,486
2003	139	111,794	14,115	18,901
2004	137	110,106	14,199	10,051

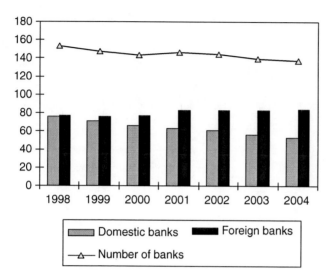

Figure 3.2   Number of banks present in the Spanish banking system

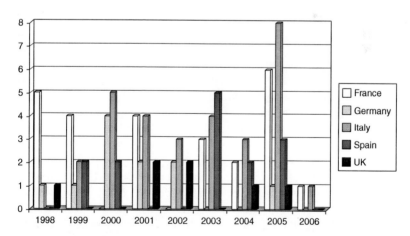

Figure 3.3   Main concentrations realized by the main European banking systems (frequency of deals)
Source: Zephyr Bureau Van Dijck data.

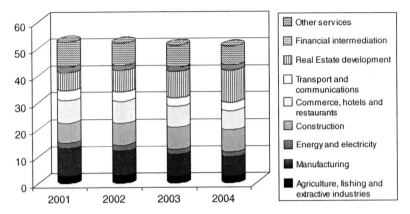

Figure 3.4   Arrangement of granted banking loans to enterprises (data in millions of euro)

As far as the structure of loans granted to the customers is concerned, the Spanish banks are mostly oriented to the financing of the corporate segment rather than the retail one (see Figures 3.4 and 3.5). In 2001, the loans granted to the enterprises amounted to 52.5% of the total and were mostly oriented to the services sector: that is, commerce, transports and communications, real estate, financial. In the same year, the loan share granted to the retail segment was mostly invested in the real estate sector, of the furnishing and partially in the sector of consumption credit.

In comparison to 2001, 2004 records a reduction of granted loans to the enterprises equal to 3%, with a difference of the segment retail, whose financing has grown in a speculate way to support the greater demands in the real estate division.

In regards to banking profitability, a first comparison in the international panorama allows to position the Spanish banks at the top of the list for dimension of the gross profits achieved (see Table 3.3). The historical series concerning 2002 positions them in the third place with a percentage equal to 1.01%, preceded by the American and English banks. Accordingly, the historical series of 2004 positions them instead in the second place with a percentage of gross profit equal to 1.17%; although gross profit is in decrease in contrast to 2003, it is inferior only to the data of the American banks (1.99%), whose percentage of gross profit is also reduced in comparison to the previous year.

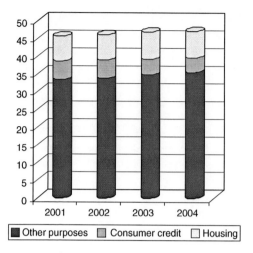

Figure 3.5 Arrangement of granted banking loans to families (data in millions of euro)

Table 3.3 Profitability of the greater Spanish banks in international comparison (data in percentage on the active total)

Countries	Earnings before tax			Interest margin			Operational cost		
	2002	2003	2004	2002	2003	2004	2002	2003	2004
USA	1.89	2.1	1.99	3.45	3.21	3.12	3.28	3.16	3.48
Japain	–0.55	–0.47	0.29	1.13	1.21	1.11	1.20	1.35	1.12
UK	1.06	1.22	1.15	2.15	1.96	1.56	2.26	2.04	2.07
Swisse	0.12	0.59	0.68	1.02	0.97	0.82	2.55	1.96	1.65
Sveden	0.69	0.77	0.98	1.48	1.44	1.35	1.44	1.37	1.24
Austria	0.46	0.53	0.69	1.80	1.71	1.80	1.92	1.85	1.84
German	–0.01	–0.12	0.09	0.80	0.81	0.71	1.37	1.26	1.35
France	0.45	0.59	0.67	0.62	0.80	0.72	1.49	1.50	1.41
Italy	0.67	1.03	1.03	3.07	2.82	2.24	3.33	3.22	2.73
Holand	0.46	0.65	0.72	1.62	1.62	1.53	1.98	1.85	1.82
Spain	1.01	1.29	1.17	2.73	2.45	2.17	2.36	2.13	1.79

Source: BRI (2005).

In view of the marginal reduction of profit derived from the typical banking activity, the greatest level of profitability of the Spanish banks emerges from a reduction of operative costs. In comparison with other international banks, the margin of interest of the Spanish banks point out an absolute bending between 2002 and 2004 of 0.6%. During the same years, the strategic paths followed by the Spanish banks have allowed a reduction of operative costs equal to 0.6% in absolute value, reaching to an inferior level of costs in comparison with the sample's average (1.86%); in the international picture, the Italian banks reveal one of the highest levels of operative costs, despite the bending of 0.6% throughout 2004.

3.3.2 The mutual savings banks

The mutual saving banks evolved from Mounts of Mercy (Montepios). They are constituted under foundations whose purpose is of a social character. These foundations carry out their own activity without profit goal thanks to the contribution and the collaboration of founding associates, public agencies and employees that compose the Administration Council, the General Assembly and the Supervisory Committee.

The government bodies of the mutual saving banks can be from mixed participation in the sense of the Ley de Organos Rectores de las Cajas de Ahorros of 2 August 1985 (so-called LORCA).[4] Regarding the current normative dispositions, the amount of minimum owner's equity necessary for the creation of a mutual saving bank is equal to 18,000 million euro (3000 million pesetas); the generated income from the business activity must be compulsorily destined to feed the social reservoirs in at least 50% of its amount (UNACC 2000).

As anticipated, the mutual savings banks are gathered in the CECA, established on a national level from the Royal Order of the Ministry of Labour, Commerce and Industry on the 21 of September 1928. The mission of the Confederation, contained in the social statute, is expressed in the following points (CECA 2004):

- to individually and collectively represent its member savings banks before public authorities in Spain and internationally;
- to provide savings banks with such financial services as they may deem appropriate, promoting and stimulating the formation of a technological infrastructure which would enable them to achieve optimum organization so as to render such services with greater efficiency;[5]
- to provide a centre for the joint study of all matters affecting savings banks;
- to provide information, technical and financial guidance and operational coordination services;
- to facilitate the operations of savings banks abroad, providing such services as they may require.

According to some recent data diffused from the CECA, the number of mutual saving banks in 2004 was equal to 46, reduced in the last four-year term by 8% as a result of the consolidation process characterizing the entire credit sector.

Facing such reduction, the division appears substantially strengthened if the trend of the last ten years is observed in terms of number of employees, capillarity of the branches' networks and spread of the automated counter machines on the Spanish territory (see Figure 3.6): in 2004, the number of employees in the mutual savings banks has grown to 34% in comparison with 1995; in the same way, in 2004, the capillarity of the branches on the national territory has grown to 43%; accordingly, the spread of the automated counter machines is increased to 101%, contributing to the improvement of the operating efficiency of the mutual savings banks from 63.59% in 1995 to 58.4% in 2004.

Because of the localization of the new network of branches and automated counter machines, the mutual savings banks have preferred the so-called "shadow zones," which are characterized by a potential market demand substantially insufficient to cover the entity of the investment deriving from the opening of a new branch/automated counter machine from a traditional bank.[6]

As it will be shown later in this chapter, the impact of the strategy of geographic expansion illustrates that the profit margins of the mutual

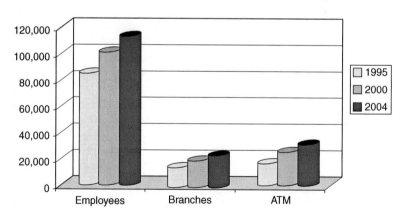

Figure 3.6 Number of employees, branches and counter machines of the mutual savings banks in Spain
Source: CECA (2004).

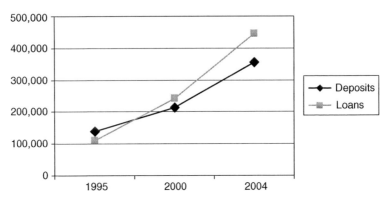

Figure 3.7 Course of deposits and granted loans to families and non financial enterprises (millions of euros)
Source: CECA (2004).

savings banks results from the remarkable increment of the volumes of loans granted alongside the equally increasing deposits (see Figure 3.7). In comparison with other European countries (United Kingdom, Denmark, Italy, France), there has been an intense debate on the Spanish mutual savings bank and the possible modification of their legal form through the process of demutualization in Spain in the last few years (Dalmaz e De Toytot 2002).

3.3.3 The cooperative credit banks

The first Spanish experience of cooperative credit bank, called Manantial de Creditos, in the capital dates back to 1865. In the following years, the cooperative phenomenon has been gradually asserted with the creation of 42 entities connected to the catholic agrarian syndicates, which merged to form the Confederacion Nacional Catolico Agraria (CNCA) in 1916. As a result of the general Law on the cooperation of 1942, the CNCA began to operate on a national level as central entity of a federal system of rural banks up until 1983, when the substantial differences between the credit cooperatives and the traditional banks created a crisis in the sector.[7]

The state took an initiative to reorganize and strengthen the sector, which made lever. On this basis, a plan was launched in 1989 to support the institution of patrimonial protections so as to guarantee the solvency and the stability of the credit cooperatives – as for example, the deposit warrantee Fund for the credit cooperatives; and the constitution of specific institutional representatives in 1989 for the entire cooperative division of credit, who represent, as it will argued later in the chapter, the current system arrangement.[8]

From 1989 onwards, the sector of the cooperative credit in Spain has been characterized by an intense development process based on a bank model which differed from the remaining credit division in terms of either of its legal form and team social or its tradition and the typicality of its business. In 2004, the number of present cooperatives in the country was equal to 85 (77 rural banks, six professional banks and two popular banks), with 4,607 branches, 17,634 employees and 1,669,676 associates demonstrating, in comparison with 1999, an increase of the distributive network of 23% – an increment of the number of employees and associates respectively equal to 27% and 35% (UNACC, 1999 and 2004).

In the denomination "cooperative banks" can be different in terms of three intermediaries: rural banks, popular banks and professional banks. At the end of the present analysis these distinctions appear insignificant, if one takes into consideration the meagre number of professional and popular banks on the Spanish territory or the business model, which is certainly similar to that of rural banks.

Under the normative profile, cooperatives in Spain are subjected to a general legal regime as it is outlined in the Law on the Cooperatives (n. 3) since 2 April 1987. Within this legal framework, cooperatives are identified as associations aiming to satisfy the financial needs of their own associates, who compose the General Assembly and the Directive Council and participate in the business life expressing their vote based on a democratic mechanism one partner/one vote.

The cooperatives carrying out the credit activity are also restricted by the national legislation detailed for the credit sector which, as it will be illustrated in the work follow-up, imposes particular economic and patrimonial bonds to guard the solvency and the development of the entire division. Besides they must follow a specific legal regime mainly outlined from the Law on the Cooperative Credit (n. 13) of 26 May 1989 and from its successive modifications. Such normative is structured in 12 articles that formulate the general principles, the purposes and the peculiarities of the cooperative bank model to which some temporary and scheduled final norms in the second part of the arranged normative are included.

The first part of the normative is dedicated to the definition of the institutional and mutualistic character of the credit cooperatives, the responsibilities and the modalities of participation of their own founding associates in the credit activities. To such aim, the main articles of the normative are the following:

- Art. 1: *"Credit co-operatives are companies incorporated in accordance with this Law with the corporate object of serving the financial needs of their members and of third parties by means of pursuing the activities proper to credit institutions. Credit co-operatives have their own legal personality. The number of members is unlimited and their liability for the co-operative's debts is limited to the value of their contributions."*
- Art. 4.1: *"Credit co-operatives may carry on all types of lending, deposit-taking and services permitted to other credit institutions, with priority attention to the financial needs of their members."*
- Art. 6.1: *"The government of Spain, upon prior report from the Bank of Spain, shall establish the minimum amount of share capital of credit co-operatives according to their territorial scope and the total number of citizens in the towns included within that territory."*
- Art. 6.2: *"Credit co-operatives shall not operate outside their territorial limits, as defined in their articles of association, without having first modified the articles and increased their share capital to adjust it to the requisite level."*
- Art. 7.1: *"All members of a credit co-operative must possess at least one registered certificate of contribution. All certificates shall have the same nominal value."*

Furthermore, the normative arranges determine organizational requirements which the cooperatives must follow, and impose an operative regime on the sector, which is deeply different from that of other banks in terms of the requirements of the business management and the allocation of the achieved profits.

According to the Law on the cooperative credit, the minimum owner's equity scheduled for the opening of a cooperative bank varies in relation to the same operating amplitude (local or regional) and to the dimension of the inhabited centre near which the bank is based: in cases of practicality on local bases, in city centres with an inferior number of 100,000 inhabitants, a minimum owner's equity requires to be equal to 25,000 million euro (150,000 million pesetas); if the practicality of the bank becomes larger on a regional level, the minimum capital demanded is equal to 130,000 million euro (approximately 800,000 million pesetas) (see UNACC 2001).

In the exercise of the credit activity the Law recognizes that the cooperatives should have wide autonomy; however, it still imposes the maximum attention to the satisfaction of the financial needs of the associates before the third parties (art. 4.1), limits the offer of financing services to third parties to a share not higher of 50% of the active total of the cooperative (art. 4.2), and constrain the distribution of the social profits arranging an annual allowance to the Fondo de Riserva Obligatorio and to the Fondo de Educacion y Promocion Cooperativa (both enrolled in the net property of the cooperative) for one equal share, respectively to 20% and 10% of the exercise of the achieved profit (art. 8).

Recently, this normative has been object of some modifications as a result of the emanation of the Ley de Medidas de Reforma del Sistema Financiero (n. 44) of 22 November 2002 (Banca Cooperativa 2003).

The normative innovations pursue the double objective to adjust the national normative frame to the communitarian directives and to support, at the same time, the competitiveness of the cooperative credit compared to the traditional banking one. In particular, the legislative measures introduced from the new discipline are made according the following directions (see Vandone 2003; 2005):

- the support of the operative diversification strategy by means of the acknowledgment of a greater degree of freedom in the share acquisition in non-cooperative society capital: before the reform, the cooperatives that acquired shareholdings for a quota superior to 10% of the owner's equity and to 40% of the share capital that carried out accessory activities to the cooperative had to demand authorization from the Ministry of the Economy; the Law of 2002 increases the limit of 10% to 25% and cancels the limit of 40%, leaving substantially the decision to realize strategies of business diversification and strengthening of the relations with the outsourcers in the respect of management aims and the stability of the business equilibriums to a single cooperative;
- the improvement of the cooperative patrimonialization's level recognizing to each cooperative the faculty to emit corporate bonds in a more flexible and immediate way, with the resolution of the Board and no longer of the General Meeting;
- the strengthening of the principle of informative transparency of the sector to safeguard the stability and the confidence of the financial markets, mainly in cases of emissions of real state values quoted on the secondary markets, by means of the publication of the annual relation and the diffusion of important information and business facts through the Internet;

- the strengthening of the organizational and internal control protections by means of codes of good government and conduct of the cooperative banks in general terms and, above all, for those which recur to financing on the financial markets;
- the improvement of the cooperatives solvency by means of a more punctual use of the informative flow produced from the Risk Centre in the process of credit risk management implemented from the single intermediary.

The identifying marks that distinguish the cooperative sector from traditional banking emerge from the normative frame. These marks are summarized in the strong localism, which detect the cooperative as a "proximity bank". Moreover, the wide knowledge of the competitive atmosphere in which the cooperatives operate, and the personal acquaintance of the customers retail served (families, professional associations, small and medium enterprises) mostly belonging to the agricultural, zootechnical, food farming, real estate sectors and of the typical financial requirements also result from the above-discussed normative frame.[9]

Under this organizational profile, the segment of the Spanish cooperative banks could be assimilated to a group of enterprises of hybrid type, based on cooperative bonds and share control between the various associates. In fact, the Spanish cooperative banks merge together in the "cooperative banking group;" that is, in an organized and coordinated block integrated by means of credit cooperatives and other societies, which operate and collaborate based on strategic lines and common directives, sharing average, resources and information and conferring unit to the action but conserving, at the same time, the sovereign spirit of the own affiliated members (Palomo Zurdo 1999).

In comparison with other European systems (Dalmaz and De Toytot 2002), the organizational arrangement of the Spanish cooperative banks is characterized by a particularly integrated and cohesive structure, which safeguards against potential threats from the intervened changes in the financial system on a national and international level.

More precisely, the group of the cooperative banks is called Gruppo Cajas Rurales and is composed of 81 out of the 85 currently present rural banks in Spain. It is put in the fifth place between the Spanish financial groups and a widespread network equal to 3,390 counter machines diffused all over the national territory above all in the rural zones.

In comparison with the mutual savings banks, the diffused localization represents a competitive advantage of the rural banks on the Spanish banking system, constituting a barrier to the income of new operators in the market segments where the Group works. It substantially presents an articulated organizational structure on three levels, of which each has different roles and functions (see Figure 3.8).[10]

The first organizational level is established from the Asociation Espanola de Cajas Rurales (AECR) that operates on national base and performs the central role of compensation of activities, helping the accomplishment of the relatively centralized operative processes. This administers the deposit warrantee Fund for the credit cooperatives – that is, the patrimonial equipments, on which the single banks must feed in regards to the law dispositions. The deposit warrantee Fund also carries out a function of coordination and representation of the Group towards the exterior.

The second and the third organizational levels are constituted by the single operative rural banks regionally and locally; they make all head to the AECR, with the exception of the higher level according to which the single banks substantially carry out the typical credit activity

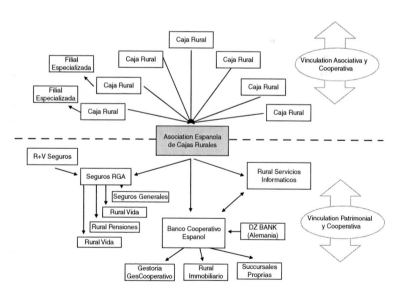

Figure 3.8 The structure of the Gruppo Cajas Rurales in Spain
Source: Palomo Zurdo (2001).

in regard of associated bonds placed from the AECR.[11] The local and regional entities are assisted by other participating societies from the Gruppo and are dedicated to the development of determined activity on behalf of the single banks.

In fact, three institutes supporting the development of specific functions directed to the attainment of synergies and cost savings to a group level belong to the Gruppo Cajas Rurales (UNACC 2001):

- the Banco Cooperativo Espanol S.A, which coordinates determined areas of financial policy, offers specific financial services to the single affiliates, acts as an operating connection between these last ones and the financial markets and carries out the role of agency in the cooperative operations;
- the Rural Grupo Asegurador, which offers insurance services to the single members of the Gruppo and is owned (30% of its capital) by the Raiffeisen und Volksbanken Allgemeine Versicherung (R+V), the fourth German insurance company;
- the Rural Servicios Informaticos, which assures that single banks will have access to advanced information technologies, and supports them in the improvement of the operating efficiency, the elaboration and the transfer of the information flows necessary to the development of specific business processes, the widening of the mass media with the customers, and the development of the virtual distributive channels.[12]

The Gruppo Cajas Rurales thus designed works like instrument of collaboration and solidarity between each of the affiliated rural banks as well as between the latter and the three specialized societies belonging to the Gruppo. It promotes a common strategy so as to support the competitiveness of the segment on the inside of the credit sector. Moreover, it coordinates the relations between the AECR, the single banks and the three specialized societies promoting intervention actions in cases of conflict or controversies between the associates as well as sanction mechanisms in situations of fraudulent behaviours from some societies. Additionally, the Gruppo institutes determinate operating bonds and patrimonial instruments to limit and ensure a cover of assumed risks from the single banks in the development of their own credit activity. Finally, it carries out specific intervention, monitoring and auditing activities in the cases in which the management of the single affiliate presents particular anomalies in the business equilibriums.

The Gruppo Cajas Rurales is therefore outlined as the model of a "federated bank," founded nearly on a "virtual fusion" between the affiliated societies, whose definition characters are inspired by decentralization, subsidiaries, solidarity, cooperation and territoriality as well as by the absence of mutual competition between the adherent members. Such a model ensures, on the one hand, independence and autonomy for the single banks, which defend the cooperative model, while it allows them, on the other hand, to gather economic advantages so as to have further dimensional growth opportunities which are hardly accessible to single banks.

Throughout the years, as a result of the process of economic restructuration that the Country has lived and the increase of typical competitive dynamics of the credit sector (see European Central Banking 2005; EU Banking Structure, 2005, October), numerous cooperative banks, which have been defending their mutual and democratic characters, have deeply changed their own competitive arrangement.

In this area, a first obvious change concerns the structure of the cooperative market, modified as a result of the weak concentration process. The federal model to the base of the Gruppo has in fact allowed the achievement of fusion operations not only in the area of the same category of banks, but also between the same affiliates. The consolidation process does not seem to be demonstrated particularly in an intense way: it has started in 2000[13] and records only three operations in 2001 and two operations in 2002 up until today (Banca di Spagna 2004).

A second change, which has affected the cooperative division, concerns the widening and strategic localization of the distributive network in more profitable geographic zones. Primary productive sectors, in particular the agricultural and zoo technical ones, have been gradually replaced by the building, industrial and commercial sectors (Banca di Spagna 2004). For these reasons, the greater capillarity of the distributive network of some cooperative banks has grown mostly in the city centres in the zones with strong tourist and commercial development.

Beside the strategies of dimensional growth and widening of the distributive network, the presence of specialized societies in the contiguous financial sectors, like insurance and real estate, also reveals the development of strategies of productive diversification by the Gruppo Cajas Rurales, the widening of their own portfolio so as to offer the retail segment complete financial service capable of satisfying the always growing and sophisticated financial requirements.

The main purpose of cooperatives comes down to the performance of financial services to associates and customers. The reason that such vocational service is preferred to a profit-based one is because the need to preserve the presence on the market and contribute to the economic development of the Country have led to a reassessment of the cooperative banking model so as for it to achieve solid business equilibriums and preserve a competitive position on the inside of the credit market.

3.3.4 Comparison of some economic indicators

With the purpose to describe the weight of the various intermediaries in the Spanish banking system, the main economic indicators achieved by the Spanish credit intermediaries – such as commercial banks, mutual saving banks and cooperative banks – are confronted throughout the last years.

The entrepreneurial formula of the cooperative bank, in conjunction with the advantages achieved through the decentralization of common activities, the productive diversification, the greater capillarity of the distributive network and the dimensional growth, express a particular competitive advantage in the Spanish banking system.

If the course of the active total of the entire banking segment is observed (see Figure 3.9), the comparison between the three credit

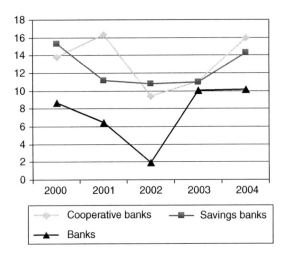

Figure 3.9   Dimensional growth for active total by typology of credit intermediary (data in millions of euro)
Source: data from UNACC.

intermediaries put to comparison point to an increasing trend of the investigated variable.[14] However, the greater increase is recorded in the segment of the cooperative banks, whose active total from 2000 to 2004 has grown to 64% while, during the same period, the active total of the mutual saving banks and banks has grown to 56% and 32% respectively.

The dimensional growth of the commercial banks has been supported mostly by external lines and, compared to other segments, has been demonstrated in a decidedly livelier way. The analysis also draws attention to a different dimension between the mutual savings banks and the cooperative banks: although the cooperative banks are numerically equal to the double quantity of the mutual savings banks, in terms of active total, they are approximately the tenth part.

As a result of the obvious dimensional increase of the sector and the expansive phase of the economic cycle that Spain has lived throughout the last years, the active part of the patrimonial state records an increment of granted loans to the customers (see Figure 3.10). Comparing 2000 to 2004, the data put in evidence the greater increment in granted loans to the customers records in the cooperative banks (88%) and in the mutual saving banks (84%); for the commercial banks the growth is clearly inferior (28%).

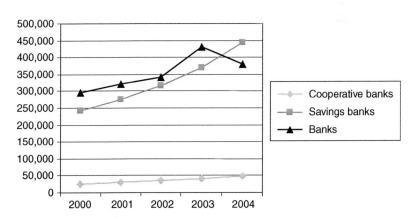

Figure 3.10 Course of granted loans to the customers by typology of financial intermediaries (data in millions of euro)
Source: data from UNACC.

The unavailability of more analytical data on the aggregated patrimonial state has not allowed the survey of the investments in shareholdings of the cooperatives toward non-financial enterprises – an act that could have rather showed the impact of the 2002 legislative innovations on the diversification strategy of the cooperative from commercial banks.

Drawing attention to the liabilities of the aggregated patrimonial state, the process of banking collection introduces an equally positive trend towards the partial cover of granted loans to the customers (see Figure 3.11). Mutual savings banks hold greater quota collection in comparison with other banks and cooperatives. The recorded variation between 2000 and 2004 is in fact equal to 65% in contrast to the 18% of the commercial banks and 62% of the cooperatives.

Despite the strong tendency to the typical disintermediation of the recent years, the entire banking system has succeeded in maintaining a positive trend of the variable. In particular, the cooperative segment continues to benefit from a wide base of collection. The analysis also points out how the customers relations represent for the cooperative segment an important competitive advantage and are necessary for the maintenance and the strengthening of the entire cooperative system.

Considered the limited resource to the capital market and the rarity in the case of share distribution in the cooperative banks, the component

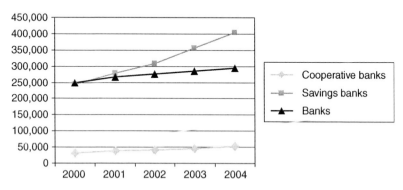

Figure 3.11 Course of banking collection by typology of financial intermediaries (data in millions of euro)
Source: data from UNACC.

of own means constitutes a further cover lever of the investments. In particular, the component of accumulated reservoirs from the cooperative banks since their foundation constitute substantially the main funding of this banking model. The trend of own means distinguished for each typology of intermediary shows a positive variation in the investigated historical series (see Figure 3.12).

In reference to the cooperative banks during the period 2000 to 2004, the growth of their own means is equal to 37%, and derives mostly from an increase in capital (101%) rather than in reservoirs (47%). In the case of the mutual savings banks, the variation of their own means is entirely generated from the allowances of several years and is equal to 47%. Finally, in the case of commercial banks, the increase in their own means is equal to 47% and is generated from the allowance of profits to reservoirs when the owner's equity has grown by 8%.

The final part of the present paragraph is dedicated to the description and the comment of some economic indicators relative to the banks under investigation (see Table 3.4). In regards to profitability, the entire division is characterized by a positive Roe in the years investigated. The mutual savings banks present a greater and more substantially stable Roe compared to the other two intermediaries. The cooperative banks also have an inferior profitability compared to the previous segment; they have widened their own profit margins from 6.2% to 7%

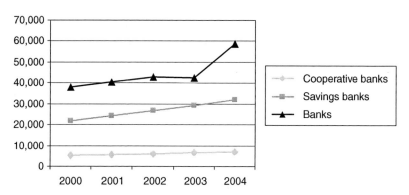

Figure 3.12 Course of own means by typology of financial intermediaries (data in millions of euro)
Source: data from UNACC.

Table 3.4   Some economic indicators by typology of financial intermediaries

Roe (%)	2000	2001	2002	2003	2004
Co-operative Banks	6.2	7.2	6.7	6.6	7.0
Savings Banks	13.2	14.5	13.8	12.9	13.0
Banks	10.3	11.7	11.3	12.0	10.5
Roe – Operational Management (%)	**2000**	**2001**	**2002**	**2003**	**2004**
Co-operative Banks	10.6	11.9	11.3	11.6	11.0
Savings Banks	21.6	22.9	20.3	22.6	22.9
Banks	24.1	23.2	20.0	18.8	18.9
Roe – Money Management (%)	**2000**	**2001**	**2002**	**2003**	**2004**
Co-operative Banks	26.3	25.8	25.4	24.2	22.5
Savings Banks	48.2	46.9	44.8	43.5	42.0
Banks	38.2	37.4	33.1	33.5	25.3
Roe – Service Revenue (%)	**2000**	**2001**	**2002**	**2003**	**2004**
Co-operative Banks	118.8	116.8	116.8	122.7	127.2
Savings Banks	129.3	126.1	123.4	129.3	131.3
Banks	152.2	132.2	134.7	129.1	146.5
Roe – Operational Result (%)	**2000**	**2001**	**2002**	**2003**	**2004**
Co-operative Banks	39.3	39.6	38.1	39.1	38.4
Savings Banks	38.1	38.8	36.7	40.2	41.6
Banks	38.8	46.9	45.0	43.5	51.0

Source: data from UNACC.

instead. On the contrary, the commercial banks show a substantially unvaried profitability between 2000 and 2004, which is, though, clearly in decrease if the two last years.

Focusing on the aggregated data of profitability of the three typologies of banks would help notice how the Roe generated from the typical banking activity points out the advantage of the mutual saving banks over commercial banks and cooperative banks. The competitive advantage of the mutual savings banks is further strengthened, if the Roe of the money management is also confronted, deriving from the typical activity of collection and employment stock in hand. Moreover, in this activity, the mutual savings banks obtain a greater remuneration regarding the other two; however, in the three cases, the margin generated from the money management has gradually lost weight as a result of the alignment of the interest rates to the European one and the tendential reduction between the assets and liabilities rates.

As a result of a tendential reduction of profit margins on the traditional credit activity, the whole banking division has gradually put into effect a strategy of widening the offered services to the customers. This is part of an attempt to increase profit through the intermediation activity. Such strategy turns out particularly effective in the case of commercial banks, which introduce an incidence of the services revenues equal to 146%; in other words, for every capital unit produced by credit intermediation nearly half of the capital from the profitability of the services activity is added.

With reference to the mutual savings banks and the cooperative banks, the profit component deriving from the services activity is positioned on more inferior levels to those of the commercial banks – following up, probably, the recent income of the cooperative banks in more ephemeral and of still limited demand from the segment retail financial activities. Nevertheless, in the investigated years, the indicator presents an increasing trend which would potentially allow profitability recovery from the cooperative segment in the future.

The analysis of a gross efficiency indicator illustrates a further advantage of the commercial banks over the cooperative segment. With reference to 2004, the calculated indicator for the banks clearly highlights an improvement in comparison to 2000. The same consideration is not valid for the mutual savings banks, whose indicator finds it hard to show a positive trend, let alone for the cooperative banks that present an operating lever anchored to clearly inferior levels to the two previous ones.

One of the main challenges that the cooperative banks are facing, beyond the dimensional increase and the business diversification, is the search of a greater efficiency in the organization of the system. Such requirement is particularly perceived in the cooperative systems articulated on three levels, like the Spanish one, in which it is necessary to integrate local realities with regional and national realities.

Nevertheless, the satisfactory economic and patrimonial equilibriums achieved up to now from the Spanish cooperative system, the organizational cohesion and the outlines of mutual guarantee held to assure the liquidity and the solvency of single affiliates inspire confidence from the Agencies of international rating. In 2004, for example, they have confirmed to the Confederation of the Spanish mutual saving banks

(CECA) the elevated rating level assigned already in 2003; in particular, Fitch Rating has assigned AA- and Moody' s Aa3. In the case of cooperative banks, the Banco Cooperativo Espanol, is placed in the A level of Fitch Rating and in the level A2 of Moody' s (Banco Cooperativo Espanol 2004).

Notes

1. The author would like to thank Professor Ricardo J. Palomo Zurdo (Universidad San Pablo – CEU de Madrid) for his comments on a previous draft of this paper.
2. The UNACC is currently a member of the European Association of Cooperative Banks, in conjunction with other associations of European category; in 2002, the UNACC was constituted by 84 associated and held a consolidated active total equal to 49,419 million euros; see Banca Cooperativa (2003).
3. The average concentration of the European banking system, measured on the share held by the first five banking groups for the active total, has increased from 37.8% in 2001 to 40.2% in 2004 (see ECB 2005). In the table of European concentrations, banks belonging to great banking systems – such as France, United Kingdom, Spain, Italy and Germany – appeared as main characters in the transactions: 64% of European concentrations were involved in the bidder or target roles. For a European comparison on the banking concentration process, see ECB (2005).
4. Some dispositions contained in the LORCA Law have been recently modified as a result of the Laws 26/2003 and 62/2003.
5. Throughout 2001, CECA has launched an implementation project of an advanced model of management and risk control, assumed from the single affiliates, in order to adjust the entire system to the regulation dispositions introduced from Basel 2; see Risk Italia (2001).
6. For a detailed analysis on the geographic expansion of the mutual saving banks see Gonzalez and Palomo Zurdo (2004).
7. For a detailed examination of the crisis of the Spanish cooperative credit sector, see Martin Mesa (1988) in Palomo Zurdo (2001).
8. For a detailed description of the contemplated actions of the reorganization Plan of the rural banks, see UNACC (2000).
9. A great share of the rural banks is mostly focused on the support of the rural atmosphere. Only in the last years, some cooperatives have been oriented to safeguard the segment against the PMI, which is located in the geographic zones of their own jurisdiction.
10. According to some authors, the structure of a cooperative group is articulated on three levels (local, regional and central) rather than on two (local and central). It would bring the attempts to centralize such activity on the top of the central societies' complex; see Dalmaz and De Toyota (2002).
11. For example, one of the bonds recently introduced by the ACER on the efficiency of the single affiliates consists of limiting their own risk exposition to 20% of the own capital; see Palomo Zurdo (2001).

12. Since 2002, the Society, which was assigned to develop a model of management and control of credit risk, was appropriated in respect of the regulation requirements introduced by Basle 2; see Rural Servicio Informaticos (2003), Convenio Basilea II, Banca Cooperativa (no. 29), p. 31.

13. The first realized merger in 2000 has involved two big rural banks for active dimension: the Caja Rural de Almeria, specialized in the agricultural credit sector, and the Caja Rural de Malaga, specialized in the real state and tourism sectors. The motivation behind the merger can be seen in the business diversification strategy and in the strengthening of the territorial protections of significant dimensions in the capital and city zone. In the operation area, an aspect worth pointing out is the post-merger management conditions: the respect of the territoriality principle of the cooperative model has, in fact, pushed the involved society to create some decentralized territorial bodies *(Consejo Asesor Territorial)* with the aim to keep the relations of every entity with the origin territory.

14. The dimensional growth in the banking sector is a generalized phenomenon on an international level. Recent research performed on the champion of international banks shows that between 1998 and 2003 European banks have grown to 86%, the American banks to 84% and the Japanese banks to 60%; see Mediobanca (2004).

References

Banca dei Regolamenti Internazionali (BRI) (2005) *Settantacinquesima relazione annuale*, Basilea.

Banca di Spagna (1999, 2000, 2001, 2002, 2003, 2004), *Informe Annual*, Madrid.

Banco Cooperativo Espanol (2004) *Informe Annual*, Madrid.

Camera di Commercio e Industria Italiana per la Spagna (1998) *L'economia spagnola*, Madrid.

Confederacion Espanola de Cajas de Ahorros, *Anuario Estadístico de las Cajas de Ahorros*, CECA, Madrid.

European Central Bank (ECB) (2005) *EU Banking Structure*, Frankfurt October.

Forestieri G., Onado, M. (1989) *Il sistema bancario italiano e l'integrazione dei mercati. Un confronto delle strutture negli ordinamenti dei principali Paesi*, EGEA, Milano.

Gonzales M., and Palomo Zurdo, R. J. (2003) *Cooperative banks and savings banks: a comparative business analysis*, CIRIEC, Madrid.

Mediobanca (2004) *Dati cumulativi delle principali banche internazionali, Milano*.

Palomo Zurdo R. J. (2001) *Las cooperativas de crédito*, Madrid, Septembre.

Palomo Zurdo R.J., and Valor, C. (2001) *Banca cooperativa. Entorno financiero y proyección social*, Madrid: Unión Nacional de Cooperativas de Crédito y Ministerio de Trabajo y Asuntos Sociales, Dirección General de Fomento de la Economía Social y del Fondo Social Europeo, Madrid.

Risk Italia (2001) *Pool di casse di risparmio spagnole per l'acquisto di un sistema di valutazione dei rischi*, Dicembre.

Uniòn Nacional de Cooperativas de Crédito (1999, 2000, 2001, 2002, 2003, 2004), *Anuario*, Madrid.

Uniòn Nacional de Cooperativas de Crédito (2001) *Banca Cooperativa entorno financiero y proyeccion social*, Wanagu Ediciones, Madrid.

Uniòn Nacional de Cooperativas de Crédito (2004) *Banca Cooperativa y Economia Social en Europa*, Wanagu Ediciones, Madrid.

Vandone D. (2003) "Le banche di credito cooperativo in Francia e in Spagna," *Cooperazione di Credito*, no. 182, pp. 469–76.

Vandone D. (2005) "Le banche di credito cooperativo in Francia e in Spagna," *Cooperazione di Credito*, no. 188, pp. 199–204.

4
The Cooperative Banking System in France

Pietro Marchetti and Arianna Sabetta[1]

4.1 Introduction

Since the mid 1990s, the French banking system has had a serious restructuring; in particular, there were some M&As whose effects influenced both banking systems' organization and *modus operandi* of the *établissement de credit* (CECEI 2004). This process is a consequence of both the evolution of international and European financial systems (for example, markets globalization), and the peculiarities of French banking sector.[2] Besides, financial and technological innovation increased and diversified the demand of financial services. It put bases for the evolution of political choices about "updating" the aims of the French banking system, which were behind the prudential deregulation and re-regulation process. At present, the banking system plays a significant role within the French economy: in fact, the banking sector contributed 2.4% of the French GDP in 2005, 2.6% in 2004, and 2.7% in 2003 (CECEI 2005).

The cooperative credit system plays a key role within the French banking sector. Its main features are the strong territorial links and excellent knowledge of local custom. This is due to the decentralized organizational structure of the French cooperative banks. Together with commercial banks, mutual and cooperative banking groups are the second type of French credit intermediaries qualified, by banking law, to carry out any banking transaction in the observance of limits put by laws, regulations or statutes. Commercial banks consider cooperative banks as dynamic and also privileged competitors by banking regulation (Labye-Lagoutte-Renversez 2002). According to the Annual Report of Banque de France (31 December 2005), cooperative banks have 30.9% of checking deposits and 36.3% of credits towards residents and 60% of French bank offices (CECEI 2005).

This chapter is divided into three sections. The first section analyzes features, regulators and the structure of French banking system as well as the profitability and efficiency indicators of French banks. The second section, dedicated to the cooperative credit sector in France, analyzes its institutional and legal aspects as well as the structure of the French cooperative network. In particular, we describe in detail the four mutual and cooperative banking groups in France, and we examine the evolution of their dimensional, economical and patrimonial results between 2003 and 2005. Finally, the third section provides a dimensional and economical comparison between cooperative and commercial banks in terms of the evolution of the banks' number and market share for deposits and loans; then, this section illustrates the guidelines followed by international rating agencies to attribute cooperative banks' rating; and finally, the third section provides a comparative analysis of the four cooperative banking groups with reference to the main results achieved on 31 December 2005.

4.2 The French banking system

4.2.1 Institutional organization and features of the French banking system

The French banking system lived for a long period in a protected circuit where the presence of nationalized and para-governmental banking groups gave it a precise physiognomy (Martin 1996). The Government participated not only through the detainment of some control, but also through a direct intervention in the definition of ease financing mechanisms, "reserved" only by some particular intermediaries categories (Fusco-Pasca 2003). In France, as well as in other European countries, the liberalization process started with a cut in the restrictions of credit allocation and with some choices about the monetary policy that since 1986, when they have been entirely put into the hands of the central bank, have been realized through the maneuver on the interest rates and the legal reserves.[3]

The years immediately after the second post-war period and those until the first half of the 1960s were characterized, in the credit field, by an interventionist public policy, having as purpose the economic reconstruction of the post-war period: in fact, the main credit corporations refer to the French Government (Crédit Lyonnais, Société Gènérale, Banque Nationale pour le Commerce e l'Industrie, Comptoir National d'Escompte). In the period 1965 to 1985, the governmental role in banking decreased. The banking system quickly developed mainly at the beginning of the 1960s, when the market growth allowed banks to prominently widen their net, which led to the outbreak of bank accounts' collection and volume (Giraudo 1986). The disengagement of Government in the banking field happened between the 1980s and the first half of the 1990s and finished in November 2002 with the cession of Credit Lyonnais shares.

During the return process of public banks to the private sector, a precise strategy has been followed so as to preserve banking organization stability through the creation of a "hard kernel" of shareholders from which the foreign institutes have been excluded or marginalized (IMF 1999; Fusco-Pasca 2003). Privatization coincides with the concentration and reorganization of the banking field besides with the increase of market indebtedness. In this period there was also the decrease of legislative texts about the credit system: through the issue of the 1984 Banking Act, a unitary normative description has been organized, with the aim of strengthening the competition and opening the wide field of para-banking jobs to banks.

In fact, banks can propose insurance contracts, with capitalization and retirement programmes, while insurance agencies can offer customers many different financial products, such as loans, worth management and financial consulting. Moreover, financial intermediation deeply changed after the introduction of the Act 96-597 of 2 July 1996 (*Loi de modernisation des activités financières*) in French banking ordering. This Act introduced the European directive of 10 May 1993 about investment services, which has defined a new category of intermediaries (*entreprises d'investissement*) and unified the conditions for investment services, whatever is the intermediary's category (*établissement de crédit* or *entreprises d'investissement*). In this way, the importance of traditional international banking intermediation (deposits collection and credits concession) diminished, while the business one (finance securitization) increased.

The development of market-based finance was simplified not only through the development of information technologies (IT),[4] but also due to the fact that the French Government prepared, since the mid 1980s, those rules necessary to give satisfactory completeness characteristics to the market, which helped make the non-banking intermediaries' growth easier. On the one hand, the French Government's aim was to create a single capital market opened to all the different traders not only for cash but also forward (Filosa 2006). On the other hand, the French Government wanted to make the public sector financing easier (IMF, 1999).

However, the personal property market development is not similar to the intensity in disintermediation of the banking field. Reasons that lead to such kind of phenomenon are two: the participation of French banks in the enterprises' financing "through the market" due to the development of finance securitization; and the strong social ties between banks and *entreprises d'investissement*, which enable banks to actively participate in intermediation in the personal property market and thus contain, in this way, their tendency to disintermediation (Filosa 2006). Therefore, the French banking system currently follows the 1984 Banking Act, which introduced the European directives into the French law (about principle of mutual acknowledgment, free plant and performance of investment services, home country control principle) and the secondary norm emanated by competent organs.[5]

The introduction of the Banking Act 84-46 of 24 January 1984 was the first of several stages that have led to an organic reform of the French credit system and marked the passage from structural vigilance to a kind of vigilance based on prudence. As regards the financial system on the whole, reforms aimed increasing the regulation towards financial fields before either scarcely regulated or not regulated at all. The Banking Act covers all banking activities, such as collections, employs, and management of payment means. It is applied to all the credit institutions that carry out bank transactions, apart from the legal form (company, cooperative or special statute), the nature of the capital owners (public or private) or the kind of activity (universal or specialized); and it sends back to competent authorities the definition of concrete conditions of the banking system operation.[6] The institutional order of the French financial and banking system includes different supervisory authorities, whose operations refer to a polycentric model (Fusco-Pasca 2003).

Through the Act 2003-706 of 1 August 2003 about financial security and the decree 2004-850 of 23 August 2004, regulation powers in banking and financing have been normalized so as to change the structure of supervisory authorities: the competence of issuing secondary norm passed from Comité de la Réglementation Bancaire et Financière (CRBF) to the Ministry of Economy, Trade and Industry. The following is a list of supervisory authorities with reference to supervised institutions:

- **Commission Bancaire** (CB) is the institution in charge of the supervision on credit institutions and investment trusts; it supervises the respect of the rules and has the power to sanction; its chairman is the Governor of Banque de France;

- **Comité des Établissements de Crédit et des Entreprises d'Investissement** (CECEI), presided by the Governor of Banque de France, is the organization in charge of issuing authorizations necessary to run a banking and financial activity in those cases in which the owners and legal form of credit institutions and investment trust change;
- **Autorité des Marchés Financiers** (AMF) was funded in 2004 after the unification of Commission des Opérations de Bourse (COB), Conseil des Marchés Financiers (CMF) and Comité de la Réglementation Bancaire et Financière (CRBF). AMF is an independent public authority with a legal personality; it issues authorizations to the portfolio management societies, consults the investment of trusts' programmes, and supervises financial markets ensuring their transparence and guaranteeing the investors' information;
- **Commission de Contrôle des Assurances des Mutuelles et des Institutions de Prévoyance** (CCAMIP), funded in 2003, controls the insurance and reinsurance of institutions and the public welfare organs;
- **Comité Consultatif de la Législation de la Réglementation Financières** (CCLRF) has an advisory jurisdiction on the norms in the banking, financial and insurance fields; its chairman is the Director General of Treasury and Economic Policy;
- **Comité des Entreprises d'Assurance** (CEA) allows the insurance activity to carry on.

4.2.2 Structure of French credit system: evolutions and tendencies

The French banking and financial system is characterized by a coexistence of organs with different juridical forms: beside the simple joint-stock companies (or *societés anonymes*) and partnerships – whether unlimited or limited – there are cooperative companies subject to different statutes (for example, banks of Crédit Agricole are subject to the Code Rural; Banques Populaires are subject to the Act of 1917; and banks of Crédit Mutuel are subject to the writ of 1958) and public institutions.

The Code Monétaire et Financier (Article L. 511-19) distinguishes *établissement de crédit* into five categories:

- **Commercial banks** can carry out all banking transactions and offer investment services after receiving an authorization.
- **Mutual or cooperative banks**[7] can carry out all operations in the respect of the limits imposed by law, regulations and statutes. These

banks don't act as independent institutes, but are grouped in big pyramidal structures. They have an institution on the top that does not necessarily have a cooperative function and that can have controlling interests on credit institutions with full operativity.

- **Financial societies** can carry out only authorized operations and are generally specialized in only one working field (consumer credit, real estate and personal property leasing, lease with purchase option and others).
- **Municipal cash trusts** are credit institutions with social purposes under the responsibility of municipalities.
- **Specialized financial institutions** are credit institutions with a mission of public interest committed by Government. These institutions cannot collect funds among the population or with a deadline lower than two years except under specific authorization.[8]

Following an explicit political point of view, the French banking system has a three-pole structure: public, cooperative and private; authorities favour the first two to the detriment of the private pole.[9] In fact, authorities give to the cooperative pole (savings banks and mutual banks) functions of public interest as well as the option of not contending some economic advantages compared to commercial banks. In particular, mutual banks distribute saving products that have tax breaks and/or managed rates: this leads to a distortion of competition in the French banking market and, despite liberalization, obstructs the full realization of a *level playing field* between different operator categories (Crespi-Rossi 2005). Moreover, during the unification process, Government and supervisory authorities privileged the growth of the cooperative pole. They followed a strategic scheme, which aimed to develop the cooperative banks' market power.[10] In fact, about half of the French banks have reference to the not-contended pole, made of mutual banks or banks controlled by cooperative organizations (Fusco-Pasca 2003).

A consequence of this trend is the increasing concentration of the French banking system (see Table 4.1) that, on a European level, has

Table 4.1   Market share (%) of the main five banks among the total system

	1990	1995	2000	2001	2002	2003	2004	2005
France	42.5	41.3	46.9	47.0	44.6	46.7	49.2	53.5
EU-Average	—	—	57.1	59.8	59.8	59.5	59.2	59.7

Source: CECEI (2005); ECB (2005, 2006).

an average concentration with an index, calculated on the basis of the active shares of the first five banks among the whole banking system, during the last 15 years oscillating between 40% and 50% (CECEI 2005; ECB 2005). The first ten multi-functional French groups control 80-90% of the market. System concentration is based not only on costs' decrease and scale economies, but also on social purposes. The aim is to promote the creation of solid national banking groups able to face the competition of foreign financial groups and privilege the mutual pole (IMF 1999; Group of Ten 2001).

The immediate consequence of the concentration process is a light reduction in the credit intermediaries' total number: in France at the end of 1984 they were 2.001, while at the end of 2005 the number of *établissement de crédit* was equal to 855 units, with a decrease by 57.3% (CECEI 2005). We want to emphasize that, during the restructuring and reorganization processes, the mutual and cooperative banks rationalization process had an important rule due to the necessity to adequate their organization to a different financial and economic background and to the chasing international competition. On the contrary, the employees' number and the fully working desks' number didn't remarkably change; on the other side, the automated teller machine (ATM) and the point on sales (POS) developed. The dimensional development dovetailed with a diversification in the business, that led to a growing quote of revenues generated by services and negotiation profits (Landi 2004).[11]

As a matter of fact, French credit institutions followed a capillarity strategy of distribution network and a strategy of the production processes diversification. They thus created a background necessary to the adoption of the universal bank model in which the organization centre is often a result of mergers among big banks or unions of mutual organizations, while some specific services are in the hands of companies created *ad hoc* or deriving from the buyout of other companies. Therefore, keeping territorial capillarity of both mutual and public banks contrasted the rationalization deriving from the private banks concentration. Moreover, in order to develop market penetration without weigh on costs, French intermediaries followed a multi-channel strategy first via the telephone, and then via the Internet by developing some distribution models that use the Internet to have access to information by customers on one hand, and virtually introduce banks to them on the other hand (Crespi-Rossi 2005).

Finally, studying the structure of French banks, it's important to consider the internationalization of the *établissement de crédit* and their opening to the entrance of foreign institutions. In fact, French intermediaries boast an old history of settlement in other countries, a heritage of the colonial conquests: there have been foreign branch offices of the main credit institutions we know since the last century. During the following years, overseas French intermediaries became more and more important. At the end of 2001 the importance of branch offices and subsidiaries abroad constituted almost one-fifth of the total intermediated funds of the French credit system. During the last years, they achieved really positive results in terms of profitability, generally higher than the domestic market operations, contributing for 12.2% to the configuration of net banking income and for 13.3% to the formation of gross operating income (Commission Bancaire 2002).

In 2005 the activity of branch offices and subsidiaries abroad further developed on a social base; and by the end of the year, it represents about 20% of the *établissement de credit* bearing interests (Banque de France 2006). Those areas in which there is a big effort in the spread process can be located in Asia (Pacific area), in the United States, and in the last few years in Eastern Europe; in the European Union, on the other hand, they are mostly in the United Kingdom, and there are also a few of them in Germany, Italy, Spain and Luxemburg (CECEI 2004). The modalities followed during the internationalization process were manifold: from the participation in foreign societies to partnership agreements in the creation of common societies; from the participation to projects for the development of specific business areas to the buyout of local banks or specialized societies. On the contrary, the penetration of foreign intermediaries in the French banking system (amounting to 161 units at the end of 2005) is somewhat restricted as to the intermediated masses volume: in fact, at the end of 2005 market share for loans is equal to 8.8% and for deposits is 8.2%. But the foreign penetration is quite consistent in terms of desks' and employees' number, respectively equal to 1.647 and 32.143 units in 2005 (CECEI 2005).

4.2.3 Profitability and efficiency indicators of French banks

During the 1980s, the *établissement de crédit* results have been influenced by increasing competition and the diversification of banking activity: as a consequence of disintermediation, net interest margins were contracted, while, at the same time, margins deriving from fees increased. This trend also continued during the period 1991-94, when the rising risks typical of banking activity affected the profitability of the

French banking system: the growth in credit demand and the enhanced default rate of small and medium enterprises (SMEs) had some recoils on financial statement of the *établissement de crédit.* In 1993, the economical slowdown and the decrease in the banks' funds had as a direct consequence the credit demand concentration. However, in 1995, the situation improved: there was a reversal thanks to economical revival, and better management of the *établissement de crédit* due to the rationalization of the organizational structures and a better coordination inside the groups. This reorganization process has been realized through internal mergers, which contributed to the improvement of the profitability and efficiency of the *établissement de crédit.* In fact, French banks proved to be particularly careful about the costs control: the ratio between operational costs and net banking income changed from 74.2% in 1994 to 64.4% in 2005.

Despite of the internal restructuring, the number of employees and desks continue to influence the French banks' costs, which have hardly changed. Profitability was positively influenced by the evolving market activities, which have changed the importance of fees on the net income; and, general, by the profit sources diversification strategies, which have changed the profit itself: the revenues deriving from asset management on behalf of a third party and from *bancassurance* represent more than one-tenth of the French banking incomes of the main organizations (Fusco-Pasca 2003). The Corporate & Investment Banking field contributes for a fourth to the creation of the net income. However, the Retail Banking (domestic and international) is the main source of revenues for French banks (Banque de France 2006), although during 2005 its contribution decreased (becoming 59.5% of net banking income compared to 61% of the previous year). Also, the risks management suffered from the structures' organizational rationalization, affecting the credit institutions' solvency in a positive way. Moreover, the emphasis that the supervisory authorities placed on the internal controls' quality tools of competitive advantage in the first half of the 1990s contributed to the spread of a control culture, which allowed credit institutions to get important developments about transparency and efficiency. In fact, under the pressure of supervisory authorities, the funds' consistency and the solvency of the French banking system enhanced. In effect, together with an efficient risks' management, it allowed French banks to support the economic and financial shocks that affected the worldwide economical and financial system at the beginning of the twenty-first century (Noyer 2004).

4.3 The cooperative credit sector in France

4.3.1 Institutional and legal aspects of the French cooperative credit

Cooperative banks first developed in nineteenth-century Germany. Ever since, they spread in most Western European systems, including France (Guinnane 1997). By virtue of the Banking Act 84-46 of 24 January 1984, which is now integrated into the *Code Monétaire et Financier*, cooperative banks in the French cooperative credit sector can receive deposits by any natural or legal person and grant loans to non-shareholders in the observance of statutory conditions (UNACC 2004). In particular, under Article L.511-19 of the *Code Monétaire et Financier*, cooperative banks are qualified to receive checking and short-term deposits and carry out all the banking transactions in the observance of limits put by laws, regulations or statutes. So, cooperative banks can carry out transactions connected with their activity, acquire equity holdings in undertakings and carry out non-banking operations to the same legal conditions of commercial banks (CECEI 2005).

In the past, the French banking law made difficult the establishment of cooperative banks. In fact, an Act of June 1941 defined which organizations were suitable to be "registered as banks" and, on the basis of this definition, listed the firms authorized to practise banking activities. That meant French cooperative banks could practise their business only if they were provided with special statutes which allowed them to distinguish from "registered banks". Each statute developed in a particular way until the 1984 Banking Act, which caused the so called "banalization" of the French credit system; that is, a common legal framework for all credit institutions (Rinella 1996). In other words, many of the normative differences which distinguished different banks collapsed. In effect, all the banks were subjected to the same legal regulation, which kept some residue of special discipline only in its fulfilment of standards. Since French cooperative banks are, banks in every respect, they are subjected to general banking rules, with some very small integration justified by their particular legal form. Also, as cooperative firms, they are subjected to the Act 47-1775 of 10 September 1947 about cooperative organizations' statute. As variable capital companies, French cooperative banks are subjected to the Act of 24 July 1867.

Moreover, in France the mutual principle was deeply attenuated, at least from some points of view, for the economic effectiveness. This process, with particular regard to the cooperatives of the banking sector, determined the extension of the social basis over the limits of a homogenous and limited group, the opening of cooperative banks' services to non-shareholders, and the attenuation of cooperative principles of financial management, such as the limited interest on capital and the "unrecoverability" of reserves during social life (Rinella 1996).

Taking into consideration that the cooperative credit sector in France represents about half of the French credit system, we can draw attention to the fact that the French mutual and cooperative banks don't act as independent organisms, but they group themselves into large pyramidal structures with a top central organ, not necessarily cooperative, that could hold controlling interests in fully operative credit institutions (Fusco-Pasca 2003). Each central organ, according to the Article 21 of the Banking Act 84-46, represents associate credit institutions towards the Banque de France, the Comité des Etablissements de Crédit et des Entreprises d'Investissement (CECEI from now on) and the Commission Bancaire, coordinates their strategies and organization, assures their groups' cohesion and good functioning of the associate credit institutions, and adopts all measures necessary to ensure the liquidity and solvency of each institution and group on the whole.

Besides, these central organizations supervise the application of laws and regulations. Not only can they practise administrative, technical and financial controls on the organization and management of associate credit institutions, but they can also place sanctions accordingly. From an economic point of view, the centralization of the production of banking services under a unified brand allows the achievement of considerable scale economies (Le Scornet 2002). Corporate governance structure of cooperative banking groups provides for regional banks own shares of central organizations and local banks own shares of regional banks, while only particular subjects own shares of local banks. Except for the central organ, not necessarily cooperative, all the other components of the group are based on the "one head, one vote" principle, typical of the cooperative companies (UNACC 2004). The European credit cooperative organizations, including the French one, have a hierarchical system, resembling an "inverse pyramid", which allows the achievement of productive and distributive structures that are efficient and consistent with their cooperative mission: the development of complex or innovative products and services is centralized, while customers' proximity is ensured by local banks' network; that is the first step of this structure and determines upper steps' decisions.[12]

Such a decentralized structure on different levels (local, regional, and national ones) allows European credit cooperative organizations to be in direct contact with the economic environment. Most of customers are member-stakeholders themselves, which directly take part in the bank's management, which guarantees a very close relationship with their reference territory, both local and regional (De Bruyn-Ferri 2005). French cooperative credit "network" systems developed on the basis of a common strategic and organizational model, since its origin based on the complementarity's principles of the support's structures at different operational levels. They aimed at achieving scale economies and developing synergies otherwise unlikely to be get-at-able by any individual bank. During the last two decades, because of the markets' liberalization and integration phenomena, the original model of the cooperative credit system based on the principle of complementarity was modified towards a more integrated structure, with a progressive centralization of strategic and operational functions and resources on upper levels. The aim of scale economies' achievement often seems to have prevailed over the need to maintain a complete decisional and entrepreneurial autonomy of cooperative local banks, and attribute strong powers of direction and control to central organisms (Revell 1995).

Moreover, centralization also took on institutional relevance and was specifically regulated by authorities. So, the whole decisional mechanism inside network takes on a "circular" character: on one hand, the company's needs are transferred to upper levels by the economic democracy instruments typical of cooperative banks; on the other hand, the first level's powers of direction and control on banks aim to increase their autonomy, especially from a prudential point of view to protect the stability not only of the group but also of each bank. Horizontal combinations on a local level aim at researching the best company's dimensions, often following an overvaluation of the scale economies' effects. They also lead to a considerable growth of the first level organizations which can impose their decisions not only on the second level associations but also on the third ones, and so a weakening of national organizations. Central organisms consequently could maintain their power only by increasing their hierarchically subordinate levels more quickly than lower organizations, and making the latter economically dependent to them.

4.3.2 Structure of cooperative credit system in France

It has been so far established in this chapter that French cooperative credit institutions belong to "networks" with a central organism regulated by the Articles L.511-30 – L.511-32 of the *Code Monétaire et Financier*. At present, French mutual and cooperative banks are grouped into four networks (CECEI 2005):

- A network of **Banques Populaires**, which has legally integrated the Crédit Coopératif network[13] since January 2003, and eight Caisses de Crédit Maritime Mutuel and Société Centrale de Crédit Maritime Mutuel, all associate to Banque Fédérale des Banques Populaires since August 2003;
- A network of **Crédit Agricole**, formed by regional and local banks of Crédit Agricole, associate to Crédit Agricole S.A;
- A network of **Crédit Mutuel**, constituted by federal and local banks of Crédit Mutuel with a general or agricultural vocation, all associate to Confédération Nationale du Crédit Mutuel;
- A network of **Caisses d'Epargne**, whose statute has been based on the cooperative model only since 1 January 2000,[14] formed by Caisses d'Epargne et de Prévoyance, associate to Caisse Nationale des Caisses d'Epargne et de Prévoyance.

The French cooperative credit system has its barycentre at a regional level (Schraffl 1995), since territorial responsibility of the first level units coincides with a regional dimension. Crédit Mutuel, Crédit Agricole and Banques Populaires are characterized by strongly centralized systems to which prudential coefficients are applied on consolidated basis at a regional level.[15] In fact, in 1990s, there was a strong vertical integration within these systems at a regional level. The tendency was to adopt the consolidation mechanism, which would then control and guarantee the system too. So the centralization model adopted by French cooperative banking groups expresses itself in a regional dimension. This actually constitutes the first operational level because autonomous local banks do not exist more. On the basis of this model, the national Central Banks have not adopted the consolidation mechanism. However, now, this has changed because they take on a relevant role of coordination and strategic direction at different levels (Di Salvo 2002). Since 1984, the centralization process has further intensified in the two main French cooperative credit systems (Crédit Mutuel and Crédit Agricole). They now seem like pyramidal systems at three bipolar levels,[16] but with a considerable rank of horizontal and vertical integration (Schraffl 1998). The principle of a unitary management has been applied to regional banks and there are thus two levels systems towards authorities:

- At a regional level, primary units each one with its agencies network at a local level (Caisses de Crédit Agricole and Caisses de Crédit Mutuel);
- At a national level, a banking institution at the top and a national federation.

Together with this transformation, there was a wide and generalized horizontal combination of the second level structures, reducing by a third the number of regional central banks (and for Crédit Mutuel the number of relevant regional federations too) in order to avoid following local mergers each other (Schraffl 1999). So they kept the (though limited) autonomy of each local bank on one hand, and facilitated the control of the regional central bank on the other hand. The abovementioned waves of regional combinations followed each other in order not only to centralize human, technological and financial resources, but also to level an inevitable territorial heterogeneity typical of all the cooperative credit systems (Schraffl 2000). From an operational point of view, local banks have to:

• Undergo inspections and revisions by their federation or regional bank;
• Conform to the binding instructions of their upper level and suffer possible sanctions;
• Distribute only products and services made inside their banking group;
• Send all liquidity not used to grant loans to their regional bank;
• Subject staff to the vocational training offered by their upper level;
• Obtain the approval of director's appointment by their upper level.

In order to maintain banking control, Crédit Mutuel and Crédit Agricole partly adopted the typical model of Banques Populaires, whose primary units were always regional institutions with local agencies. Recent results achieved by mutual and cooperative banking networks demonstrate effectiveness of this model: in all EU Countries these networks got market shares and improved their results and capitalization level (Piot 1997). Finally, these four mutual and cooperative banking groups, in variable proportions, now manage an important banking component of common law:[17] Crédit Agricole Group by Crédit Lyonnais, Crédit Mutuel Group by Crédit Industriel et Commercial (CIC), Banques Populaires Group by Natexis-Banques Populaires, and Caisses d'Epargne Group by Ixis Corporate & Investment Banking. Besides, branches of these banks can be associate to the central organism too and become members of network themselves (CECEI 2005). In succession, we analyze organizational structures of the four mutual and cooperative networks in the French banking system and we examine their dimensional, economical and patrimonial evolution during the period 2003–5.

4.3.2.1 Banques Populaires

The network of Banques Populaires was born in 1972 after its previous name *Crédit Populaire de France*, which is still partly used, was modified. The Group turns its business to professionals, SMEs, and families. Its organizational structure is based on tree levels:

- On the first (cooperative) level, there are 21 Banques Populaires, of which 19 are regional banks,[18] with a well-defined territorial responsibility, and two are national banks with a particular vocation: Casden-Banque Populaire[19] and, since 30 January 2003, Crédit Coopératif[20] that funds non-agricultural organisms of social economics. Moreover, since August 2003,[21] Crédit Maritime Mutuel, with eight regional banks and one central bank, became a member of the Group. However, it does not have the status of a popular bank and its responsibility is limited to the fishing sector and related activities.

- On the second (federal) level, there is Banque Fédérale des Banques Populaires (BFBP) – changed in a public company after the Act 2001-420 of 15 May 2001 on new economical regulations – whose capital stock is almost wholly owned by the first level popular banks. At the same time, BFBP is both the new central organ of the Group and the holding company of Natexis-Banques Populaires (CECEI 2005). Previously, the financial and technical central organ of the Group was Chambre Syndicale des Banques Populaires.

- On the third (listed-company) level, there is Natexis-Banques Populaires, a banking and financial institution not really cooperative, listed on the primary market of Euronext Paris, which represents the pivot of international and financial business of the Group. Its range of corporate banking services and its international presence[22] were increased in 2002, after the acquisition of Coface, a company specialized in insurance and banking sectors.

Therefore, the Group combines the cooperative culture of regional Banques Populaires and Casden-Banque Populaire with a global and international approach of the funding, investment and service's activities by Natexis-Banques Populaires (Vandone 2003). There are also 76 mutual guarantee companies – that is, financial companies (operating in artisan, estate and other professional sectors) associate to the regional banks and whose activity is guaranteeing loans to the Group's member-stakeholders. Furthermore, the Group includes many institutions, which are not legally associate to the BFBP; rather, they are branches of the regional popular banks or Natexis-Banques Populaires, or else associate to Crédit Coopératif: those institutions are 14 banks, 34 financial companies and four investment companies (CECEI 2005). At present, the Banques Populaires Group is the fifth banking group in France with its total equity amounting to €13,699 million in 2005 and its market share for loans[23] being 8.3%. By the Crédit Coopératif's control, the Group became both a domestic and international leader of the social economics. On 31 December 2005, the Group included 6.8 million clients, more than three million member-stakeholders (of which over 1.500.000 were regional banks' member-stakeholders), 45,530 employees (of which 13,432 were for Natexis and its branches) and had 2807 branches in France.

From the consolidated financial statements of the Group during the years 2003-05 (see Table 4.2), we find a steady growth of economical and patrimonial results. In particular, consolidated net banking income, equal to € 8,242 million in 2005 (increased by 7.8% compared with 2004 and 8% from 2003 to 2004), comes about two-third from local retail banking business[24] (in particular, local retail banking contributes for 63%; that is, € 5194 million) and one-third from

Table 4.2 Main indicators, and economical and dimensional results of the Banques Populaires Group

Dimensional results	2003	2004	2005
Regional banks	21	20	19
Branches	2,605	2,692	2,807
Employees	43,224	44,509	45,530
Member-stakeholders	2,450,000	2,770,000	3,100,000
Clients	6,300,000	6,600,000	6,800,000
Economical results (€ million)	**2003**	**2004**	**2005**
Net banking income	7,066	7,646	8,242
Gross operating income	2,270	2,545	2,852
Net income, Group share	853	1,059	1,522
Customer deposits	98,945	98,253	104,483
Loans and advances to customers	111,800	120,584	146,603
Total assets	237,163	250,404	288,711
Shareholders' equity, Group share	8,504	11,684	13,699
Tier 1 Capital	12,217	13,421	14,634
Indicators	**2003**	**2004**	**2005**
Cost-income ratio	68.9%	66.7%	65.4%
ROE	10.6%	11.9%	13.5%
Tier 1 ratio	8.2%	8.4%	8.5%

Source: Banques Populaires Group's Rapport Annuel (2003, 2004, 2005).

Natexis-Banques Populaires (for 37%). Gross operating income of the Group amounts to €2,852 million in 2005 (+12.2% in relation to 2004 and +12% from 2003 to 2004) and consolidated net income attributable to equity holders of the parent improved from €853 million in 2003 to €1,059 million in 2004 (+24%) until €1,522 million in 2005 (+27.3% compared with 2004). In particular, at the end of 2005, €971 million (about 64%) of net income came from local retail banking business. Cost-income ratio is 65.4% in 2005, with a significant improvement (–3.5%) during the period 2003–5. The Group's profitability improved too: from 2003 to 2005 ROE increased to 13.5% in 2005. Finally, the financial structure of the Group was very solid: in 2005 Tier 1 Capital amounts to €14,634 million, with an increase by 18% compared with 2004, and Tier 1 ratio is 8.5%, one of the highest levels in the banking sector.

4.3.2.2 Crédit Agricole

Although the Crédit Agricole Group aimed to satisfy agricultural financial needs,[25] its customers and responsibilities increased with time. Crédit Agricole Mutuel is considered as a cooperative bank aiming at a demutualization strategy:[26] its purpose is to continue to improve itself into the retail banking business in Europe and, in order to obtain that, it has pursued an external growth politics in recent years both in France and abroad.[27] Crédit Agricole is organized in a double vertical structure formed by two national institutions, and regional and local banks, which carry out ordinary banking transactions and, even if associate to their relevant central institutions, they are autonomous banks responsible for their management and development.

The Crédit Agricole Group is hierarchically structured on tree levels:

- On the basis, there are 2,583 local banks[28] with 5,700,000 member stakeholders, associate to regional banks of which local ones own a majority stake.[29] Local banks keep their members' and customers' proximity and they manage loans and guarantees operations.
- On intermediate level, there are 41 regional banks, which were created by the Act of 7 November 1899 (*Loi Viger*). They are autonomous and associate to their central organ, wholly responsible for managing and controlling a certain geographical area.[30] Main regional banks' member-stakeholders are their associate local banks, and some agricultural and food cooperatives. After the 1984 Banking Act, each regional bank, together with its associate local banks, identifies itself as a mutual and cooperative bank. So the real banking business is

located on the regional banks level (with their 7,142 bank offices and 16.1 million clients), while the local banks can only receive and immediately transfer deposits to their regional bank (CECEI 2005).

• Over these regional and local structures, there are two national institutions: Crédit Agricole S.A., known as Caisse Nationale du Crédit Agricole (CNCA)[31] until 2001, and Fédération Nationale du Crédit Agricole (FNCA).

Crédit Agricole S.A. is a banking institution in every respect, apart from the Group's central organ. As such, it ensures the cohesion and proper operation of the Crédit Agricole network, still delegating the local banks' control to the regional ones. It coordinates and makes easier the rural banks' business, as well as promotes mutual credit in agricultural population. As the Group's central bank, Crédit Agricole S.A. operates as a clearing house for the Group's financial unity, and carries out all the banking and financial activities abroad by its foreign branches and subsidiaries (CECEI 2005). Fédération Nationale du Crédit Agricole (FNCA) established in 1945 after the regional and local banks' initiative to balance the State presence (by CNCA) into the Group. Therefore, after the "mutualization" of CNCA in 1988, FNCA ought to have lost its original role, while it kept carrying out its collateral functions with CNCA. In particular, FNCA represents the regional banks and the Group in discussions with the French authorities, trade associations (AFEC, GIE Carte Bancaire, entrepreneur unions, Conseil de l'Agriculture Française and rural associations), and other cooperative and mutual organizations and international organisms. The FNCA also provides advice and assistance services to the regional banks, by its Federal Commissions qualified in law, tax, R&D, marketing, international relationships. Instead, in the Group's structure there are not regional federations: on this level, the regional banks themselves carry out assistance services to the local banks.

Therefore, from an organizational point of view, Crédit Agricole is an imperfect bipolar system on three levels: on operational level, regional banks are the most strategic. In fact, local banks have a rather limited managerial autonomy because they have to adapt themselves to the upper level's instructions (Di Salvo-Schraffl 2002). Moreover, in France and Monaco the Crédit Agricole Group includes a number of institutions not associate to Crédit Agricole S.A. but its own or regional banks' branches. This number increased year after year, following the Group's acquisition of Banque Indosuez (then called Calyon) and its branches in 1996, Banque Sofinco in 1999, Crédit Lyonnais and its branches in

2003, and the financial company Finaref. There are eleven banks, 32 financial companies, and six investment companies in the Group on the whole (CECEI 2005).

Crédit Agricole is one of the largest banks worldwide for its total equity's amount and balance sheet, has a fundamental role in financing national agriculture and private individuals, and offers a diversified range of financial and insurance services to an international level and its large clients. Crédit Agricole is a solid and decentralized group, which financial, commercial and legal cohesion keeps in step with responsibilities' decentralization in. On 31 December 2005, in France and the 66 countries it is present abroad, the Crédit Agricole Group had 136,848 employees (of which 62,112 were for Crédit Agricole S.A. and its branches), 9,072 bank-offices (of which were 7,142 for the regional banks), and over 21 million clients. The Group is the first bank in France for its total equity amounting to €51,235 million in 2005, and the first one in regards to market share for loans (24%).

During the period 2003–5 and especially in 2005, all main results improved (see Table 4.3). In particular, net banking income (equal to €25,949 million in 2005) increased by 8.6% compared with 2004 was consolidated because of the extremely positive performances of the regional banks (providing with €12,255 million, over 47% of total net banking income), and the recovery of all the Crédit Agricole S.A. business lines after its deep reorganization following Crédit Lyonnais integration into the Group. On 31 December 2005, the gross operating income of the Group amounted to €9,588 million (+15.2% in relation to 2004), of which 52% provided by the regional banks (that is, €4,993 million); the consolidated net income attributable to equity holders of the parent was equal to €5,983 million, increased by 37.4% compared with 2004 and over 64% from 2003 to 2004. We highlight a notable contribution of the regional banks to consolidated net income: in fact, regional banks contribute for about 47% of consolidated net income, in particular they provided €2,816 million in 2005 (+14.2% compared with 2004). Total assets of the Crédit Agricole Group substantially improved in the years 2003-05: at the end of 2005, they amounted to €1,170,349 million (+13.4% in relation to 2004 and +4.4% from 2003 to 2004).

Moreover, in 2005, 28% of total assets (that is, €323,565 million) were provided by the regional banks network. Shareholders' equity analogously improved during this three-year period (+15.1% in 2005 compared with 2004 and +8.6% from 2003 to 2004), and it

Table 4.3 Main indicators, and economical and dimensional results of the Crédit Agricole Group

Dimensional results	2003	2004	2005
Regional banks	44	43	41
Branches	9,110	9,057	9,072
Employees	136,414	135,502	136,848
Member-stakeholders	5,700,000	5,700,000	5,700,000
Clients	21,000,000	21,000,000	21,000,000
Economical results (€ million)	**2003**	**2004**	**2005**
Net banking income	23,886	23,895	25,949
Gross operating income	8,294	8,322	9,588
Net income, Group share	2,757	4,354	5,983
Customer deposits	366,960	377,981	397,860
Loans and advances to customers	370,895	409,785	455,380
Total assets	875,238	913,773	1,170,349
Shareholders' equity, Group share	40,976	44,501	51,235
Tier 1 Capital	31,391	33,802	37,900
Indicators	**2003**	**2004**	**2005**
Cost-income ratio	65.3%	64.1%	63.1%
ROE	10.6%	13.6%	15.8%
Tier 1 ratio	7.6%	7.9%	7.9%

Source: Crédit Agricole Group's Rapport Annuel (2003, 2004, 2005).

amounted to €51,235 million in 2005. Cost-income ratio of the Group decreased by 2.2% from 2003 to 2005, and it was equal to 63.1% in 2005; in particular, the regional banks achieved an excellent level of efficiency, with a cost-income ratio of 59.3% in 2005 (–0.5% in relation to 2004). Also the Group's profitability improved: on 31 December 2005, ROE of the Crédit Agricole Group was the best of the whole banking sector and it was equal to 15.8%, with an increase by 5.2% compared with 2003. Instead, during the period 2003-05, Tier 1 ratio was rather steady: it was 7.9% in 2004 and 2005, while 7.6% in 2003.

4.3.2.3 Crédit Mutuel

Cooperative banks of the Crédit Mutuel Group fully enter into *Raiffeisen* tradition: originally established in Alsatian according to the German law (that was more favourable to cooperation than the French one), they refer to the cooperative and mutual logic. From an organizational point of view, Crédit Mutuel is like an imperfect bipolar system on three levels (Schraffl 1999). These three levels of organization – local, regional and national – operate on a decentralized basis: therefore, the entire Group's functioning is based on the subsidiarity principle, according to which the upper level takes over when the lower level's ability is exhausted. Local banks, which are closest to clients and member-stakeholders, are thus responsible for the principal functions of branches; while regional federations and the national confederation deal with those responsibilities local banks do not carry them out alone.

In particular, the Group's organizational structure is divided like this:

- On the first level there are 1,920 local banks (regulated by the Act of 1947 and ordinance of 16 October 1958)[32] with 6,700,000 member-stakeholders and 10.5 million clients (CECEI 2005). Even if each of them is associated to a federal bank, local banks are legally autonomous and collectively joint liable at regional level. Each local bank has a board of director and a supervision committee, both whose members are elected by shareholders' meeting according to the rule: "one head, one vote". Managerial autonomy of each local bank is usually limited to gathering deposits and granting loans under a certain *plafond*.[33] In regards to products' and services' selling activity, local banks are like "branches" of the federal banks, even if they are formally provided with legal autonomy: in fact, local banks have to offer their clients (formed only by member-stakeholders or third persons by the regional bank's authority received) all the products and services centrally promoted (Schraffl 1999).

- On the second level, there is a regional organization formed by 18 regional federations and 14 largely decentralized federal banks. Local banks are associated to one regional federation (professional and trade union structure of the regional group) and are member of one federal bank (financial structure of the regional group). Regional federations are associations that practise the control on local banks by proxy of the national confederation, and promote the local banks' development, and act for them to third counter-parties. Federal banks are credit institutions. They deal with the clearing of credit and debit standings among local banks, the management of their excess resources, and the execution of operations, which local banks cannot do because of their nature or size. Regional federations and federal banks are managed by representatives that local banks elected. Together with the 18 regional federations, there is also the federation of Crédit Mutuel Agricole et Rural (CMAR), with a national vocation, which is the second institution financing the French rural sector (Pflimlin 2005).

- On the third (national) level, there are two central organizations: Confédération Nationale du Crédit Mutuel (CNCM) (provided for by the Act of 1901 and established by the ordinance of 16 October 1958), as a public service's institution, and Caisse Centrale du Crédit Mutuel (CCCM), with a financial vocation (CECEI 2005).

CNCM is an association with an administrative vocation, which includes all the regional federations. According to the 1984 Banking Act, it is the national central organ responsible of the system on the whole. Both 19 regional federations (CMAR, the rural one, included as the central one) and CCCM are members of the confederation. Since CNCM represents Crédit Mutuel before the State, it assures the financial, technical and administrative control on the organization and management of each federal bank of Crédit Mutuel and CMAR. CCCM is the top national bank of the Group, and coordinates regional groups and carries out banking services to federal and local banks, placing excess liquidity of its associate banks on market and assuring financial solidarity inside the Group without any direct relationship with customers. Instead, in regards to the Group's banking operational structure, its barycentre is situated on federal banks: regionally, the centralization of decisional powers has achieved its top as regards both associative and business functions (apparently clearly divided)[34].

In practice, the cooperative credit system of Crédit Mutuel is operationally structured as a complex of "regional banking groups" with a common central organ at national level. The top of each regional banking group is formed by a federal bank which, apart from practising the ordinary banking business, coordinates the associate banks' activities and gives them binding instructions, deriving from concerted decisions with its associates. Moreover, the level of centralization within different regional groups is not uniform in all regions: in some regions (for example in Bretagne) there is a strong vertical combination rate, in others (as generally in East regions) a significant attenuation of the federal bank's role. The reasons of this disparity are not evident from objective organizational data, but they are exclusively linked to historical, social and economic factors, which analogously influenced the other sectors of cooperation like agricultural and retail ones (Schraffl 1999). The Crédit Mutuel Group includes also several credit institutions, not legally associate to the national confederation ex Article L.511-31 of the Code Monétaire et Financier, but branches of the federal banks: so, there are 25 banks, 14 financial companies and seven investment companies (CECEI 2005).

The number of the Group's branches increased very much following the acquisition of Crédit Industriel et Commercial (CIC) by Banque Fédérative du Crédit Mutuel (BFCM) of Strasbourg, a commercial branch of the Centre Est Europe regional federation.[35] The Crédit Mutuel-CIC Group, specialized in retail banking, combines the strengths of Crédit Mutuel (a mutual and cooperative bank with an extensive local and regional presence) with those of CIC, which is a commercial bank with some 40 bank-offices outside France. The Group provides all banking services (a complete range of savings products and many diversified credits, from home financing to consumer credit) not only to individuals, but also to local communities, associations, professionals and firms, in France and abroad.[36] Moreover, the Group provides all financial products (investment companies, mutual funds, asset management) and many services in insurance, tourism, leasing, financial engineering[37] and venture capital. A further reinforcement's element of the Crédit Mutuel Group's integration comes from the new multi-channel network that gave a substantial contribution to efficiency: in fact, Crédit Mutuel is now the fifth banking group in France for its performance (CECEI 2005).

Crédit Mutuel-CIC is the second-largest retail bank in France: on 31 December 2005, it had 5,022 branches and 57,000 employees (1,940 branches and 29,639 employees only for CIC) and 14.2 million clients; and the Group's market share for loans was 16.3% and for deposits was 12.3%. In particular, market shares of only the Crédit Mutuel banks (which have about 3,100 branches and 33,610 employees) are respectively 9.4% for loans and 7.7% for deposits. The Group is the number-two in retail banking network for consumer credit in France, as well as in electronic banking, home financing, farmers and agriculture; in the bancassurance sector, the Group ranks first for non-life and fourth for life insurance.

From the consolidated financial statements of the Group[38] (see Table 4.4), we find a very limited growth, or even a fall during the period 2003–04 because of the worsening of Crédit Industriel et Commercial (CIC) and insurance sector. However, in 2005 there is a clear recovery of all results. In comparison with the light drop (–0.4%) of the net banking income from 2003 to 2004, in 2005 consolidated net banking income amounts to €9,633 million, with an increase by over 10% in relation to 2004. From 2003 to 2004, gross operating income decreased too (–5.4%), and it highly improved in 2005 (+21.2% in relation to 2004) when it amounted to €3,617 million. In 2005, the Group benefited from growth in all areas of business and consolidated net income

Table 4.4 Main indicators, and economical and dimensional results of the Crédit Mutuel-CIC Group

Dimensional results	2003	2004	2005
Regional banks	18	18	18
Branches	4,760	4,990	5,022
Employees	55,690	56,760	57,000
Member-stakeholders	6,100,000	6,500,000	6,700,000
Clients	13,500,000	13,900,000	14,200,000
Economical results (€ million)	**2003**	**2004**	**2005**
Net banking income	8,796	8,754	9,633
Gross operating income	3,155	2,984	3,617
Net income, Group share	1,304	1,494	2,389
Customer deposits	133,886	143,550	148,230
Loans and advances to customers	144,787	158,397	188,407
Total assets	355,005	387,886	436,390
Shareholders' equity, Group share	16,152	17,959	20,530
Tier 1 Capital	15,297	18,188	19,600
Indicators	**2003**	**2004**	**2005**
Cost-income ratio	64.1%	65.9%	62.5%
ROE	11.2%	10.6%	13.7%
Tier 1 ratio	9.6%	10.5%	10.2%

Source: Crédit Mutuel-CIC Group's Rapport Annuel (2003, 2004, 2005).

reaches €2,389 million (+60% compared with 2004, and +14.6% from 2003 to 2004), topping the €2 billion mark for the first time. Total assets increased by 9.3% during the years 2003-04; in 2005 shareholders' funds rose too (+14.6% in relation to 2004) and reached €20,530 million. We can also highlight the Group's productive efficiency and strong financial solidity: in fact, in 2005 cost-income ratio was 62.5%, improved by 3.4% from 2004; in 2005, Tier 1 ratio was equal to 10.2% (and it supported ups-and-downs during the period 2003-2004) and ROE is 13.7%, with a growth from 2004 when it was equal to 10.6% (–0.6% compared with 2003).

4.3.2.4 Caisses d'Epargne

These organisms, commonly known as Caisses d'Epargne (or savings banks), are officially called Caisses d'Epargne et de Prévoyance and they distinguish themselves from the National Savings Bank managed by the French Post. Their origin is ancient: the first Caisse d'Epargne is of 1818. According to the Act 99-532 of 25 June 1999, the *sui generis* private law status of the French savings banks transformed into its cooperative status alongside the changes in their national organizational structure[39].

At present, the Caisses d'Epargne Group is structured on three levels:

- Locally, there are 440 local savings companies (Sociétés Locales d'Epargne – SLE) – that is, cooperatives, which do not directly carry out banking activity but hold 80% shares in Caisses d'Epargne (CECEI 2005). At first SLE's mission is to promote equity dispersion of savings banks on the market, thus assuring a real proximity to their local territory.

- Regionally, there are 29 savings banks (Caisses d'Epargne), with a cooperative status, which can carry out all banking activities and are entirely responsible for managing the Group's brand. These banks refund and coordinate the Group's regional sector. At least seven SLEs have to own stakes (not over 30% each one) in every savings bank.

- Nationally, there are two organisms: Fédération Nationale des Caisses d'Epargne (FNCE) and Caisse Nationale des Caisses d'Epargne (CNCE). FNCE is a professional organ in the form of association that combines all 29 regional savings banks and coordinates relationships between banks and their member-stakeholders; it defends common interests to State and internationally and defines the Group's strategies about financial supports to social and local economics (Projets d'économie locale et sociale – PELS)[40] and general interest works.

According to the Banking Act, CNCE is the central organ of the Caisses d'Epargne network, apart from the central bank of the Group. CNCE holds 20% shares in each Caisse d'Epargne, in the form of mutual investment certificates which attribute a right on earnings but not a right of voting. CNCE's equity, equal to €7.3 billion on 31 December 2005, is divided between savings banks (for 65%) and Caisse des Dépôts et Consignation (for 35%), which is the latest Group's strategic shareholder (CECEI 2005). As the Group's central organ, CNCE has to supervise the network's cohesion and good functioning, ensure the savings banks' liquidity and solvency, define products and services supply, coordinate the Caisses's commercial policy, and finally negotiate and subscribe national and international agreements on behalf of the Group. As the Group's central bank, CNCE centralizes the excess resources of regional banks and branches and acts on the financial markets on behalf of the Group, funding large corporate firms and large projects.

After the partnership agreements in 2001 and 2004 between the Caisses d'Epargne Group and Caisse des Dépôts et Consignation (CDC), CNCE became the holding of an important network of companies dealing with real estate and insurance sectors. At the end of 2005, Caisses d'Epargne Group consisted of 74 credit institutions associated to CNCE, of which 29 were savings banks, 14 banks, 28 financial companies and two specialized financial institutions (as regional development corporations). Following the acquisition of the investment bank Ixis in 2004, the Group became a big and multi-business universal bank: now it provides its 26 million clients with a wide range of investment, corporate finance and asset management solutions, and other services to investors. In 2005 the Investment Banking Division[41] of the Group contributed for 26% to consolidated net banking income and 25% to net income.

The Group's real core business is represented by the Commercial Banking Division, which contributed for 61% to consolidated net income in 2005. On the 17th November 2006, general meetings of the Caisses d'Epargne Group and Banques Populaires Group approved the creation of Natixis, which is a joint venture destined to unify both Groups' subsidiaries, specialized on Corporate & Investment Banking and other financial services. Natixis is expected to become the major financial institution in France and one of the most important Group inside the international banking sector (CECEI 2005). On 31 December 2005, the Group includes 3.1 million member-stakeholders, of which 98% are individuals and only 2% are legal persons, territorial authorities and employees. The Caisses d'Epargne network consists of 54,400 employees, 4,700 branches and over 26 million clients: in practice, one of two French individuals is a client of Caisses d'Epargne.

As it is evident from the consolidated financial statements in the years 2003–05 (see Table 4.5), there is a positive improvement of the Group's economical and patrimonial results. Specifically, the 29 Caisses d'Epargne represent historical foundation of the network and certainly contribute to the improvement of the Group's performance with their activity dedicated to local economics. In particular, consolidated net banking income increased by 4% during the period 2003-04 and 6% from 2004 to 2005. At the end of 2005, it amounted to €10,301 million, of which €5,961 million (about 58% of total net banking income) were provided by the 29 regional savings banks (+2% compared with 2004,

Table 4.5 Main indicators, and economical and dimensional results of the Caisses d'Epargne Group

Dimensional results	2003	2004	2005
Regional banks	32	29	29
Branches	4,700	4,700	4,700
Employees	44,700	52,800	54,400
Member-stakeholders	3,000,000	3,100,000	3,100,000
Clients	26,000,000	26,000,000	26,000,000
Economical results (€ million)	**2003**	**2004**	**2005**
Net banking income	9,335	9,742	10,301
Gross operating income	2,599	2,595	2,758
Net income, Group share	1,375	1,656	2,071
Customer deposits	202,835	214,103	218,416
Loans and advances to customers	168,565	188,501	202,421
Total assets	487,780	543,911	594,132
Shareholders' equity, Group share	16,611	18,022	19,416
Tier 1 Capital	14,527	18,396	18,994
Indicators	**2003**	**2004**	**2005**
Cost-income ratio	72.2%	73.4%	73.2%
ROE	10.9%	10.0%	11.9%
Tier 1 ratio	9.6%	10.1%	9.6%

Source: Caisses d'Epargne Group's Rapport Annuel (2003, 2004, 2005).

despite the adverse period for term savings passbooks). Instead, the gross operating income of the Group was rather steady for the period 2003-04, then improved (+6%) and at the end of 2005 it amounted to €2,758 million, over 72% of which (€1,989 million) are provided by the 29 Caisses d'Epargne (+3% in relation to 2004). But during the period 2003-05 the most significant improvement was related to the consolidated net income (+20% from 2003 to 2004, and +25% in the years 2004-05), amounting to €2,071 million at the end of 2005, over 70% of which were provided by savings banks (that is, €1,467 million, +20% compared with 2004).

Total assets of the Group were equal to €543,911 million in 2004 (+11.5% in relation to 2003) and €594,132 million at the end of 2005 (+9% compared with 2004). The Caisses d'Epargne Group is the fourth banking group in France for shareholders' equity, amounting to €19.4 billion in 2005 (+8% in relation to 2004, and +8.5% from 2003 to 2004). Moreover, Tier 1 ratio was equal to 9.6% in 2005. In regards to the profitability and efficiency indicators of the Group, both cost-income ratio and ROE worsened in 2004 compared with 2003, but improved in 2005: in fact, at the end of 2005, ROE was equal to 11.9% (+1.9% in relation to 10% in 2004) and cost-income ratio is 73.2% (–0.2% compared with 2004). Finally, at the end of 2005 we observe a considerable profitability of the Commercial Banking Division, equal to 16%; on the contrary, cost-income ratio of the same division was 74% in 2005 (but, inside the division, cost-income ratio of the 29 regional Caisses d'Epargne was equal to 66.6%, with a decrease by 0.6% in relation to 2004), while cost-income ratio of the Investment Banking Division was 69.6%.

4.4 Main conclusions: a comparative analysis

Changes in financial markets, both on the supply-side and demand-side, offer new challenges for all banks, especially the cooperatives. Growing integration in the European financial markets produces more competitive banking structures in the face of globalization with considerable benefits to clients. Therefore, the banking consolidation process ought to improve the banks' different "models", and favour the natural interlocutors of customers' determined segments; for example, in the case of cooperative banks, it is the relationships with SMEs and families. As Fratta Pasini observed, during the "1st Convention on Co-operative Banks in Europe" organized by the EACB (European Association of Co-operative Banks) on 1 December 2005 in Brussels: «European co-operative banks, in order to widen their own efficiency and vitality further on, would continue to adapt themselves to legal, technological and market changes, and keep their own localism's business model, that is a model in which a "patient" capital, i.e. free from immediate aims of profitability's maximization, and as an expression of a democratic governance in bank, becomes an instrument to achieve significant economical and social results for the whole community, through intense and lasting relationships with all stakeholders» (Fratta Pasini 2005).

Moreover, international rating agencies recognize that cooperative banks are financially sound and good managed. Not only does this helps them to stabilize the European financial system and make it more competitive, but it is also the solution by which they can constructively contribute to its dynamic modernization and a complete restructuring (EACB 2005). In particular, agencies like Standard & Poor's and Moody's and FitchRatings believe that differences in the bank's organizational approach and decentralization level (centralized structures on two or three levels) definitely have an impact on the methodological approach they adopt to estimate the cooperative banks' rating (Le Bras 2005). But should each network be considered as a unique bank or as a set of different and more or less independent local banks? Ratings' assignment would be facilitated by packages of reciprocal securities among banks associated with the same cooperative network, inside which each bank has to ensure liquidity and solvency for all the other associates (Dalmaz-De Toytot 2002).

In this case, all the associate banks have the same rating ("of group"), since it reflects the cooperative group's dependability on the whole. For example, regional banks of Crédit Agricole have the same rating of Crédit Agricole S.A. Instead, if banks of the same cooperative network do not adopt reciprocal security's schemes, rating agencies examine other elements, and this could cause significant differences of rating among banks of the same group. So, we outline the principal credit ratings of the French cooperative banking groups as follows (see Table 4.6). For each international rating agency, we respectively indicate the long-term rating, outlook, and short-term rating. As we have previously observed, in the last 20 years, the French banks' combination process was considerable and led to the reduction of banks to more than half, especially in the case of mutual and cooperative banks, which decreased from 663 in 1984 to 124 in 2005 (−81.3%).

Since 1996, even mutual and cooperative banks are involved in the general restructuring process of the French banking sector. In regards to the cooperative sector, this process is two-fold in that it involves grouping local and regional banks around a same central organ in order to optimize the group's organization as well as exploiting a wealth of resources to productively diversify and externally grow the group. Both processes were realized by distribution agreements and M&As (see Table 4.7), apart from the *ex novo* establishment of apposite organisms (CECEI 2005).

But even if the aggregation, external growth and internal rationalization processes of the French cooperative banking sector implied a substantial

Table 4.6 Credit ratings of the French cooperative banking groups

	Standard & Poor's	Moody's	FitchRatings
Banques Populaires	AA− /stable/A1+	Aa3/stable/P1	A+/stable/F1
Crédit Agricole	AA− /positive/A1+	Aa2/stable/P1	AA/stable/F1+
Crédit Mutuel	A+/positive/A1	Aa3/stable/P1	AA− /stable/F1+
Caisses d'Epargne	AA−/stable/A1+	Aa2/stable/P1	AA/stable/F1+

Source: official data, updated December 2006.

Table 4.7   Main M&As concerned with the French cooperative banking networks

	1996/1997	1998/1999	2000/2001	2002/2003	2004/2005
Banques Populaires		**1999** Take-over of *Natexis*		**2003** Mergers of *Crédit Cooperatif* and *Crédit Maritime*	
Crédit Agricole	**1996** Take-over of *Banque Indosuez*		**2001** First listing of *Crédit Agricole S.A.*	**2002** Take-over bid on *Crédit Lyonnais* (privatized in 1999) by *Crédit Agricole S.A.* **2003** Take-over of *Crédit Lyonnais* by *Crédit Agricole S.A.*	
Crédit Mutuel		**1998** Take-over of the *CIC* Group during privatization			
Caisses d'Epargne		**1999** Adoption of the cooperative status and take-over of *Crédit Foncier de France*	**2001** Establishment of a common holding, *Eulia,* for the competitive activities of *Caisses d'Epargne* and *CDC*		**2004** Take-over of *Eulia* and absorption of *CDC Ixis* by *Caisse Nationale des Caisses d'Epargne*

Source: CECEI (2005).

reduction in the number of associate credit institutions, during the last decade in France the mutual and cooperative branches' number was rather steady (from 14,906 in 1995 to 15,992 in 2005, for about 60% of total branches), and the number of cooperative banks' employees even increased (+14.3%, from 155,562 in 1995 to 177,741 in 2005), seeing that as follows (Figure 4.1).

In addition, mutual and cooperative banks' market shares for both deposits and loans (see Figure 4.2) were highly strengthened by the early 2000s. While lately the market share for deposits was reduced, the market share for loans did not increase much.

The comparison between commercial and mutual and cooperative banks would show that the loans-deposits ratio is over the unit only for commercial banks (see Figure 4.3).

Besides, in terms of the evolution of the profitability and efficiency indicators (see Figure 4.4), the cost-income ratio improved in the French banking system on the whole in the last decade. This is particularly evident in the case of commercial banks: in 2005 the cost-income ratio was 64.4% on average, decreased by 3% in relation to 2000 (67.4%) and 5.8% compared with 1995 (70.2%).

After the strong reduction's period of 1992-97, the ROE of the whole French banking sector has been steadily over 10% since 1998: in 2005 ROE was 11.9% on average, increased from 9.8% in 2000 (+2.1%) and 1.1% in 1995 (+10.8%). The French banking system has a significant place internationally: in 2005 the French banking groups were amongst the hundred banking groups worldwide. In regards to the cooperative credit sector, Crédit Agricole is the only French mutual banking group among the first ten world groups – being sixth – with its total equity's amounting to $60.6 billion, and it

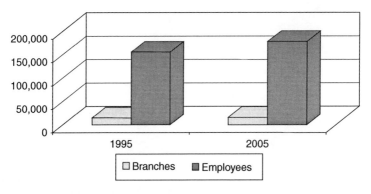

Figure 4.1 Evolution in the number of branches and employees in the French cooperative banking sector
Source: Banque de France (1995, 2005).

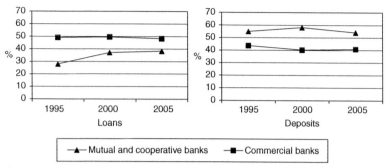

Figure 4.2   Market shares for deposits and loans: a comparison
Source: Banque de France (1995, 2000, 2005).

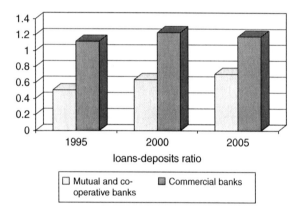

Figure 4.3   Evolution in the loans-deposits ratio
Source: Banque de France (1995, 2000, 2005).

is the second in Europe. Among the other French cooperative banks, Crédit Mutuel is number 25 worldwide (with over $23 billion), Caisses d'Epargne is 26th, and Banques Populaires is just below (The Banker 2006).

In conclusion, we propose a comparative analysis of the four French cooperative banking groups in relation to their main results on 31 December 2005 (see Table 4.8).

Crédit Agricole is distinguished within the French cooperative credit system on the basis of its performance: as above-mentioned, it is sixth worldwide for its total equity amount. Its cooperative structure

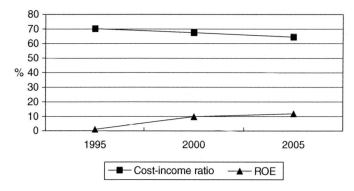

Figure 4.4 Evolution in the profitability and efficiency indicators in the French banking system
Source: Commission Bancaire (1995, 2000, 2005).

includes 2,583 local banks, which, grouped together in 41 regional banks,[42] provide a wide range of banking and financial products and services, by its 7,142 branches with financial subsidiaries of the holding Crédit Agricole S.A.

Regional banks have a fundamental role in almost all the French retail banking areas: they have a market share by 24% for individuals (about 16.1 million clients) and 34% for SMEs (Banque de France 2005). Moreover, the regional banks of the Crédit Agricole network substantially contribute to the Group's results: specifically, in 2005 regional banks contributed for over 47% (that is, €12,255 million) to consolidated net banking income and for 52% (that is, €4,993 million) to gross operating income; their net income amounted to €2,816 million – that is, 47% of the Group's total net income. In 2005 the Crédit Agricole Group granted over 45% (that is, €455,380 million) of all loans to the private sector by the four French cooperative networks. This is due to the consumer credit and retail banking sectors of the regional banks and Crédit Lyonnais, as well as the corporate & investment banking sector of Calyon. The Crédit Agricole Group's deposits to the private sector, which amounted to €397,860 million (that is, over 45% of all deposits to the private sector by the four French cooperative networks) at the end of 2005, were mainly formed by current accounts and savings deposits of the regional banks and Crédit Lyonnais.

Moreover, at the end of 2005, the total assets of the Group amounted to €1,170,349 million. This was much better than the other French mutual and cooperative networks. Regional banks provided no less

Table 4.8   The French cooperative credit system on 31 December 2005

	Banques Populaires	Crédit Agricole	Crédit Mutuel	Caisses d'Epargne	ALL
Regional banks	19	41	18	29	107
Local banks	–	2,583	1,920	440	4,943
Branches	2,807	9,072	5,022	4,700	21,601
Employees	45,530	136,848	57,000	54,400	293,778
Member-stakeholders	3,100,000	5,700,000	6,700,000	3,100,000	18,600,000
Clients	6,800,000	21,000,000	14,200,000	26,000,000	68,000,000
Total assets (€ million)	288,711	1,170,349	436,390	594,132	2,489,582
Market share for assets (% of ALL)	11.60%	47.01%	17.53%	23.86%	100.00%
Deposits (€ million)	104,483	397,860	148,230	218,416	868,989
Market share for deposits (% of ALL)	12.03%	45.78%	17.06%	25.13%	100.00%
Loans (€ million)	146,603	455,380	188,407	202,421	992,811
Market share for loans (% of ALL)	14.76%	45.87%	18.98%	20.39%	100.00%
Cost-income ratio (%)	65.4%	63.1%	62.5%	73.2%	66%*
ROE (%)	13.5%	15.8%	13.7%	11.9%	13.7%*
Tier 1 ratio (%)	8.5%	7.9%	10.2%	9.6%	9%*

* Average value.
Source: Different cooperative banks' Annual Reports (2005).

than 28% of the total assets – that is, €323,565 million. In addition, the cost-income ratio of the whole Group was 63.1% in 2005, and the cost-income ratio of the regional banks was 59.3% (–0.5% compared with 2004). Finally, in 2005 the best level of profitability in the cooperative banking system is achieved by Crédit Agricole, whose ROE is 15.8%.

Under the Crédit Agricole Group's performance, there are 29 Caisses d'Epargne, i.e. cooperative banks deeply rooted on the regional level. They are the third banking network in France with their 4,337 branches, 5,920 ATMs, and 26 million clients. Saving banks are dynamic actors of local economics. Together with the other banks of the Caisses d'Epargne Group, they provide an extensive range of products and services adapting to all the specific needs of customers. They strive to offer the best products and services for each need, ranging from asset management, lending, and payment instruments to real estate financing and insurance.

The Caisses d'Epargne Group is a specialized bank in regional development with a decentralized banking structure. It is active in the social sector by acting in a strict contact with local authorities, public health sector, real estate companies, and local organizations; and providing them with several products and services to finance their projects, simplify their management, and maximize their investments. The Group has also an essential role in the public-private-partnership (PPP). As a bank based on solidarity and social commitment, the Caisses d'Epargne Group contributes to social cohesion by developing social and local economics' projects (PELS)[43] and working against all forms of dependence and social exclusion by founding a basis for social solidarity (Foundation Caisses d'Epargne pour la Solidarité). The 29 Caisses d'Epargne represent a historical foundation of the network. Despite the worse remuneration of term savings passbooks, in 2005 the net banking income of regional savings banks increased by 2% compared with 2004 and amounted to €5,961 million, about 58% of the whole Group's net banking income. During 2005 regional savings banks increased their lending by 7.6%, especially housing loans (+19%) and consumer credits because of the growing demands of revolving credit cards. Also deposits rose by 4.6%, despite the adverse period for life insurance and savings deposits.

Since the limited growth of operational costs (+1%) in 2005, the gross operating income of regional savings banks amounts to €1,989 million (+3% in relation to 2004), over 72% of the entire Group's result. Consequently, the cost-income ratio of the 29 Caisses d'Epargne is 66.6%, has improved by 0.6% compared with 2004 and less than 73.2% of the Group, because of the higher costs derived from the Investment Banking Division and specialized companies in asset management (Ixis AMG) above all. Therefore, on 31 December 2005 regional savings banks provided a net income equal to €1,467 million (+20% compared with 2004), which was over 70% of the whole Group's net income (that is, €2,071 million in 2005). Instead, the ROE of the Caisses d'Epargne Group (that is, 11.9% in 2005) was the worst of the four French cooperative banking networks.

The Crédit Mutuel-CIC Group, specialized in retail banking, is the third French cooperative bank: it combines strengths of Crédit Mutuel, a mutual and cooperative bank with a wide local and regional presence, with those of CIC, a commercial bank with about 40 bank-offices abroad.[44] Crédit Mutuel, the Group's central pivot, is a cooperative bank which focuses its activity on clients, who are also its member-stakeholders. (On 31 December 2005, there were respectively 10.5 million clients and 6.7 million members.)

On the basis of the Group's organizational structure, the 1,920 local banks are grouped into 18 regional federations, which subdivide their responsibilities inside a national confederation. These three levels of organization – local, regional and national – operate on a decentralized basis in accordance with the principle of subsidiarity; this means that decisions are taken as close to the actual area of implementation as possible. Local banks, which are the closest to members and clients, are thus responsible for the principal functions of bank branches, while regional federations and the national confederation deal with those functions they are not equipped to handle on their own. In 2005, Crédit Mutuel, the fifth banking group in France for its total assets, achieved a market share for deposits equal to 7.7% (and 12.3% in all, CIC included) – that is, €92,794 million – and a market share for loans by 9.4% (and 16.3% in all, CIC included), that is, €108,652 million. Moreover, in 2005 the Group has the lowest cost-income ratio (that is, 62.5%) of the four French cooperative banking networks, and its ROE is 13.7%, which is only lower than that of Crédit Agricole.

From the Annual Report of 2005, we cannot distinguish the contribution of Crédit Mutuel cooperative banks to the entire Group's economical and patrimonial results. This is because Crédit Mutuel-CIC is not listed and so it does not have to detail its balance sheet.

Finally, the 19 regional banks which are deeply linked to their local territory within the Banques Populaires Group, alongside the two national banks CASDEN Banque Populaire and Crédit Coopératif, deal with local retail banking that provides about two-third of the whole Group's net proceeds, while one-third is provided by Natexis Banques Populaires. So, with their 2,807 branches, over 3 million members and 6.8 million clients since the end of 2005, Banques Populaires are one of the best French banks for local retail banking. In particular, during 2005 in the local retail banking business of Banques Populaires (Natexis excluded) net fees and commissions from client transactions improved (+6% compared with 2004) with an increase by 4.5% of net banking income that was equal to €5,194 million on 31 December 2005 (and represented 63% of the entire Group's net banking income).

Therefore, at the end of 2005, net income provided by local retail banking business amounted to €971 million, almost 64% of total net income.

Also, the cost-income ratio of cooperative Banques Populaires was 65.2%, which was more or less homogenous to that of the Group (65.4%), with a decrease by 0.7% in relation to 2004 and one of the best of the French retail banking sector. In regards to local retail banking, at the end of 2005 loans to personal clients amounted to €97.5 billion, with a growth by 10% compared with 2004, especially due to equipment financing (+8.8%) and home loans (+13.7%). Specifically, loans to corporate and small business clients increased by 6.7% (that is, €42.8 billion), and loans to personal clients rose by 12.3% and amounted to €51.9 billion – that is, 53.3% of total loans distributed by the Group. Finally, on 31 December 2005 customer deposits for local retail banking amounted to €85.5 billion (+6.7% in relation to 2004) and, among this total, demand deposits amounted to € 33.5 billion (+11.3% compared with 2004), nearly 40% of the total. In particular, in 2005 personal deposits were equal to €52.3 billion (+6.1% in relation to 2004), while deposits to corporate and small business clients were €26.8 billion (+12.4%). Instead, retail certificates of deposit and savings bonds decreased by 8.8%, and they were €6.4 billion at the end of 2005. The cost-income ratio of the Group was 65.4% and ROE was 13.5% in 2005.

Notes

1. This paper is the result of a co-operation between the authors. In particular, Arianna Sabetta has contributed to Section 4.2, while Pietro Marchetti has contributed to Sections 4.1, 4.3 and 4.4.
2. Up until the mid 1980s, the French banking system was characterized by a great fragmentation of the banking regulation which bound banks' actions and strategies very much, contributed to the heterogeneity of banking intermediaries, and shaped banking activity as a public service.
3. Since 1972, the monetary policy tools were based on quantitative credit control techniques. After deregulation, and the Banking Act of 1984, the monthly goals of credit volumes progress were abolished and extra stocks were suppressed. In 1985, besides deposit stocks, progressive stocks on the employment in banks were introduced; furthermore, credit institutes were asked out to issue debentures in order to enhance credit supply, without causing a dilatation of the monetary mass.
4. The influence of this factor on banking and financial markets leads to financial innovation, which is a remarkable enlargement of financial products characterized by their increasing replacement and liquidity due to the financial markets development. Products innovation is also strictly related to the

evolution of management techniques, such as transformation, transfer, and financial risks coverage. Finally, information technologies lead to the development of new supply channels and banking and financial services' channels which adopt automatic desks and channel in the distance (Landi 2004).

5. The Act 92-665 of 16 July 1992 modified the Banking Act to introduce in the French juridical order the principles included in the second European directive about banks and the Act 95-597 of 2 July 1996 took in the European directive about investment services.

6. The Bank of France, Post Office and Caisse des Dépôts et Consignation (CDC) are not included in the Banking Act.

7. Since 2000, savings banks are also included; they have to use a part of their profits for social initiatives, such as solidarity, fight against social ostracism, and promotion of social saving.

8. See Fusco-Pasca 2003: 12.

9. The cooperative pole's credit institutes had a privileged access to the privatized public banks and, along with the public pole, enjoy a law about the savings products distribution that use fiscal advantages; moreover, the compensation rate is established by Authorities not taking care about market situations. The most important one is the *Livret A* distributed only by Post Office and savings banks. This special system, despite of the deep liberalization in the French banking field, represents an important factor of competition distortion.

10. For example, the relinquishment of participation in Crédit Lyonnais from State to Crédit Agricole. Observing evolutionary trends of the French banking market, we can see that the size enlargement is a strategically relevant element to sustain the competition.

11. The consequence of the interest margin reduction is the adoption by all the European banks of a strategy that privileged a profit expansion instead of a reduction in the production process and costs.

12. In fact, all the European cooperative credit systems take form in a network of banks' model. The local units of all these systems, including those that are more integrated, keep their legal autonomy and operational responsibility of the local market. But they differ in their bigger or smaller level of adopted horizontal and vertical integration, especially on the basis of economic reasons: some systems (like Rabobank in Netherlands) are organized as "groups", others (like Popular Banks and Raiffeisen Banks in Germany) as "integrated systems" with internal collaborations (Schraffl 1999).

13. Up until 2003, the Crédit Coopératif network existed, too; its 11 credit institutions were associate to Caisse Centrale de Crédit Coopératif, its central organ until 2 August 2003 (owing to the promulgation of the Act 2003-706 of 1st August 2003), and merged by Crédit Coopératif in October 2003. Credit institutions, which are associate to Caisse Centrale de Crédit Coopératif, currently benefit by an association convention with Crédit Coopératif, and so they can use of guarantee system of Banque Fédérale des Banques Populaires (CECEI 2005).

14. According to the Act 99-532 of 25 June 1999 (*Loi relative à l'épargne et à la sécurité financiére*), these credit institutions have abandoned the legal form of no-profit corporation and have adopted the cooperative model since 2000.

15. After the first UE-Directive on banking coordination of 1977, these systems modified their organizational structures to benefit regionally by obtaining banking control through the application of solvency and liquidity coefficients on a consolidated basis. In order to have banking control (by the Commission Bancaire), the 1984 Banking Act provisions for each cooperative banking groups have a responsible central organ (that is Caisse Nationale du Crédit Agricole, Confédération Nationale du Crédit Mutuel, and ex Chambre Syndicale now Banque Fédérale des Banques Populaires), and prudential coefficients on a consolidated basis applied regionally because members of these central organisms are just regional banks.

16. "Bipolarism" is imperfect for Crédit Agricole because there are no regional federations at its intermediate level.

17. Until a few years ago, mergers and acquisitions (M&A) and filialization seemed unthinkable phenomena in the cooperative sector, especially on the central level (Schraffl 2000). But nowadays, all main European cooperative groups, French included, consolidated their equity basis by the acquisition of an existing but not cooperative banking group, keeping their cooperative style as possible.

18. Those are cooperative credit companies which operate on a regional basis granting loans to their members without any limitation. Their branches and offices have legal personality.

19. Caisse d'Aide Social de l'Education Nationale (Casden) is a cooperative credit company which grants loans only to its members; that is, those subjects which operate in national education, culture and research sectors, by the regional popular banks network.

20. The system of Crédit Coopératif is made up of a number of different cooperative credit institutions: Groupe Crédit Coopératif, Sociétées financières coopératives which operate in microfinance and in favour of SMEs, and Crédit Maritime Mutuel. Groupe Crédit Coopératif which is made up of Crédit Coopératif cooperative banks (since 2003 belonging to the Banques Populaires Group), and Banque du Batiment et des Travaux Public (BTP-Banque) and other institutions specialized in specific segments of financial markets. Its aim is to promote the development of movements and companies of social economics. These are, on the one hand, cooperatives, associations, mutual companies, saving institutions, private with which individuals identify, and, on the other hand, those generally affiliated to associations and local community.

21. This is when the French Financial Security Act of 1 August 2003, in particular its Article 93, came into force.

22. In fact, Natexis-Banques Populaires and Coface are established in 68 Countries.

23. Moreover, it is the first for granting micro-loans in France.

24. The 19 Banques Populaires regional banks, strongly linked with their local territory, deal with local retail banking business, together with the two national banks, Casden and Crédit Coopératif.

25. Traditionally considered as the "green bank", Crédit Agricole enjoyed an absolute monopoly of granting soft financing to agriculture until 1988.

26. "Demutualization" is the transformation of mutual and financial organizations, specialized in mortgage credit and subject to the "one

head, one vote" principle, in business corporations subject to the rule of proportional and *pro quota* capital rights. First examples of this phenomenon date back to the 1960s, when demutualization invested all German retail cooperatives.

27. In France, the Group acquired Sofinco and Finaref, two of the most consumer credit institutions, apart from Crédit Lyonnais in 2003; in Europe the Group was an active part of the Banca Intesa creation; in Latin-America the Group took on the Banco Bisel control, the third Argentine private bank.

28. Crédit Agricole local banks were created by the Act of 5 November 1884 as the first cooperative banks in France. They are regulated by provisions of Code Rural and Code Monétaire et Financier.

29. Since the end of 2001, Crédit Agricole S.A. owns a 25% stake in each regional bank, with the exception of Caisse Régionale de Crédit Agricole Mutuel de la Corse.

30. In particular, the French metropolitan territory is divided into 95 departments, and so each regional bank has exclusive responsibility of one or more departments. Most of Banques Populaires and Federal banks of Crédit Mutuel, and a considerable number of Crédit Agricole regional banks have responsibility of more departments (CECEI 2005).

31. Created by the Act of 5 August 1920 as a public law institution controlled by State, Caisse Nationale du Crédit Agricole was privatized and mutualized in 1988; now regional banks own 73% CNCA share capital and CNCA is a listed company since 2001.

32. According to the decree 58-966 of 16 October 1958, local banks of Crédit Mutuel are obliged to adhere to one regional federation, which practises their revision by proxy of public powers; and regional federations have to adhere to a national confederation. So the Group's relationships are regulated by legal provisions, and since the beginning Crédit Mutuel takes form in a rigid bipolar system on three levels.

33. Higher loans have to be approved by the regional bank, or concerted in pool with the same one, or else transferred to the regional bank according to the subsidiarity principle.

34. Since the association, and not top bank, is responsible to national Authority, there is a sort of interests' commingling, typical of almost all the bipolar cooperative credit systems. Moreover, the informative flow among local bank, federal bank and national bank is undoubtedly more effective and quick compared with that one among local bank, regional federation and national confederation (Schraffl 1999).

35. Features of CIC are compatible with Crédit Mutuel. In fact, CIC was originally a network of private regional banks, established by regional Authorities to fund local economics, and then nationalized in 1981. So the market and managerial style of CIC is very similar to that of the cooperatives because they are based on localism. Therefore, in the future, the CIC's cooperative quality will grow stronger to make parallel these two networks that will operate on the basis of the decentralization principle, while at the same time they will be using the existing complementarities among the relative market segments (like retail banking, corporate lending, insurance), assigning wealthy private individuals and SMEs to CIC and

families, traders and craftsmen to Crédit Mutuel. CIC's local agencies will
be coordinated by its regional banks, as it was the case in the past, while
the local banks of Crédit Mutuel will be assisted by its regional banks and
federations (Schraffl 2000).
36. Outside France, Crédit Mutuel is present in Luxemburg, Belgium and
Germany, while CIC is in the UK, Luxemburg, Singapore, Switzerland and
USA.
37. French financial engineering products, regulated by the 1992 Act, can widen
the investors' number, apply private or public capital market, and assign to
some investors (members included) a right on earnings. The use of these
financial products is obviously optional and the choice depends on the
managerial decisional power. Inside Crédit Mutuel, these products were used
only in determined occasions (Pflimlin 2002).
38. From *Rapport Annuel* of 2005, we cannot observe the contribution provided
by the Crédit Mutuel cooperative banks to the entire Group's results. This
is because Crédit Mutuel-CIC is not listed and does not have to detail its
balance sheet.
39. The new cooperative status of savings banks, established by the Act 99-532,
required a wide equity base; for this reason, savings banks opened to public
the share subscription since 1 January 2000.
40. According to the Act 99-532, French saving banks created Foundation
Caisses d'Epargne pour la Solidarité. Each savings bank has to assign a part
of its excesses to PELS's funding: this is unique within the French banking
system. General features of PELS's funding are annually defined by FNCE.
Instead, CNCE fixes their technical, legal, financial and accounting methods. Finally, each savings bank defines PELS will fund. For example, PELS are
concerned with education, health, cultural patrimony, and so on (Vandone
2003). In 2005 the Group funded 2,556 PELS for a total amount of about
€51.5 million.
41. It includes IXIS Corporate & Investment Bank (IXIX CIB), IXIS Asset
Management Group (IXIS AMG), CIFG (IXIS Financial Guaranty), and
CACEIS – a joint venture established for 50% with Crédit Agricole S.A. in the
summer of 2005, which combines IXIS Investor Services and Crédit Agricole
Investor Services and deals with safekeeping, asset management and other
services to investors.
42. In the last years, the Credit Agricole Group's regional banks reduced from 94
in 1998 to 41 in 2005.
43. During 2005 Caisses d'Epargne funded 2,556 PELS, for a total amount of
about €51.5 million.
44. As above-mentioned, Crédit Mutuel Centre Est Europe took the CIC's
control by Banque Fédérative du Crédit Mutuel in 1998.

References

Banque de France (1995) *Rapport Annuel*, Paris.
Banque de France (1999) *Bulletin de la Banque de France*, no. 61, Janvier, Paris.
Banque de France (2000) *Rapport Annuel*, Paris.
Banque de France (2005) *Rapport Annuel*, Paris.

Banque de France (2006) *Bulletin de la Banque de France*, no. 151, Juillet, Paris.

CECEI – Comité des Établissements de Crédit et des Entreprises d'Investissement (2004) *Rapport Annuel*, Paris.

CECEI – Comité des Établissements de Crédit et des Entreprises d'Investissement (2005) *Rapport Annuel*, Paris.

Commission Bancaire (1995) *Rapport Annuel*, Paris.

Commission Bancaire (2000) *Rapport Annuel*, Paris.

Commission Bancaire (2002) *Rapport Annuel*, Paris.

Commission Bancaire (2005) *Rapport Annuel*, Paris.

Crespi F., Rossi S. (2005) "Sistemi finanziari esteri e modelli organizzativi: il caso della Germania, della Spagna e della Francia", in S. De Angeli (a cura di), *Banca universale o gruppo creditizio?* Roma: Bancaria Editrice, pp. 149–203.

Dalmaz S., De Toytot A. (2002) "Le banche cooperative europee continuano ad evolversi", *Cooperazione di credito*, no. 176/177, pp. 279–291.

De Bruyn R., Ferri G. (2005) "Le ragioni delle banche popolari: motivi teorici ed evidenze empiriche", *DISEFIN Working Papers*, no. 1/2005, Genova.

Di Salvo R. (2002) "La 'governance' des systèmes bancaires mutualistes et coopératifs en Europe", *Revue d'Economie Financière*, no. 67, pp. 165–179.

Di Salvo R., Schraffl I. (2002) "La *governance* cooperativa: modelli strutturali e funzionali dei sistemi creditizi cooperativi europei", *Cooperazione di credito*, no. 175, pp. 7–49.

EACB – European Association of Cooperative Banks (2005) *Activities Report*, Brussels.

ECB – European Central Bank (2005) *EU Banking structures*, October, Frankfurt.

ECB – European Central Bank (2006) *EU Banking structures*, October, Frankfurt.

FBF – Fédération Bancaire Française (2005), *Rapport Annuel*, Paris.

Filosa R. (2006) "Stile di vigilanza e struttura finanziaria," in M. De Cecco, G. Nardozzi (a cura di), *Banche e finanza nel futuro: Europa, Stati Uniti e Asia*, Roma: Bancaria Editrice, pp. 219–31.

Fratta Pasini C. (2005) *Co-operative values and local development in Europe*, EACB Convention, 1 December, Brussels.

Fusco G., Pasca P. (2003) "Il sistema creditizio francese", *Quaderni di ricerche dell'Ente per gli Studi Monetari, Bancari e Finanziari Luigi Einaudi*, n. 41, Roma.

Giraudo A. (1986) "Cinque grandi sfide per il sistema bancario francese", *Bancaria*, no. 9, pp. 49–51.

Giraudo A. (1987) "Le privatizzazioni in Francia come sfida per il sistema bancario", *Bancaria*, no. 1, pp. 33–34.

Group of Ten (2001) *Report on consolidation in the financial sector*, January, Basel-Washington, DC.

Groupe Banques Populaires (2003) *Rapport Annuel*, Paris.

Groupe Banques Populaires (2004) *Rapport Annuel*, Paris.

Groupe Banques Populaires (2005) *Rapport Annuel*, Paris.

Groupe Caisses d'Epargne (2003) *Rapport Annuel*, Paris.

Groupe Caisses d'Epargne (2004) *Rapport Annuel*, Paris.

Groupe Caisses d'Epargne (2005) *Rapport Annuel*, Paris.

Groupe Crédit Agricole (2003) *Rapport Annuel*, Paris.

Groupe Crédit Agricole (2004) *Rapport Annuel*, Paris.

Groupe Crédit Agricole (2005) *Rapport Annuel*, Paris.
Groupe Crédit Mutuel (2003) *Rapport Annuel*, Paris.
Groupe Crédit Mutuel (2004) *Rapport Annuel*, Paris.
Groupe Crédit Mutuel (2005) *Rapport Annuel*, Paris.
Guinnane T. (1997) "Motivazioni ed ispirazione originaria delle cooperative di credito: il modello Raiffeisen", *Cooperazione di credito*, no. 156/157, pp. 185–207.
IMF (1999) "France – Selected issues", *IMF Staff Country Report*, no. 99/139, May, Washington, DC.
Labye A., Lagoutte C., Renversez F. (2002) "Banques mutualistes et systèmes financiers: une analyse comparative Allemagne, Grande-Bretagne, France", *Revue d'Économie Financière*, no. 67, pp. 85–109.
Landi A. (2004) "I nuovi assetti del sistema bancario europeo e le dinamiche concorrenziali", *Cooperazione di credito*, no. 183/184, pp. 29–43.
Le Bras A. (2005) *European cooperative banking groups: a ratings perspective*, EACB Convention, 1 December, Brussels.
Le Scornet D. (2002) "L'évolution récente et l'avenir du mutualisme dans le domaine de la santé en France", *Revue d'Economie Financière*, no. 67, pp. 199–210.
Martin H. (1996) "L'evoluzione del settore bancario in Francia: situazione e prospettive", *Studi e Note di Economia*, no. 3, pp. 91–122.
Noyer C. (2003) *Présentation du Rapport Annuel de la Commission Bancaire pour 2003*, Paris.
Noyer C. (2004) *Présentation du Rapport Annuel de la Commission Bancaire pour 2004*, Paris.
Pflimlin E. (2002) "La formazione del capitale proprio nel Crédit Mutuel", *Cooperazione di credito*, no. 178, pp. 373–380.
Pflimlin E. (2005) "L'engagement du Crédit Mutuel dans le microcrédit", *IRU-Courier*, no. 2, pp. 23–27.
Piot B. (1997) "Il sistema delle relazioni tra le banche di credito cooperativo e i soci: il quadro normativo europeo", *Cooperazione di credito*, no. 156/157, pp. 209–222.
Pleister C. (2005) *Cooperative banks in the Europe of 25*, EACB Convention, 1 December, Brussels.
Revell J. (1995) "L'efficienza e il ruolo delle istituzioni centrali nel sistema del credito cooperativo", *Cooperazione di credito*, no. 148, pp. 345–356.
Rinella A. (1996) "Soci e mezzi propri nelle cooperative di credito di alcuni paesi europei. Il quadro di riferimento normativo", *Cooperazione di credito*, no. 154, pp. 649–675.
Schmidt R.H., Hackethal A., Tyrell M. (2001) "The Convergence of Financial Systems in Europe", *Working Paper series: Finance & Accounting*, no. 75, Frankfurt.
Schraffl I. (1995) "La politica di rete delle banche cooperative europee", *Cooperazione di credito*, no. 147, pp. 49–59.
Schraffl I. (1998) "Aspetti strutturali e funzionali delle federazioni nazionali di alcuni sistemi creditizi cooperativi", *Cooperazione di credito*, no. 160/161, pp. 503–544.
Schraffl I. (1999) "Modelli di integrazione dei sistemi bancari cooperativi", *Cooperazione di credito*, no. 164/165, pp. 303–331.

Schraffl I. (2000) "Quando chi acquista è una banca cooperativa", *Rivista delle banche di credito cooperativo*, no. 1/2, pp. 84–85.

The Banker (2006) *The top 1000 world banks*, London.

UNACC (2004) *Banca Cooperativa y Economía Social en Europa*, Madrid.

Vandone D. (2003) "Le banche di credito cooperativo in Francia e in Spagna", *Cooperazione di credito*, no. 182, pp. 469–473.

5
The Peculiarity of the UK Case: Mutual Building Societies

Valeria Stefanelli

5.1 Introduction

In regards to European cooperative credit, the English situation is the most diverse when considering the prevailing cooperative model that is on the market and the resulting competitive solutions it has implemented. The cooperative sector in the UK is that of mutual building societies, a particular category of reciprocal financial enterprises specialized in lending mortgages and subject to the "one man – one vote" principle. These building societies are governed by a special single text, even if they have substantially the same functions as banks. In recent years, the greater competitiveness of the financial markets and the changes in the regulatory framework have led to the demutualization of the majority of the mutual building societies, which resulted in a change in their structure.

The second section of this chapter describes the origins and the main characteristics of mutual building companies in the UK with reference to specific regulations. It highlights their differences from commercial banks. The third section focuses on the reasons behind building societies' decision to demutalize and its impact on the cooperative sector whose more than two-thirds have implemented demutualization since the 1980s. The fourth section of the chapter is an account of the state of the art of mutual building societies in the UK with which this chapter concludes.

5.2 The origins and main characteristics of the mutual building Societies

In the British Isles, cooperative banking has a different institutional model to that of Europe. It is made up of mutual building societies created in the eighteenth century and associated with a revivalist Christian movement that became popular among the working class and the lower middle class segments of society (Fonteyne 2007). In the UK, the term building society first arose in the eighteenth century from working men's cooperative savings groups. By pooling savings, members could buy or build their own homes. The original building society was formed in Birmingham in 1774. Most shut down when all their members had a house. The last building society closed at the end of the 1980s (Heffernan 2003).

In the early nineteenth century, a new form of building society came into being: it is the permanent Building Societies that continually took in new members as previous building's form. The main legislative framework for the Building Society was the Building Society Act of 1874, with subsequent amending legislation in 1894, 1939 and 1960.[1] During the period of greater development, hundreds of building societies were on the English market; there was at least one in almost every city offering its members financial support house buying. In subsequent decades, the number of building societies gradually decreased as a result of the process of concentration of the market which has produced significantly larger building societies through the merging of the smaller ones. Box 5.1 contains an historical overview of Building Societies in the seventeenth and eighteenth centuries.

Box 5.1 The history of building societies in the seventeenth and eighteenth centuries

The first known society was Richard Ketley's, at the Golden Cross Inn, Birmingham. The earliest societies were 'terminating', and wound-up when all their members had been housed. They were confined to the Midlands and the North of England.

The Jubilee of the industry: there are over 250 societies in existence throughout the country.

The Great Reform Act, which extended the franchise to owners of property worth 40 shillings a year, resulted in a rapidly increased growth of the industry.

The first legislation dealing specifically with the industry was the Regulation of Benefit Building Societies Act, which officially recognized societies for the first time. It came about partly because the Government wished to encourage building society saving – the Savings Bank rate of 4.5%, subsidized by the Treasury, had proved embarrassingly expensive. A barrister was appointed to certify societies' rules and offer advice. Later he became known as the Chief Registrar of Friendly Societies.

Societies began to accept savings from members who were not necessarily potential home owners.

James Henry James produced a leaflet, which outlined a new idea for "permanent" building societies. The first known permanent society was The Metropolitan Equitable.

The Liverpool and London Building Society Protection Associations were formed, to safeguard the industry from increasing legislation designed to extract more tax revenue from the industry. There are over 750 societies in existence in London and 2000 in the provinces.

The Royal Commission on Friendly Societies included building societies in its enquiries. Many had retained the features of members balloting for loans, thus attracting gamblers as well as genuine house-buyers.

The Commission's Report, plus amendments from the Association, resulted in the Building Societies Act. The Chief Registrar's Report on Friendly Societies now included a separate annual section on building societies.

A Building Societies Act dealing with the question of arbitration was passed, enabling societies to take erring members to court rather than employing arbitrators.

The spectacular collapse of the largest building society in the country (The Liberator Permanent Benefit) due to the financial activities of its founder.

Source: Caledonia Centre for Social Development (2001).

5.3 The choice of demutualization of the building societies: motivations and effects

Due to demutualization of one third of the building societies in the 1980s, a long process of change has begun. Box 5.2 contains a historical overview of Building Societies in the nineteenth and twentieth centuries.

Box 5.2 The history of building societies in the nineteenth and twentieth centuries

There are 1723 societies with 626,000 members and total assets of over £76 million. The Building Societies Protection Association was renamed into The Building Societies Association with 310 member-societies.

A split in the industry caused by the 'Code of Ethics' resulted in the Association being wound up and the formation of a new Building Societies Association, but with a splinter group called the National Federation of Building Societies.

The Building Societies Act, passed with the cooperation of the Association and the Government, restricted the mortgage security that building societies could accept. The Building Societies Act, ensuring liquid funds were both liquid and safe, increased the power of the Chief Registrar and restricted size of loans, particularly to corporate bodies.

The Building Societies Act – a consolidation of all previous legislation – proved too restrictive in the 1980s.

The New Building Societies Act gave wider powers to societies in the field of housing and personal banking services, and established the Building Societies Commission as societies' regulator.

Abbey National passes a resolution enabling it to convert to plc. and have a bank status. This was an option given under the Building Societies Act 1986. From July 1989 the Abbey National is no longer a building society.

A new central trade body for mortgage lending institutions was established in 1989. The Council of Mortgage Lenders was promoted by four trade bodies – the Association of Mortgage Lenders, the Association of British Insurers, The Building Societies Association and the Finance Houses Association – with the BSA withdrawing from most mortgage and housing matters.

Cheltenham & Gloucester Building Society converted to plc and obtained bank status. They became part of the Lloyds Bank Group – the first example of a society using the provisions in the 1986 Act to be taken over by an existing organization.

In March, the Building Societies Act 1997, which made substantive amendments to but did not replace the Building Societies Act of 1986, was enacted. The 1997 Act introduced a more flexible operating regime for societies. It increased the powers of the Building Societies Commission in line with the new powers granted to societies and included a package of measures to increase the accountability of building societies' boards to their members.

The industry's largest society, Halifax Building Society, converted to plc and obtained bank status along with four other societies.

Legislation changed to increase the number of members required to propose a resolution for consideration at an annual general meeting, nominate a candidate for director, and require a special general meeting.

The Financial Services and Markets Act of 2000 – providing for a single legislative framework for regulation of financial services in the UK – came into force on 1 December 2001. The Financial Services Authority became societies' regulator and substantive amendments were made to the Building Societies Act of 1986

Source: Caledonia Centre for Social Development (2001).

Demutualization is the process by which a customer-owned mutual organization changes its legal form to that of a shareholder-owned company, which is usually a listed joint-stock company. As part of the demutualization process, members of a mutual organization usually receive a "windfall" payout as shares in the successor company, as cash payment or as a mixture of both. Some authors identify increasing competition in the retail financial market, the crisis of real estate and deregulations as some of the reasons underlying the choice of demutualization of building societies (Pflimlin 1998; Coles 1999).

Firstly, the diversification strategy implemented by the various financial countries has increased competitiveness by reducing the competitive advantages resulting from the specialization of the sector. At the same time, the productive diversification has increased the complexity of the products, which are divided ever more into derivatives, with a loss of immediacy in buying choices for the clients. Moreover, the distribution process of more complex financial products requires that financial intermediaries invest higher sums when choosing the sales and customer assistance channels. Secondly, the recession period that in the 1990s characterized the real estate market, such as the business area typical of building societies, contributed to worsening the conditions of the economic survival of the these societies on the market.[2]

In this context, British banking laws changed to enable building societies to offer the same banking services of normal banks. The management of a number of societies still felt that they were unable to compete with banks, and as a result of these concerns a new Building Society Act passed allowing building societies to demutualize. If more than 75% of members voted in favor, the building society would then become a limited company and members' mutual rights would be exchanged for shares in this new company. A number of the larger societies made such proposals to their members and were all accepted.[3]

Demutualization gave building societies' members the opportunity to benefit from the conversion of the mutual organizations into shareholder-owned companies (Schraffl 1999). It is important to look into some empirical studies, which aim to evaluate the impact of demutualization on building societies (Fonteyne 2007). For example, Mercer Oliver Wyman (2003) finds that demutualized building societies in the UK significantly decreased their cost-to-asset ratios two years after demutualization. His analysis, however, does not indicate whether this really reflects improved efficiency or is merely the mathematical result of faster balance sheet growth after demutualization and a switch to a different business model. Davis (2001) argues that demutualization is much more favourable to older members than to younger ones because the value of future benefits offered by the cooperative is much higher for the latter. Shiwakoti (2005) finds that the demutualization of building societies in the UK appears to have led to faster growth in management compensation without a corresponding improvement in management performance. Lastly, some authors stress that the process of demutualization should not be interpreted as a means to eliminate from the market an outdated business model. Rather, they argue, substantial changes are needed in order to revitalize the market of building societies and overcome the shortcomings in the governance mechanisms that have traditionally characterize this sector (Llewellyn 1999).

5.4 The mutual building societies in UK

Building societies are organizations, owned by their members, which pay interest on deposits and lend money on the security of property to enable members to buy their own homes. In the UK, mutual building societies are represented by the Building Societies Association (BSA) and are registered and regulated by the Financial Services Authority. There are 59 building societies in the UK. During the last ten years, the number of building societies decreased due to 18 mergers concluded inside the market (BSA 2007).

The main legislative framework for the UK building society is The Building Societies Act of 1986, which gave building societies what, at the time, was a completely new legal framework compared to the initial comprehensive building society legislation in 1874. That Act has been subsequently amended on numerous occasions, and was substantively revised by the Building Societies Act of 1997 and by the Financial Services and Markets Act of 2000 (BSA 2003).

The amended 1986 Act sets out detailed provisions in relation to the constitution of building societies, limits on raising funds from sources other than individuals and lending other than fully granted by residential property, and restrictions on powers, management of building societies, accounts and audit, mergers, and transfers of business. The 2000 Act includes in regards to building societies, provisions for the powers of the Financial Services Authority, regulated activities, authorization and permission, approved persons, rules and guidance (BSA 2003).[4]

The Building Societies Act defines a building society as a "mutual institution"; this means that most people who have a savings account or mortgage are members and have certain rights to vote and receive information, as well as to attend and speak at meetings. Each member has one vote, regardless of how much money he has invested or borrowed or how many accounts he might have. Each building society has a board of directors who run the society and who are responsible for setting its strategy (BSA 2008a).

As explained by the Building Societies Association, people and institutions investing in building societies can be divided into two categories: the depositor and the investing member (or shareholder). Depositors are not members of the society and have no say in its running. Shareholders, as members, have the right to receive information on the activity of the society, including the summary financial statement, and notification of the annual general meeting and any special general meeting. Shareholders can vote in elections for the board of directors, attend annual general and other meetings and, providing that the correct procedures are followed, propose motions or stand for election themselves.

Depositors are not members of the society and have few of the rights of shareholders. Depositors for example, need not be notified of the annual general meeting as they are not entitled to attend that meeting or vote on matters under consideration. Also depositors are not automatically sent a copy of the summary financial statement, although generally copies of this document are available from societies on request. Theoretically, depositors enjoy a greater level of security than shareholders, although in practical terms this distinction is largely irrelevant. In the extremely unlikely event of a building society becoming insolvent, depositors will receive all of their money back before any distribution is made to shareholders. If there is a shortfall of funds shareholders will bear this shortfall rather than depositors.[5]

Building societies are different from banks, which are companies (normally listed on the stock market) and are therefore owned by their shareholders. Societies have no external shareholders requiring dividends and are not companies. This normally enables them to run on lower costs and offer cheaper mortgages, better rates of interest on savings and better levels of service than their competitors. The other major difference between building societies and banks is that there is a limit to the proportion of their funds that building societies can raise from the wholesale money markets. A building society may not raise more than 50% of its funds from the wholesale markets. The average proportion of funds raised by building societies from the wholesale markets is 30% (BSA 2008b).

About 15 million adults have building society savings accounts and over 2 million adults are currently buying their own homes with the help of building society loans. Building societies have diversified in recent years and a number of services now offer, among others, current accounts, credit cards, cash machines, travel money, unsecured loans, and various types of insurance and estate agency services. So, actually, building societies compete with banks for most banking services especially mortgage lending and deposit accounts. Building societies have total assets of just under €475 billion and, with their subsidiaries, hold residential mortgages of around €365 billion, approximately 20% of the total outstanding in the UK. Societies hold just under €307 billion of retail deposits, accounting for about 20% of all such deposits in the UK. Building societies employ over 50,000 full and part-time staff and operate through more than 2,100 branches in 2007 (BSA 2008a).[6]

Building societies frequently appear in the best buy tables for mortgages and savings products. This is because they are owned by their customers, so they do not have to pay dividends to shareholders. They can therefore offer more attractive rates of interest.

Building societies support local projects and communities with different activities; as for example financial education and volunteer and charitable work. Financial education involves the support advertising within newsletters, programmes or handbooks for villages, clubs and groups, sponsorships of events or groups and organizations, and donations towards events or the purchase of equipment for use within the community. Accordingly, volunteer and charitable work entails holding functions during the Christmas season such as mince pie and sherry/coffee mornings, visits from Father Christmas for children, and fancy dress days.

The GFK NOP Financial Research Survey, which is independent research commissioned by the Building Societies Association, shows that building societies provide better service and higher customer satisfaction than other financial service providers. The Survey found that at building societies, 71% of savers were extremely or very satisfied, compared to just 56% of people saving with all other institutions. When it comes to mortgages, 72% of customers were extremely or very satisfied of building societies, versus 62% who said the same of other providers. It shows evidence of an additional way that building societies return the benefits of their mutual structure to the customers that own them – through higher levels of service. Customers who experience poor service or uncompetitive rates at their financial service provider should be aware that building societies tend to offer a fairer, more trustworthy and more satisfying alternative that is also better value for money (BSA Customer Service Survey 2007).

Therefore, in 2007, building societies have enjoyed another strong year as high interest rates and attractive products have encouraged people to save with societies. The continuing economic uncertainty and volatility in stock markets have provided further incentives to put money in cash savings. Building societies had net receipts of €1,142 million in February 2007, and this showed an increase of 72% by the same month the following year. Conversely, net lending by building societies is down compared to this same time last year; this suggests that the lower levels of activity in the housing market reported for 2007 may be continuing into 2008 (BSA 2008a).

5.5 Conclusion

The aim of this paper is to present the characteristics of the cooperative banking sector in the UK, through an historical survey of the driving forces behind the birth of the cooperative movement and the typical developments of the present market environment. Generally speaking, the UK cooperative credit sector is very particular, compared to its European counterpart, and can be identified in terms of its size in the building society segment, which consists of organizations owned by their members that pay interest on deposits and lend money on the security of property to enable members to buy their own homes.

Building societies are different from banks, which are companies (normally listed on the stock market), and are therefore owned by their shareholders. Building societies have no external shareholders requiring dividends and are not companies. This normally enables them to run on lower costs and offer cheaper mortgages, better rates of interest on savings, and better levels of service than their competitors. The other major difference between building societies and banks is that there is a limit to the proportion of their funds that building societies can raise from the wholesale money markets.

Building societies originally appeared to meet the financial requirements of local communities (most frequently for geographical or professional reasons), offering a number of advantages to their members (for example, subsidized loans for first-time home buyers). In any case, the importance of building societies increased significantly over the years, thanks to the existence of a supportive regulatory environment up until the end of the 19th century. They remained small establishments, so as to prevent the dilution of the notion of common interest and its ensuing advantages; however, they offer a diversified range of products such as current accounts, credit cards, cash machines, travel money, unsecured loans, and various types of insurance and estate agency services. Building societies compete with banks for most banking services especially mortgage lending and deposit accounts.

Increased competition on the lending market – in the wake of globalization and financial innovation trends – and the transformation of the regulatory framework have driven a number of building societies to take the path of demutualization, thus inevitably leading to the downsizing of the sector. Besides those who justify the decision by building societies to demutualize (purely to ensure more favourable economic and financial conditions for their members), there are also several authors who propose not to interpret this choice as a solution for getting rid of the building societies' competitive lending model and recommend the introduction of substantial changes to revitalize their market.

Notes

1. A "terminating" society is one "which by its rules is to terminate at a fixed date, or when a result specified in its rules is attained"; a "permanent" society is one "which does not have among its rules a fixed date or specified result by when is to terminate". For further details on the specific case of building societies see the Building Society Act of 1874.
2. Factors leading to the recession of the real estate market can be found in the reduced public means of purchasing the first house, the preference of the market to rent rather than to buy, the falling birth rate. and the resulting decrease in number of potential first house buyers (see Coles 1999).
3. Coles (1999) describes the Bradford & Bingley Building Society's story on its conversion in 2000. Heffernan (2003) reports some information about demutualized building societies which occurred from 1989 to 2002.
4. For any other details on the amended Building Societies Act, see BSA (2003), The Building Societies Act 1986 – A BSA Summary Fourth Edition.
5. On this topic the Building Societies (Funding) and Mutual Societies (Transfers) Act of 2007 (a recent Act of Parliament) could change this arrangement (see BSA 2008b).
6. The data in euro have been converted using 1.4611 as the average £/€ exchange rate in 2007.

References

Building Societies Associations (BSA) (several years) *Annual Report*, London (available at http://www.bsa.org.uk, accessed 28 January 2009).

Building Societies Associations (BSA) (several years) *Statistics*, London (available at http://www.bsa.org.uk, accessed 28 January 2009).

Building Societies Associations (BSA) (2007) *Customer Service Survey*, London (available at http://www.bsa.org.uk/docs/consumerpdfs/comm_report.pdf, accessed 28 January 2009).

Building Societies Associations (BSA) (2008a) "Building Societies continue to attract record savings," London, (available at http://www.bsa.org.uk, accessed 28 January 2009).

Building Societies Associations (BSA) (2008b) "Depositors and Shareholders in a Building Society," London (available at http://www.bsa.org.uk, accessed 28 January 2009).

Caledonia Centre for Social Development (2001) "The History of Building Societies in the UK," (available at http://www.caledonia.org.uk/papers/History-of-Building-Societies.doc, accessed 28 January 2009).

Coles A. (1999) "Come ridare nuova vita al mutualismo. Il caso delle building societies britanniche," *Cooperazione di Credito*, no. 164/5, pp. 217–228.

Davis K. (2001) "Credit Union Governance and Survival of the Cooperative Form," *Journal of Financial Services Research*, 19: 197–210.

Fonteyne W. (2007) "Cooperative Banks in Europe," International Monetary Found, Working Paper, no.7159.

Heffernan S. (2003) "The effect of UK Building Societies conversion on pricing behaviour," Cass Business School, City of London, Working Paper, March.

HM Treasury (2006) "Consultation on legislative changes to the Building Societies Act 1986, November" (available at http://www.hm-treasury.gov.uk/media/6/7/consult_em_bsa_rp_a_reg07.pdf, accessed 28 January 2009).

Llewellyn D. (2000) "Il futuro del mutualismo nel Regno Unito. Il governo d'impresa nelle organizzazioni mutualistiche e nelle Plc," *Cooperazione di Credito*, no. 169, pp. 433–450.

Pflimlin E. (1999) "La demutualizzazione delle cooperative finanziarie in Europa," *Cooperazione di Credito*, no. 164/5, pp. 209–215.

Oliver Wyman (2003) "Mutuality Matters, Perspectives – Retail practice," June. (available at http://www.oliverwyman.com, accessed 24 September 2008).

Schraffl I. (1999) "Dalle riviste estere, Osservatorio Estero, Modelli di integrazione dei sistemi bancari cooperativi. I casi di Radobank, del Crédit Mutuel e del Crédito Agrícola Mútuo" *Cooperazione di Credito*, no. 166, pp. 303–331.

Shiwakoti R. K. (2005) "Building Societies' Demutualization and Managerial Private Interest," Kent Business School Working Paper, no. 94.

Toporowski J. (2002) "La Banque Mutuelle: de l'Utopie au Marché des Capitaux – Le Cas Britannique," *Revue d'Economie Financière*, vol. 67, pp. 45–56.

6
Cooperative Banking in the Netherlands: Rabobank Network

Matteo Cotugno

6.1 Introduction

The Dutch economy is characterized by a considerable opening towards international trade and an unemployment rate among the lowest in the European Union. Historically, its strategic economic sectors are linked to the world of agriculture and fishing, and recently to the petrochemical and pharmaceutical sectors. The banking system has played a decisive role in the development of the country. In particular, the cooperative credit system affected the the agricultural sector. Owing to its definitely unique characteristics, the Rabobank Network is a success story in credit cooperation, having reached such a point as to rank among the three leading Dutch banking groups.

This first section of this chapter aims to describe the peculiar features of the Dutch economic and banking system, by paying particular attention to the trend of the major macroeconomic indicators and the characteristics of the banking system (concentration, development, and so forth). In subsequent sections, the chapter will analyze the organizational and control setup of the Rabobank Network, as well as its competitive positioning. The final section will compare the Dutch banking system with the Rabobank Network in order to outline the distinctive features of these two different banking business models.

6.2 The Economic and Banking System in the Netherlands

The Dutch economy has one of the best economic developments worldwide (the 2005 Report on the human development index ranks the Netherlands ninth in the world). It is also distinguished by its *per capita* income since it had 29,000 USD *per capita* by the end of 2003

(ICE Report 2005). The growth of the Gross Domestic Product (GDP) in the past decade has been slightly higher than the figure reported on average by the European countries (+2.2% Netherlands against +2% Eurozone, IMF 2006). Therefore, the real economy fundamentals prove positive: in particular, the unemployment rate has been structurally lower that the figure reported on average by the European countries. There is no certainty as to the price trend in recent years, as it proves lower than the European average due to a limited domestic demand, from both the household and the public sector.

The national finances are especially sound; in particular the public debt/ GDP ratio falls fully into the Maastricht parameters as it was 53% in 2005. Besides, the deficit/GDP ratio proves under control, being 1.5% in 2005. On the whole, the Dutch economy is extremely sound, as shown by the triple A rating awarded by the Fitch agency to the country. Within a definitely favourable macroeconomic framework, the banking system operates with a concentration level which is among the highest in the world. In fact, the five top-ranking banks hold between 75% and the 80% of the market shares. In particular, ABN Amro, Rabobank, ING/Postbank, Fortis and SNS hold nearly 75% of the shares in regards to the consumer credit market and 73% with reference to the loan market. The concentration tends to rise in respect of deposits: 79% of the market is covered by the five top-ranking banks referred to above. Such a situation is reason for concern for the supervisory authorities as far as the competition, efficiency and stability of the Dutch financial system is concerned (Groeneveld and Boonstra 2005).

Ever since 1999, the banking system has been characterized by a slight decrease in the number of institutions (see Table 6.1) in the face of the growing diversification of the distribution channels, especially in the case of the direct channels connected with technology (Internet banking). In fact, the direct channel (through brokers), has increased from 38% in 1985 to 62% in 2002. This may be taken as evidence of a definitely evolved market where a relevant share of the distribution of financial products occurs through a non-banking channel. For instance, further to the establishment of BIJfinance, Vendex KBB – the most important Dutch distribution chain – has succeeded in securing a slice of the loans and insurance products market by making the most of its outlets.

Although the high concentration level would seem likely to suggest a particularly high level of satisfaction of the Dutch customers, a rather recent KPMG study rules out such a suggestion: while most European customers are relatively satisfied with their bank (min. 56%, max. 86%, mean 77.5%, standard dev. 9.69), the Dutch prove to have the highest level of customer satisfaction (see Figure 6.1). A likely explanation of

Table 6.1   The Dutch credit system

	1999	2000	2001	2002	2003	2004	2005
Section I – Credit institution supervised pursuant to section 6 of the Act							
Universal bank	100	104	101	93	93	94	96
Security credit institutions	12	12	12	11	10	10	8
Savings banks	21	4	4	4	4	4	4
Mortgage banks	4	4	4	4	4	4	4
Electronic money institution	–	–	–	–	1	1	1
Section II – Branches of credit institution established in non-EU							
Universal banks							
Electronic money institution	10	10	10	10	8	7	6
Section III- Branches of credit institution established in EU							
Universal banks	21	25	23	22	23	25	26
Electronic money institutions							
Section IV- EU credit institution offering cross-border Services in the Netherland							
Universal banks	214	262	289	308	315	353	380
Electronic money institutions	–	–	–	–	–	1	1

Source: De Nederlandsche Bank (2005), *Statistical Bulletin*, September.

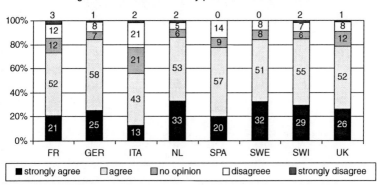

Figure 6.1   Customer satisfaction regarding banks
Source: KPMG (2004).

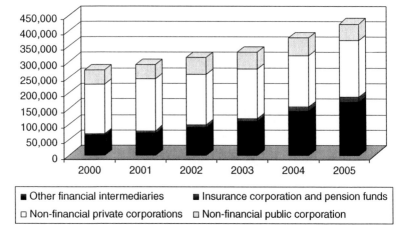

Figure 6.2   MFI loans granted to corporate customers
Source: DNB data (2005).

this phenomenon could be the possibility to gain the scale economies which, in an excessively pulverized market, would otherwise be lost.

The analysis of the volume of loans granted to customers by the MF institutions[1] in the period 2000-05 points, on the whole, to a significant and rather balanced growth in all the sectors (see Figure 6.2).

The average yearly growth rate for the entire corporate segment was 9.11%, with a particularly significant level of growth for the "Other financial intermediaries." As a rule, this segment includes the Special Purpose Vehicles set up for the securitization operations. In this case, such a showy increase in the loans granted to this type of customers witnesses a substantial increase in synthetic securitization rather than traditional securitization operations.[2]

Even the amount of the loans granted to private customers by the MFI has increased by a 9.24% average yearly rate (see Figure 6.3). The highest growth was reported by the consumer credit sector, which witnessed 13.3% average yearly rate of growth against 9.83% increase in real estate financing.

6.3 The Cooperative Credit System in the Netherlands

Within the Dutch banking system, a leading role is played by the cooperative credit system with its definite propensity for the food & agricultural sector. Organized in a single national network, nowadays Rabobank comprises 248 independent local cooperative banks with

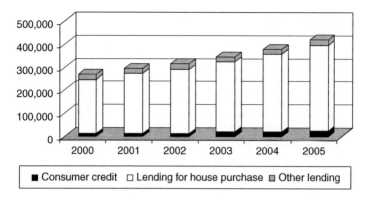

Figure 6.3   MFI loans granted to private customers
Source: DNB data (2005).

over 3000 branches throughout the national territory; it has 1.55 million members, serves 9 million private individuals and corporate clients, and its assets exceed 500 billion Euro.

6.3.1 The origins of Rabobank Netherland and its current organizational Setup

The origins of the Rabobank Network date back to 1898, when 46 local credit cooperatives saw to the establishment of two separate banks, which were to engage for the most part in cooperative credit to the agricultural sector. The first cooperative network, the so-called Coöperatieve Centrale Raiffeisenbank, had its headquarters in Utrecht and was strongly inspired by the tradition of the German cooperative bank based on the Raiffaisenbank model. The second bank was represented by a type of agricultural consortiums closely interconnected with farmers' associations (Catholic Boerenleenbank) based in Eindhoven. The Coöperatieve Centrale Raiffeisenbank became operational in the northern part of the Country, inhabited for the most part by Protestants, unlike the Catholic Boerenleenbank, whose area of operations was prevalently located in the south of the Netherlands.

These two movements could be traced back to extremely different ideological bases: on the one hand, the German cooperative tradition inspired by Wilhelm Raiffeisen; on the other hand, a cooperative system inspired to a considerable extent by Catholic values. While the ideological motivations were different, the two cooperative movements shared the same field of action: to limit the dependence of local farmers on the high interest rates charged by commercial banks. In fact, banking competition in small agricultural areas was practically inexistent. This caused commercial banks that settled in any given territory to charge interest rates on loans that were exorbitant for a population that, as a rule, was relatively poor. On the other hand, owing to high structural costs, the local commercial banks used to offer a very low remuneration on deposits.

Within this context, the cooperative movement found fertile ground, giving rise to several banks that, a little at a time, joined the two groups until they reached a peak of 1300 local cooperatives. In 1970, a report issued by the two cooperative credit groups (Gezamelijk Bericht) announced the project of a merger that was to lead, two years later, to the establishment of the present-day group, Coöperatieve Centrale Raiffeisenbank – Boerenleenbank BA, (Rabobank Netherland) with two headquarters, one located at Eindhoven and the other at Utrecht.

From a legal point of view, the cooperative companies of the Netherlands fall within the category of partnerships, which may be likened to associations under private law. The purpose of a cooperative enterprise is to promote or strengthen the private economies of its members (Schraffl 1999). The Dutch law does not provide for any official supervision with respect to cooperatives in general, while it has laid down distinctive supervisory provisions that apply to credit cooperatives. In fact, the adoption of Directive 77/780/EEC through the law of April 13, 1978 makes it mandatory for any existing or newly established Dutch banks, organized as cooperative associations, to affiliate with a single central institution (Kredietinstelling) that, in the Dutch case, is indeed represented by Rabobank Netherland. This characteristic makes the Rabobank Group a centralized national cooperative network, in the same way as the Crédito Agrìcola Mùtuo Network is in Portugal and the Okobank Group in Finland (Di Salvo R., Sharffl I., 2002).

Coöperatieve Centrale is therefore entrusted with control and supervisory functions with respect to the individual local banks, while the De Nederlandsche Bank shall only carry out its supervisory controls on the latter, considering it as a single bank with a number of branches spread throughout the territory.[3] Therefore, crucial relevance is attached to the consolidated balance sheet of the Group that, in addition to being the fundamental vehicle for conveying financial communications to stakeholders, is also the basis for calculating the capital requirements for supervision purposes. The current organizational setup of the Rabobank Group may be viewed as a two-tier (local and national) system. In particular, from a strictly operational point of view, the central level (Rabobank Netherland) and the peripheral level, comprising local cooperative banks, the Lokale Rabobanken (Local Rabobanks or Local Member Banks), are clearly identifiable.

Indeed, from an organizational point of view, a number of "intermediate levels," which are to allow the two poles of the system to get closer together, may also be identified. In fact, there are nine Rabobank regional offices, which carry no banking activities, as well as Province Member Committees (Kringe), which organize themselves in a superstructure at a national level that joins together the delegates of the individual Province Committees, the Centrale Kring Vergadering (CKV – Central Delegates Assembly). The corporate governance views these superstructures as strong centers of democracy that rebalance a network that, on the surface, would seem to have a top-down organization. In fact, while the recommendations made by the Central Bank are the fruit of a considerable policy-making and general control power, they recover their democracy as they fall within an underlying strategic direction determined by the Central Delegates Assembly. The recommendations become mandatory only in case of financial straits of a member bank and any failure to comply with them results merely in penalizations in terms of refunding rate by the Central Bank.

The Local Member Banks (at present, 248) are legally independent banks that subscribe shares of the Rabobank Netherland capital in proportion to their total assets. The central organization sees to the issue of the representative shares of the corporate capital (cooperative shares) and, besides, holds the equity participations directly in a comprehensive series of subsidiaries (not necessarily cooperatives), which allow the local banks to provide their customers with complex and competitive products thanks to the outsourcing of their production and the recovery of efficiency at a group level thanks to the exploitation of scale economies (see Figure 6.4).

In particular, the leading companies of the Rabobank Group are:

- Rabobank International, for corporate banking, investment banking and private banking;
- Robeco Group NV, for assets management;
- NV Interpolis, for supplementary insurance and pensions;
- De Lage Landen International VB, for leasing, factoring and commercial financing;
- Gilde Investment BV Management, for merchant banking.

The strategic policy of the Group underwent considerable changes with the passing of time. In fact, its operations may be broken down in a

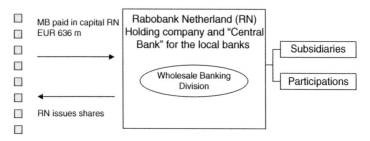

Figure 6.4 The Rabobank Netherland cooperative system
Source: Rabobank Netherland, www.rabobank.com.

number of phases. There was an initial period of development, going from the unification of the Raiffeisenbank with the Boerenleenbank towards the end of the 1980s, when the operational centralization of the central organization was very strong, just like the centrifugal tendency towards a multiplication of local banks. Starting from the 1990s, the operational delegations and the discretion in credit lines became more evident, while the process leading towards a progressive reduction of Local Member Banks became extremely evident (see Table 6.2).

In fact, the number of member banks had reached its peak in 1989, with a total of 889 affiliated banks. Notwithstanding the above, the number of branches has grown significantly in recent years, allowing the preservation of a distinctive feature of cooperative banks: their widespread distribution throughout the territory and, in particular, in rural areas.

The system of cross-guarantees worked out by Rabobank Netherland guarantees the utmost solvency of the cooperative group. In particular, it provides for two guarantee levels, one locally and one at an intra-group level (see Figure 6.5). The first level takes the form of a joint responsibility of the member banks in the case that one of them meets with financial difficulties. The second level brings in the Central Rabobank organization that, should a local member bank meet with difficulties, sees to its refunding on favorable terms, disburses subsidies or discounts on interest based on a special "Clearing regulations for the guarantee of profits and the strengthening of assets." These regulations govern the types of intervention by the central organization based on a pre-established case record of financial problems (balance difficulty, loss on credits, and so forth). The costs incurred for the financial reorganization of a member bank are prorated based on the total applications of the individual affiliated companies.

Table 6.2 Employee, client data and rating of the Rabobank Group

	2000	2001	2002	2003	2004	2005
Member banks	369	349	328	288	288	248
Offices:						
–branches	1,648	1,516	1,378	1,299	1,299	1,249
–contact points	2,618	2,697	2,800	2,965	2,965	3,031
Cash dispensing machines	2,889	2,979	2,981	3,062	3,062	3,116
Foreign offices	137	169	222	244	244	267
Employees						
–total number	58,120	58,096	57,055	56,324	56,324	50,988
–full-time equivalents	52,173	51,867	50,849	50,216	50,216	45,580
Employee satisfaction	83%	84%	85%	85%	85%	81%
Client data						
Members (x 1,000)	825	1,108	1,360	1,456	1,456	1,551
Membership/customer ratio	9.7%	13.2%	16.0%	16.7%	16.7%	17.7%
Rating						
Standard & Poor's	AAA	AAA	AAA	AAA	AAA	AAA
Moody's Investor Service	Aaa	Aaa	Aaa	Aaa	Aaa	Aaa
SAM-rating (corporate social responsibility)	64%		74%			80%

Source: Rabobank Netherland, www.rabobank.com

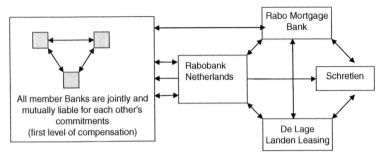

←→ *Denotes intra-group credit support (second level of compensation)*

Figure 6.5   The cross-guarantee scheme of Rabobank Netherland
Source: Rabobank Netherland www.rabobank.com.

As a rule, each one of the 248 member banks is organized into departments or segments, which generally coincide with customer segments character-ized by the homogeneity of the financial needs to be managed. In particular, there are the Client Advice, Financial Advice, Business Advice, Corporate clients, and Businesses Administration segments. As a rule, the first three divi-sions correspond to the retail, private and corporate divisions of a commercial bank. On the other hand, the Business Administration segment deals with a series of back-office services such as the preliminary paperwork for loans, risk management, management control, and so forth. Each segment is managed by an executive who only answers to the General Manager.

The General Manager is the person responsible for the management of the member bank, takes part in the "regional circle meeting" and, in given cases, in the meetings of the Central Delegates Assembly – CKV. Besides, the General Manager chairs the executive board of the member bank (Raad van Bestuur) and the Compliance Board (Raad van Toezicht). The local banks do not issue shares on the capital market in order to finance themselves, since they require their members, which most of the times coincide with their customers, to subscribe the cooperative shares (Rabobank Membership Certificates). In fact, in order to be granted a loan, it is mandatory for the applicant to have the legal status of a member, while this is not required for customers who only want to make deposits into the local bank. The "ordinary" customers entertain their relations directly with the member bank of the relevant territory, which decides in its credit autonomy. If the amount of a loan exceeds the credit autonomy of the member bank, the latter needs to refer to the Central organization for decisions. On the other hand, the corporate clients, represented by nearly 500 enterprises engaged in agribusiness at a national level, entertain direct relations with Rabobank Netherland.

6.3.2 Competitive positioning, operations and future prospects

Rabobank Netherland is the leading banking group in the Netherlands in the agribusiness sector, with 90% share of the market. Its cooperative arrangement allows it to make the most of its banking-type organizational structure. On the one hand, a widespread territorial distribution allows it to get to know and interpret at best the financial needs of its customers and to serve them in the best possible manner thanks to a strong independence of local banks. On the other hand, a concentrated structure that produces high-level banking services permits to make the most of the considerable scale economies for given products, whose decisive success factor is to reach a pre-established critical mass.

From an operational point of view, Rabobank Netherland carries on important functions on behalf of its member banks. As previously pointed out, the supervision over the network banks is performed directly by the central organization, which checks that each individual member bank has a minimum regulatory capital equal to 8%. More specifically, the aim set out in the group strategy is the attainment of 12% equity, even with a view to allowing retaining the Triple A rating.[4] Whenever a member bank drops below the 8% capital requirement, the Central Organization shall see to its refunding. In that case, the member bank shall be required to return the capital as soon as the coefficient exceeds 12%.

The Central Organization is also entrusted with the task of acting as "clearing house" with respect to liquidities exceeding management requirements, without prejudice to the obligation of each individual member bank to deposit at least 25% of its liquidity in the Central Organization. The latter produces for its member banks, either directly or through its controlled companies, sophisticated financial services to meet the financial requirements of the most demanding customers. The Central Organization makes a series of recommendations to member banks to ensure a unitary management. It should be borne in mind that this gives rise to a sort of circularity in the governance arrangement, whereby the classical top-down model typical of commercial banks and – at the opposite end – the bottom-up model find a way to coexist thanks to the assistance of intermediate government bodies.

Furthermore, the Central Organization is responsible for the administrative management of all the personnel of the group, offers technical, legal and managerial assistance and sees to the tax optimization of the network. In particular, it is some time since the Dutch tax law has been in favour of admitting a consolidated statement for taxation purposes. In such a way, the burden of taxation may be optimized thanks to the possibility of offsetting losses, if any, produced by a few member banks. The Rabobank products portfolio has undergone a considerable evolution in recent years, thereby ensuring a definitely assertive competitive positioning of the Group with respect to the most sophisticated enterprises. In particular, the completion of the range of products has proved indispensable to guarantee the best coverage of customers. This may be exemplified by the merchant bank, specialized in the acquisition of equity stakes in companies operating for the most part in the agribusiness sector and the Venture Capital Group, in case of entry into start-up share capital.

The mission that Rabobank is determined to pursue differs with respect to what is generally proposed by commercial banks. In particular, Rabobank does not view the maximization of shareholder value as its highest goal (Rabobank Annual Report 2005). Instead of the classical distribution of dividends to shareholders, Rabobank distributes its profit to its members through the organization of a series of local initiatives that transfer part of the profits to its members (cooperative dividend). In order to guarantee the maximum satisfaction of customers and members alike, Rabobank's goal is profit optimization rather than profit maximization.[5]

A recent national meeting of the local Rabobanks (Central Delegates Assembly – CKV) on 22 March 2006 has led to the launch of the Strategic Framework for 2005-2010 (see www.rabobank.nl). This framework is founded on a number of principles that may be summarized as follows:

- The Rabobank group, in spite of its recent adoption of an international territorial expansion strategy, must keep on focusing on the national economy, with specific reference to the food and agricultural sector, and small and medium-sized enterprises.
- Rabobank legal status as a cooperative bank is unquestionable, while exceptions may be made for Group subsidiaries.
- The Triple A rating is and remains a strategic objective. The operational management, the risk management policies and the coverage of financial needs must be such as to guarantee the preservation of the maximum rating.
- The legal independence of Rabobank remains a pivotal element of its strategy. In any merger, Rabobank will only accept a majority interest.

The force and the cohesion of Rabobak are represented by the coexistence of principle whose root lie in the past and the need to run a business aimed at curbing cost and standing up to competition. The banking group is leader in Netherland for banking sector and aspires to international growth in the rest of the world.

6.4 A comparative performance-related analysis

It is important to examine the major economic indicators reported by the Dutch credit intermediaries (commercial banks and cooperative banks) over the last few years. The analysis in this section takes into consideration the Dutch banking system as a whole, including Rabobank Netherlands. Lately, the dimensional growth of the Dutch banking system, measured in terms of total assets variation, has been remarkable, with average yearly rates approximating 11% (Figure 6.6). Rabobank Netherland has reported a slightly lower rate (8.2%), which was mostly due to a considerable discrepancy of the 2005 figures. On the other hand, that fiscal year was affected by the passage to the IAS-IFRS, which was adopted by the entire Dutch banking system, as laid down in the Regulation (EC) no. 1606/2002. (Even Rabobank Netherlands has drawn up the 2005 balance sheet according to the IAS-IFRS.)

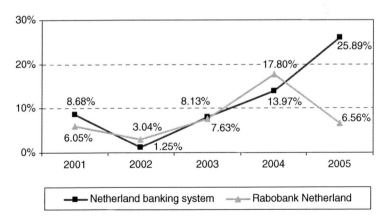

Figure 6.6 Total assets growth (percentage variation with respect to the previous year)
Source: Central Cooperative Bank balance sheets and DNB statistics.

In addition to the variation resulting from the corporate management, close attention must also be paid to the variation that may be ascribed to the transition from the *Dutch GAAP* to the IAS-IFRS. The growth of the balance-sheet assets has been financed in a balanced manner by Rabobank Netherland. Due to the allocation of the resulting profits, the latter has reported average yearly equity growth rates of 10.4% against 7.7% reported by the banking system (see Figure 6.7). It goes without saying that this trend has clear repercussions on the degree of leverage: Rabobank has witnessed the gradual reduction of the leverage level in consequence of an equity growth exceeding the assets growth, unlike the banking system in general that experienced a leverage increase owing to the fact that it did not succeed in growing from the point of view of equity at the same rate as from the point of view of assets.

The analysis of the economic-financial performance in a classical sense is affected by the above-mentioned strategic approach in respect of the distribution of profits that, quite naturally, "anticipates" the distribution of margins to members owing to the effect of the cooperative dividend. Therefore, it is no surprise that the outcome, in terms of ROE (Return on Equity – Net Result/Equity), is systematically below the figure reported on average by the Dutch banking system (see Figure 6.8). In particular, with the exception of 2002, when the Rabobank ROE was higher than the one reported by the Dutch banking system, every other year pointed to a differential in terms of return on equity that ranged from 155 bp (2001) to 545 bp (2005).

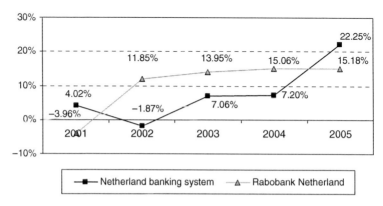

Figure 6.7 Total equity growth
Source: Central Cooperative Bank balance sheets and DNB statistics.

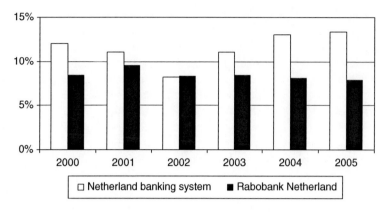

Figure 6.8 ROE Comparison
Source: Central Cooperative Bank balance sheets and DNB statistics.

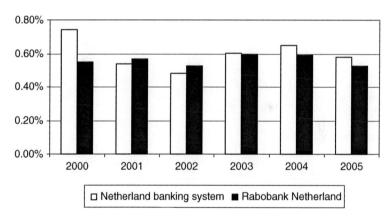

Figure 6.9 Comparison in terms of ROA
Source: Central Cooperative Bank balance sheets and DNB statistics.

The comparison in terms of ROA (Return on Assets) – (Operating Result/ Total Asset) highlights a result that is less penalizing for Rabobank Netherland (see Figure 6.9). The trend of the indicator witnesses a level of profitability of the characteristic Rabobank management that is approximately in line with the figure reported by the system. This datum seems to highlight that, owing to the special policies of the cooperative network, the ROE is unable to single out the "real" economic performance since the distribution of margins to the members are "paid" at a higher level of the profit and loss account.

Focusing the analysis on the Risk Adjusted Return on Capital, the RAROC for the group is 14% thanks to a cautious credit policy. In particular, the probability of a weighed average default of the whole portfolio is 1.04%, with an economic capital to be held to absorb credit losses that is 49%.[6] As for the rest of the economic capital, 23% is held to absorb the interest risk, 10% the operating risks, and 13% the business risk (which is, however, not relevant for the purposes of Basel 2).

A more in depth analysis of the accounting returns, having recourse to the ROE breakdown in keeping with the model developed by the DuPont Corporation, allows observing the areas of formation of the return on equity:

$$ROE = \frac{NeR}{E} = \frac{NeR}{GrR} \times \frac{GrR}{OpR} \times \left[\frac{IM}{TA} \times \frac{IntM}{IM} \times \frac{OpR}{IntM} \right] \times \frac{TA}{E}$$

Legend:

IM   = Interest Margin
IntM = Intermediation Margin
OpR = Operational Result
GrR   = Gross Result
NeR = Net Result
E   = Equity
TA   = Total Assets

The return on equity results from the iteration of different variables. In the first place, variables connected with the bank characteristic management, or rather the formation of the interest margin (expressed through the Interest Margin/Total Assets ratio) and the intermediation margin (Intermediation Margin/Interest Margin). Secondly, the operating costs are taken into consideration through the Operational Result/ Intermediation Margin ratio. Thirdly, the fiscal and extraordinary components are taken into consideration (through the Net Result/Gross Result ratio and Gross Result/Operational Result ratio, respectively). Finally, the bank leverage is taken into consideration through the Total Assets/Equity ratio (Boscia 2002).

Table 6.3 ROE analysis relative to Rabobank Netherland

Year	NeR/GrR	GrR/OpR	IM/TA	IntM/IM	OpR/IntM	TA/E	ROE
2000	73.03%	100.00%	1.34%	1.69	24.25%	21.11	8.45%
2001	71.96%	97.22%	1.39%	1.67	25.14%	23.31	9.51%
2002	73.95%	88.67%	1.44%	1.59	25.98%	21.48	8.36%
2003	69.48%	99.26%	1.49%	1.54	20%	20.28	8.39%
2004	65.93%	100.00%	1.32%	1.61	27.91%	20.77	8.10%
2005 (*)	77.67%	100.00%	1.27%	1.47	28.55%	19.21	7.91%

(*) The balances are struck according to the IAS-IFRS
Source: Rabobank Netherland data, *Annual Reports*, various years.

Table 6.4 ROE analysis relative to the Dutch Banking System

Year	NeR/GrR	GrR/OpR	IM/TA	IntM/IM	OpR/IntM	TA/E	ROE
2000	75.22%	93.20%	1.44%	1.93	26.78%	23.08	12.05%
2001	77.50%	109.17%	1.41%	1.80	21.32%	24.12	11.06%
2002	72.29%	95.96%	1.50%	1.66	19.28%	24.88	8.26%
2003	72.91%	99.99%	1.45%	1.65	25.12%	25.13	11.02%
2004	75.31%	99.99%	1.33%	1.71	28.44%	26.72	13.04%
2005(*)	83.59%	99.99%	1.08%	1.85	29.09%	27.51	13.36%

(*) The balances are struck according to the IAS-IFRS
Source: Rabobank Netherland data, *Annual Reports*, various years.

Tables 6.3 and 6.4 permit to observe, with reference to the Rabobank's characteristic management with respect to the Dutch banking system that:

- for Rabobank, the interest margin/total assets ratio during 2000-03 has been higher than the average reported by the system; however, in the last two years there has been a reversal of this trend;
- the contribution to the formation of the service component return (mostly commissions) has been systematically lower in Rabobank than other banks within the Dutch banking system.

Instead, the incidence of operating costs is inconstant and no clear trend is perceivable. In particular, in the last two years the incidence of operating costs was lower within the Dutch banking system than in the Rabobank group. In regards to the incidence of the items connected with the extraordinary and tax management, it is interesting to note that, particularly with reference to the latter variable, the taxation in the Rabobank group has been more penalizing than in the Dutch banking system taken as a whole.

The element that characterizes the Dutch cooperative credit system is the leverage level (Total Assets/Equity), which is constantly lower than the figure reported on average by the banking system. This stresses that the management focus is not the shareholder but the customer and, after all, the typical cooperative credit policies whereby profit is put on reserve make the Rabobank structure much more solid than the rest of the banking system from the point of view of capital and reserve. Quite naturally, this penalizes the ROE but, as shown in the Group summary table (Table 6.3), this has allowed Rabobank to maintain for long time the Triple A rating awarded by Standard & Poor's and Moody's, as well as a high value with respect to the rating of the bank's social responsibility.

Focusing the attention on the interest margin formation, the average percentage cost of the sources of financing may be compared with the average return on earning assets. In such a way, the gross spread may be determined. It may be noted that the gross spread dynamics is reversed with respect to what was noted in respect of the unitary interest margin (IM/TA). In particular, in the course of the past three years, Rabobank Netherland has reported a higher gross spread than the Dutch banking system (see Figures 6.10 and 6.11).

For a complete analysis of operating costs, is possible to calculate a efficiency indicator, such as the Operating Expenses/Total Assets ratio or, exclusively with reference to staff costs, like a Staff Cost/Total Assets ratio (see Figures 6.12 and 6.13). With reference to the former, it may be noted that Dutch banking system has experienced a trend decidedly

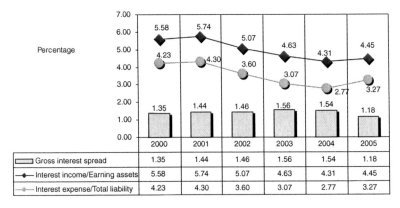

	2000	2001	2002	2003	2004	2005
Gross interest spread	1.35	1.44	1.46	1.56	1.54	1.18
Interest income/Earning assets	5.58	5.74	5.07	4.63	4.31	4.45
Interest expense/Total liability	4.23	4.30	3.60	3.07	2.77	3.27

Figure 6.10 Margin analysis relative to Rabobank Netherland
Source: Rabobank Netherland data, *Annual Reports*, various years.

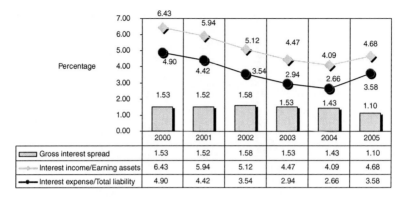

	2000	2001	2002	2003	2004	2005
Gross interest spread	1.53	1.52	1.58	1.53	1.43	1.10
Interest income/Earning assets	6.43	5.94	5.12	4.47	4.09	4.68
Interest expense/Total liability	4.90	4.42	3.54	2.94	2.66	3.58

Figure 6.11 Margin analysis relative to the Dutch banking system
Source: De Netherlandsche Bank data.

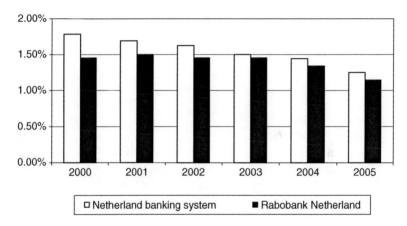

Figure 6.12 Operating expenses/total assets
Source: De Netherlandsche Bank data and Rabobank Netherland data.

on the decrease, with a mean yearly variation rate of –6.8%. Even Rabobank has reported a decreasing trend, but it was slower, with a yearly average of –4.3%. Throughout the period under consideration, Rabobank has reported a systematically lower ratio than the average value for the Dutch banking system.

The situation does not change to any considerable extent when reference is made to staff costs, even though Rabobank has reported slight ratio increases in the years 2000–03. While the reduction of the indicator has

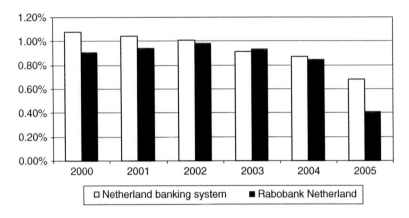

Figure 6.13   Staff cost/total assets
Source: De Nederlandsche Bank data and Rabobank Netherland data.

been particularly sharp in 2005, this should be interpreted with due caution in the case of being contaminated by the transition to the IAS-IFRS.

6.5 Conclusion

The Dutch economy ranks at the top in terms of its economic development and *per capita* income, with a triple A country rating. The fundamental sectors of the economy, particularly food and agribusiness, have been able to count on the financial support of one of the leading Dutch banking groups: Rabobank Netherland. Organized in the form of a national centralized network, Rabobank Netherland was established in 1972 further to the merger of two cooperative groups and works within one of the most concentrated banking systems in the world.rabobank Netherland is organized on two levels of governance, a central one and a local one, with "intermediate levels" at a provincial and a regional level that allow managing the group as an organic whole. The local banks are independent and their participation in the capital of the supra-local organization is on a pro-quota basis. The product-specialized companies provide complex financial services to member banks allowing them to benefit from appropriate scale economies.

From the point of view of supervision, Rabobank is considered a single bank and, therefore, it is up to the supra-local organization to ensure the capital adequacy of the local organizations. A complex system of cross guarantees permits to increase the solidity of the group that has been awarded the triple A rating since a number of years. Rabobank's levels of profitability, measured in terms of ROE, are lower than those reported by the banking system, and this may be attributable to the result distribution policies. In terms of ROA, the levels of Rabobank are not too different from those of the banking system. Rabobank systematically shows a lower leverage level than the banking system, reaching levels of efficiency (measurable in terms of operating expenses/total assets or staffs cost/total assets) that are definitely lower than those reported by the Dutch banking system.

Notes

1. The Monetary Financial Institutions include credit institutions, monetary market funds and other lesser institutions registered under a special section, as laid down in article 52 of the Act on Supervision of the Credit System 1992.
2. A traditional securitization operation provides for the assignment of assets by the originator to an SPV, which will issue securities to finance the acquisition. On the contrary, a synthetic operation does not provide for a true sale, since it will be the originator to grant a loan to the vehicle company. In December 2005, ABN Amro Bank has carried out two important synthetic securitization operations – called Smile and Shield – amounting to 6.65 billion euro and 4 billion euro respectively.
3. 1992 Act on Supervision of the Credit System, § 3 Authorization Requirements, Section 12 in accordance with EU Directive 77/780/ EEG, Article 2, section 4. The main section 12 criteria are:

   a) the credit institutions (the local Rabobank) are affiliated with a central institution (Rabobank Netherlands);
   b) the central credit institution supervises compliance by the affiliated credit institutions regarding directives governing solvency, liquidity and the administrative organization;
   c) the central institution and its affiliated credit institutions are jointly and severally liable for each other' s commitments;
   d) in the opinion of the DNB, the central institution has to be adequately empowered to give instructions to the affiliated credit institutions;
   e) the supervision of solvency of the central institution and the affiliated credit institutions is exercised on a consolidated basis.

   The Rabobank Group fulfils the section 12 criteria and is therefore treated as a consolidated entity for the supervision of solvency, liquidity and other controls.
4. The last meeting of the Central Delegates Assembly has confirmed its long-term strategic objective of maintaining the triple A rating. This objective is being pursued due to an extremely strict risk management system, which requires a confidence level for the credit standing Value at Risk of 99.99%. See Rabobank Netherlands, Annual Report, 2005.

5. In 2005, the level of customer satisfaction of its members stood at 7.4, on the increase with respect to the 7.3 figure reported in 2004. The strategic goal of the group is to get to a minimum level of 7.5 in the forthcoming years.

6. The absorbed capital is defined by Rabobank as the amount of capital to be held in order to absorb unexpected losses, based on a one-year period and a confidence level of 99.99%. For the time being, it is not possible to perform the same analysis in terms of RAROC on the banking system as a whole.

References

Boscia V. (2002) *The future of small banks in the new competitive environment. The case of the Italian banking industry*, Bari: Cacucci Editore.

De Nederlandsche Bank (2005a) *Overview of financial stability in Netherland*, no. 3, Dicember, Amsterdam.

De Nederlandsche Bank (2005b) *Statistical Bulletin*, September, Amsterdam, Available from: http://www.dnb.nl/dnb/home, [Accessed 8 July 2007].

Di Salvo R. Schraffl I. (2002) "La governance cooperativa: modelli strutturali e funzionali dei sistemi creditizi cooperativi europei," *Cooperazione di Credito*, no. 175, pp. 7–49.

European Central Banking (ECB) (2005), EU Banking Structure, October, Frankfurt.

Forestieri G., Onado, M. (1989) *Il sistema bancario italiano e l'integrazione dei mercati. Un confronto delle strutture negli ordinamenti dei principali Paesi*, Milano, EGEA.

Groeneveld J.M., Boonstra, W.W. (2005) Competition in a highly concentrated banking sector. Theoretical, empirical and practical considerations for the Netherlands, Economic Research Department, Rabobank, Available from: http://www.rabobank.com [Accessed 8 July 2007]

Istituto nazionale per il Commercio Estero (ICE) (2005) *Rapporto sui Paesi Bassi*, Rome, Available from: http://www.ice.it/paesi/pdf/paesi_bassi.pdf [Accessed 8th July 2007].

International Monetary Fund (IMF) (2006) "World Economic Outlook 2006," Washington, Available from: http://www.imf.org/[Accessed 8 July 2007].

KPMG (2004) Banking beyond borders: will European consumers buy it?, London, Available from: http://www.kpmg.com.ar/pdf/publicaciones/Banking_beyond_borders.pdf/ [Accessed 31 July 2009]

Munari L. (2000) "Customer satisfaction e redditività nelle banche," *Banche e Banchieri*, vol. 27, no. 3, pp. 195–224.

Piot B. (1997) "Il sistema delle relazioni tra le banche di credito cooperativo e i soci: il quadro normativo europeo," *Cooperazione di Credito*, no. 156/157, pp. 209–222.

Rabobank Group (Various Years) *Annual Report*, Amsterdam, Available from: http://www.rabobank.com. /[Accessed 8 July 2007].

Schraffl I. (1999) "Modelli di integrazione dei sistemi bancari cooperative. I casi di Rabobank, del Crédit Mutuel e del Crédito Agrícola Mútuo," *Cooperazione di Credito*, no. 166, pp. 303–331.

Standard & Poor's (2005) Bank credit report, Rabobank Netherland, September, The McGraw-Hill Companies, New York, Available from: www.standardandpoors.com, [Accessed 8 July 2007].

7
The German Cooperative Banking System: Volksbanken and Raiffeisenbanken

Massimo Biasin

The German cooperative banks, namely the Raiffeisenbanken and Volksbanken and their central institutions, linked together in the so called Finanzverbund, define the "third pillar" of the German banking system beside the large commercial banks (also known as *Grossbanken* like Deutsche Bank, Dresdner Bank, Commerzbank and HypoVereinsbank, recently merged with the Italian Unicredit Banking Group) and the savings banks' network (the so called *Sparkassen* and *Landesbanken*). Given a general overview of the size and structure of the German cooperative banking market, the present analysis focuses on the institutional framework of the cooperative system, both on the associative and entrepreneurship level, considering its legal and operational peculiarities. The chapter further investigates the network strategies and the business relations of and within the Raiffeisen and Volksbanken sector, taking into consideration the governance structure of the (first and second level) bank entities. This is in order to highlight the capability of the German mutual banks to act as an *Allfinanz*-banking group and not as a loose collection of individual financial intermediaries by preserving the statutory independence of the single first level bank entity.

7.1 The German cooperative banking system (*Raiffeisenbanken* and *Volksbanken*): an overview

In order to investigate the size and the relative market power of the German credit cooperative system, let's start from a general overview of the domestic banking universe. Table 7.1 summarizes the overall structure of the German banking system in terms of its balance sheet's composition by category of banks. Credit cooperatives and their central institutions, with over 30 million customers the majority of which are

Table 7.1 Assets and liabilities of German banks – million euros and percentage

	Number of reporting institutions	Balance sheet total	Cash & equivalents (2)	Lending (3)	Debt securities & treasury bills	Shares & participating interests	Other assets (4)	Amounts owed to banks	Amounts owed to non-banks	Securitized liabilities	Other liabilities	Provisions & others (5)	Subordinated liabilities	Capital (6)
All banks														
2003	2,226	7,173,403	74,339	5,166,505	1,306,215	358,355	267,989	1,990,734	2,772,552	1,611,337	349,877	71,606	92,734	284,563
2004	2,147	7,527,693	63,667	5,353,579	1,433,099	386,689	290,659	2,109,015	2,913,526	1,672,491	380,840	74,757	100,230	276,834
2005	2,089	7,794,262	67,613	5,500,133	1,512,394	446,306	267,816	2,162,622	3,017,355	1,769,725	372,465	79,847	102,936	289,312
Commercial banks (including the so called "Big Banks") (1)														
2003	327	3,820,296	30,851	2,810,121	624,446	188,417	166,461	1,064,362	1,297,354	1,002,582	224,433	43,735	48,353	139,477
2004	320	4,233,448	25,205	3,040,621	756,343	218,561	192,718	1,201,778	1,452,572	1,089,725	253,008	43,594	55,096	137,675
2005	318	4,378,216	29,081	3,113,186	805,913	254,933	175,103	1,214,063	1,513,355	1,160,628	245,289	46,150	56,778	141,953
Savings banks (Sparkassen & Landesbanken)														
2003	504	2,589,857	29,520	1,828,914	527,872	126,662	76,889	736,492	1,037,537	550,642	99,770	19,613	38,678	107,125
2004	489	2,507,144	25,113	1,773,984	510,847	123,365	73,835	706,276	1,016,079	523,402	100,119	21,957	39,174	100,137
2005	475	2,581,262	25,616	1,829,954	518,226	139,103	68,363	724,245	1,043,255	547,766	95,170	23,819	39,946	107,061
Credit cooperatives and Regional institutions of credit cooperatives (Raiffeisen- und Volksbanken; Zentralbanken)														
2003	1,395	763,250	13,968	527,470	153,897	43,276	24,639	189,880	437,661	58,113	25,674	8,258	5,703	37,961
2004	1,338	787,101	13,349	538,974	165,909	44,763	24,106	200,961	444,875	59,364	27,713	9,206	5,960	39,022
2005	1,296	834,784	12,916	556,993	188,255	52,270	24,350	224,314	460,745	61,331	32,006	9,878	6,212	40,298
Asset & liabilities as proportion (%) of relative balance sheet total														
Commercial banks (including the so called "Big Banks")(1)														
2003	327	100%	1%	74%	16%	5%	4%	28%	34%	26%	6%	1%	1%	4%
2004	320	100%	1%	72%	18%	5%	5%	28%	34%	26%	6%	1%	1%	3%
2005	318	100%	1%	71%	18%	6%	4%	28%	35%	27%	6%	1%	1%	3%
Savings banks (Sparkassen & Landesbanken)														
2003	504	100%	1%	71%	20%	5%	3%	28%	40%	21%	4%	1%	1%	4%
2004	489	100%	1%	71%	20%	5%	3%	28%	41%	21%	4%	1%	2%	4%
2005	475	100%	1%	71%	20%	5%	3%	28%	40%	21%	4%	1%	2%	4%
Credit cooperatives and Regional institutions of credit cooperatives (Raiffeisen- und Volksbanken; Zentralbanken)														
2003	1,395	100%	2%	69%	20%	6%	3%	25%	57%	8%	3%	1%	1%	5%
2004	1,338	100%	2%	68%	21%	6%	3%	26%	57%	8%	4%	1%	1%	5%
2005	1,296	100%	2%	67%	23%	6%	3%	27%	55%	7%	4%	1%	1%	5%

(1) including special purpose banks and mortgage banks; (2) balances with Central Banks; (3) to banks & non-banks; (4) fiduciary assets & equalization claims, fixed assets, others; (5) provisions for liabilities and charges & fund for general banking risks; (6)including participation rights; (7) i.e. lending of credit Cooperatives as % of credit lending amount of all banks;
Source: Deutsche Bundesbank, Monthly Report, April 2006. Adaptation by the author.

at the same time cooperatives' members (15.7 million), cover around 11 per cent of the market measured by total assets in 2005,[1] compared to a percentage of 56 per cent managed by commercial banks (including the so called big banks or *Grossbanken*); the residual part (33 per cent) is controlled by the saving institutions. The balance sheet total of the cooperative sector amounts to roughly 835 billion Euros. The market share has not moved considerably over the last three years, confirming the German banking market's relative stability given the different clientele segments served by the various bank categories.

In particular, credit cooperatives are largely devoted to traditional banking activities towards small and medium business as well as private retail clients located in rural areas and small towns, with generally a weaker presence in large urban centres. Due to customary relationship activities, cooperative banks benefit from higher retail funding (55 per cent of the total liabilities – Table 7.1 – equal to a market share of over 15 per cent of domestic deposits) compared to commercial and savings banks (with 35 per cent and 40 per cent respectively [2005 data]) which rely more heavily on securitized liabilities (commercial banks 27 per cent, savings banks 21 per cent of total liabilities versus 7 per cent of market type debt of cooperative banks including their central institutions).

As depicted in Table 7.2 covering the cost and income structure of the German banking industry, the significant business volumes with private retail clients and small and medium-sized firms of the cooperative banks lead to above average net interest margin and its relative contribution to total earnings (Deutsche Bundesbank 2005: 15-43). Over the period 2000–4, the Raiffeisenbanken and Volksbanken achieved a net interest income of 2.47 per cent of balance sheet total (equivalent to 77 per cent of total earnings), roughly equal to the margin of the savings institutions serving a similar clientele, but compared to 1.22 per cent of the commercial banks heavily involved in wholesale activities. In addition, credit cooperatives benefit from their rural or semi-rural location where financial competition is somehow lower. In turn, the net commission income's incidence on total earnings is somehow lower than those for commercial banks due to the type of clientele served.

Overall, German credit cooperatives enjoy high gross earnings as percentage of balance sheet total (see Table 7.2) but suffer from above average provisions (0.55 per cent).

The strong territorial presence of the German cooperative banks that follows their orientation towards traditional banking activities is testified by the wide branch network (12,722 offices equal to 36 per cent of the whole banking industry) and the high number of institutions

Table 7.2   Cost and income structure (2000–2005 annual average – selected indicators)[1]

	Commercial banks	Savings banks	Credit cooperatives
Net interest income (% balance sheet total)	1.22%	2.35%	2.47%
Net commission income (% balance sheet total)	0.63%	0.53%	0.62%
Gross earnings (% balance sheet total)	1.85%	2.88%	3.09%
Staff costs (% balance sheet total)	0.77%	1.18%	1.37%
Other administrative spending (% balance sheet total)	0.79%	0.78%	0.96%
Provisions (% balance sheet total)	–0.28%	–0.56%	–0.55%
Operating results (% balance sheet total)	0.23%	0.39%	0.33%
Profit for financial year (% balance sheet total)	0.05%	0.44%	0.45%
Net interest income as % of total earnings	58.8%	80.64%	76.98%
Net commission income as % of total earnings	30.55%	18.06%	19.26%

Credit cooperatives only (excluding central institutions)[2]

	2003	2004	2005
Return on equity (Roe)	n.a.	4.7%	6.9%
Return on equity pre-tax	n.a.	9.7%	11.5%
Cost/income ratio	69.4%	68.8%	70.2%
Total employees	188,435	189,748	195,101

Source: (1) Bundesverband Deutscher Banken, *Ertragslage bei den einzenen Bankengruppen, 1996–2005*;
(2) BVR, *Consolidated Annual Accounts of the Cooperative Financial Services Network, 2005, 2004, 2003*.

(2005: 1.294 units) (see Table 7.3), reflecting the local nature of the Raiffeisenbanken and Volksbanken that had been historically established at municipality level. These circumstances play an important role in downsizing the single credit cooperative company measured by total assets (see Table 7.4): in 2005 credit cooperatives had an average balance sheet total of 457 million Euros compared to 298 million of 2000 (+53.6 per cent).

One quarter of the Raiffeisenbanken and Volksbanken had a company size below 100 million Euros, while over 52 per cent was concentrated between 100 and 500 million; the remaining 24 per cent are "large" credit cooperatives totaling more than 500 million Euros of assets. As described further, the increase in size follows the dramatic reduction of the number of cooperative banks (–27.8 per cent over the period)

Table 7.3 Number and branches of German banks

All banks	Commercial banks (including the "Big Banks") (1)	Saving banks (Sparkassen & Landesbanken	Credit cooperatives and regional institutions of credit cooperatives		
			Central & regional institutions (Zentralbanken)	Credit cooperatives (Raiffeisen and Volksbanken)	

Number of banks					
2000	2,740	369	575	1,796	4	1,792
2003	2,226	327	504	1,395	2	1,393
2004	2,147	320	489	1,338	2	1,336
2005	2,089	318	475	1,296	2	1,294
Branches (2)					
2000	43,307	10,420	17,530	15,357	25	15,332
2003	36,599	8,058	15,328	13,213	12	13,201
2004	35,760	7,941	14,841	12,978	11	12,967
2005	35,041	7,778	14,530	12,733	11	12,722
	100%	24%	40%	35%	0%	35%
	100%	22%	42%	36%	0%	36%
	100%	22%	42%	36%	0%	36%
	100%	22%	41%	36%	0%	36%

(1) including special purpose banks and mortgage banks
(2) exluding Deutsche Postbank AG
Source: Deutsche Bundesbank, Monthly Report, April 2003, 2005, 2006.
Deutche Bundesbank, Time Series Database.

pursuing a precise strategy that aims to reduce the relative incidence of fixed costs and to improve efficiency of the first level banks of the Finanzverbund.

At the same time, as maintaining bank offices is extremely cost intensive, the extensive branch network and the limited company size of the Raiffeisenbanken and Volksbanken generate high administrative costs which, in turn, lead to a high cost/income ratio. Excluding their central institutions, cooperative banks have a cost/income ratio of 70.2 per cent (68.8 per cent in 2004; 69.4 per cent in 2003 – see Table 7.2). Relative high provision costs and, contrary to other European fiscal legislations, *de facto* no tax benefits granted to the cooperative banks, determine a return on equity of roughly 7 per cent (11.5 per cent pre tax Roe in 2005; 2004: 4.7 per cent and 9.7 per cent respectively). Beside possible efficiency gaps in respect to commercial banks, Roe analysis must consider the fact that due to the cooperative nature of the Raiffeisen and Volksbanken, profits are driven to shareholders not only in the form of

Table 7.4   Credit cooperatives only – distribution & average size (balance sheet total)

	2000	%	2003	%	2004	%	2005	%
Balance sheet total <25 million Euros	67	4%	–	–	–	–	–	–
Balance sheet total between 25>50 million Euros	217	12%	155	11%	132	10%	120	9%
Balance sheet total between 50>100 million Euros	368	21%	223	16%	212	16%	199	15%
Balance sheet total between 100>250 million Euros	559	31%	398	29%	374	28%	364	28%
Balance sheet total between 250>500 million Euros	346	19%	327	23%	327	25%	313	24%
Balance sheet total between 500 million>1 billion Euros	151	9%	191	14%	188	14%	189	15%
Balance sheet total between 1 billion> 5 billion Euros	79	4%	92	7%	96	7%	101	8%
Balance sheet total >5 billion Euros	5	0%	7	1%	7	1%	8	1%
	1,792	100%	1,393	100%	1,336	100%	1,294	100%
Average size (based on balance sheet total)								
Average balance sheet total (million euros)	*298*		*407*		*431*		*457*	

Source: Deutsche Bundesbank, Monthly Report April 2003, 2006.
Deutsche Bundesbanks, Time Series Database.

dividends but also in terms of better economic conditions (lower costs or higher earnings), compared to non-member clients.

7.2 The credit cooperatives' institutional framework

German credit cooperatives are independent, private banks established locally in the form of registered associations with legal personality (so called Eingetragene Kreditgenossenschaften). Within the cooperative banking sector they constitute the so called first level entities while their central institutions form the second level bank firms (for the entrepreneurship level of the cooperative sector, see the second section of this chapter). Members – individuals as well as legal entities forming a broad ownership base – are united voluntarily to meet their common economic and social needs through a jointly-owned and democratically controlled enterprise; they participate through the acquisition of capital shares authorized by the board of the cooperative union itself, generally entitling to one vote per share regardless of the (generally limited) participation held ("one member, one vote" principle) but the by-law may entitle multiple voting rights to particular members (*Gesetz betreffend die Erwerbs- und Wirtschaftsgenossenschaften* 1889: § 43).

Shareholders' liability is generally limited to the initial capital contribution plus an additional amount (*Haftungssumme*) eventually defined by the articles of association (*Gesetz betreffend die Erwerbs- und Wirtschafts genossenschaften* 1889: § 6). The solvency of the cooperative banks is also ensured by a protection scheme in form of a guarantee fund and guarantee network.[2] Although sharing the same legal and operational framework, credit unions are traditionally divided in Raiffeisenbanken and Volksbanken because of their different historical background.[3] While Raiffeisenbanken were originally founded in rural areas by farmers and field workers, Volksbanken were established in towns and urban centres by (small) business men.[4] Beside the nominal indication, both categories act nowadays as one single network sharing the same central institutions as well as regional and federal organizations.

Corporate governance and administration of credit unions are regulated by the cooperative federal law (*Genossenschaftsgesetz*) and, to a lesser degree, by statutes or by-laws (Lang and Weidmüller 2005). Business activity is submitted to the general banking law (*Kreditwesengesetz*) and to supervision by the Federal Financial Authority (Bundesanstalt für Finanzdienstleistungsaufsicht – BAFIN).[5] The governance structure consists of an executive board, which is directly responsible for all business activities of the cooperative, a supervisory board and a general assembly of the members. The general meeting (assembly) of shareholders elects the members of the board, carries out the annual closing of the accounts and is responsible for the supervision of both the executive and the supervisory board as well as for decisions of extraordinary nature (Kramer 2006).

At operational level, credit cooperatives act as full financial intermediaries with *de facto* no legal limitations or regulatory burdens different from the general rules applying to commercial banks.[6] German cooperative banks do not enjoy particular tax benefits either. In particular, due to their strong infra-sector business relations described more in detail in the following chapters, Raiffeisenbanken and Volksbanken are able to offer to their customers (members as well as non-members) the whole range of banking and financial services following an *Allfinanz*-strategy, typical of German intermediaries, by exploiting the distribution power of their branch offices (Ashhoff and Henningsen 1995: 176). Given the statutory independence of the single *Raiffeisenbank* and *Volksbank*, the peculiarity of German cooperative banks is therefore their capability of acting as a decentralized but coordinated network (without forming a banking group in the formal sense) with strong interlinked interests both at associative and entrepreneurship level.

7.2.1 The associative level: the *Verband*

The cooperative banks are organized in (7) regional and (1) national federations, called Regionalverbände and Bundesverband deutscher Volksbanken und Raiffeisenbanken (BVR) respectively.[7] The national association, resulting from the merger of the previous national associations of the Raiffeisenbanken and Volksbanken in 1972, is also member of the federal association of cooperatives encompassing all German cooperatives irrespective of their category type (*Genossenschaftsverbände in der Bundesrepublik Deutschland*, qtd. in Handwörterbuch des Genossenschaftswesens 1980: 841). Both associative levels function as political and service centres for the cooperative banks and their affiliated companies promoting the cooperative banking industry, developing strategic concepts and offering consultancy services including legal and tax support as well as consulting on general management issues and staff training.

Membership is mandatory regionally in the sense that first level banks (Raiffeisenbanken und Volksbanken) are obliged by law to become member of a co-operative auditing association (Prüfungsverband incorporated in the Regionalverbände) deputized to perform the annual audit of the financial statements as well as of the overall correctness of management of the associate cooperative banks (*Gesetz betreffend die Erwerbs- und Wirtschaftsgenossenschaften* 1889: § 53).[8] On the contrary, cooperative institutions are not obliged to become member of the national federation.[9]

Membership-fees are generally calculated in per mil of balance sheet total, while audit services are invoiced separately. As for the billing conditions, the tendency is to lower annual contributions to a minimum level towards an increased separate invoicing of the services requested. This is noteworthy because in the past membership fees tended to be given for free regardless of the effective volume of services requested by the single cooperative bank – especially regionally where the national association served more as a strategic coordination centre (Genossenschaftsverband Frankfurt 2006: 33).

It is of immediate evidence that the mandatory membership has relevant implications on the cohesion level of the cooperative sector giving regional associations a relevant role in addressing and unifying the strategic and business orientation of the first level Raiffeisenbanken and Volksbanken. In addition, as we will see, the presence of regional associations' representatives in the supervisory boards of the central cooperatives business companies (like the DZ-Bank and its affiliated entities) enforces their coordination influence over the sector (Backenköhler 2002: 52). At the same time, the tendency toward transparent pricing modalities of the services provided, exposes the cooperative associations to the competition of external service suppliers (like private consultancy firms) but simultaneously providing incentives to increase service quality and conform to market practices.[10]

However, the traditional strategic promotion role of the cooperative banking industry by the cooperative associations and the ability of the same associations to provide adequate services to their members came under pressure in the last decade. This was a consequence of stronger commercial competition in the retail banking sector, increased bank management complexity and higher regulatory standards. In turn, financial markets' dynamic forced the first level credit unions to improve their skills and competences both at commercial as well as at (risk) management stage but their limited average size hindered the process. The Finanzverbund defined and implemented over the last years a strategy involving both the associative and the entrepreneurship level (see the second section of this chapter), in order to face competition by offering products and services to the local cooperative banks at financially viable, competitive rates, and providing adequate (risk) management.

The strategy requires a strengthening of the cooperation within the cooperative sector. In turn, given the autonomy of the single credit unions, this relies on the economic incentives and convenience of the local institutions to pursue the defined goals. The main steps of the strategy may be summarized as follows (Bundesverband der Deutschen Volksbanken und Raiffeisenbanken, 1999; DG Bank 1999: 7):

- assigning to the national association (BVR) strategic competences and defining a clearer job division between national and regional associative levels;
- standardizing information processes and platforms and consolidating regional service companies;

- centralizing the credit cooperatives' protection scheme management;
- rationalizing the local banks' structure also *via* mergers in order to increase average size and thereby reducing the incidence of fixed costs (see the second section of this chapter);
- strengthening the separation between (central) production and (local) distribution momentum of banking services and products of asset broker type (see the second section of this chapter).

The first three goals aim at strengthening the coordination capacity of the national association so as to achieve an ideal separation of duties between national and regional associations. This involves the allocation of the responsibility of defining the strategic orientation of the cooperative movement on federal level, as it was suggested by the local banks through their regional associations and at the BVR's general meeting; it also entails the implementation of the so called "competence centres" in the (main) areas of information technology, staff training, product development & marketing; payment systems, legal and tax services, risk management and internal control procedures – the so-called "V Control," a computer-supported whole bank controlling system designed to improve business and risk diversification for the individual banks (Bundesanstalt für Finanzdienstleistungsaufsicht 2005: 92).

In turn, the operative implementation of those service facilities and procedures is performed locally by the regional cooperative associations interfacing the local credit banks. Those competence centres should pursue economies of scale in developing at central stage the necessary know-how otherwise non obtainable at economic and efficient conditions at local level; representatives of the Raiffeisenbanken and Volksbanken participate in the working groups established within each competence centre in order to bring in the operational needs of the category and act as interlink between associative and entrepreneurship circuits (Krüger 2004: 6).

At the same time, the number of *Regionalverbände* has gradually been reduced in order to limit possible overlaps of infrastructures and cost duplications between regional associations. This probably as part of an idealistic attempt to form a single association that should favour a strong central coordination of the cooperative sector by serving the local banks through regional subsidiaries (Backenköhler 2002: 52). In parallel, regional associations have consolidated the average size of their service companies via supra-regional mergers of the controlled business units with those of neighbouring associations. The national association is also in charge for the management of the credit cooperatives' protection scheme. The safety net is intended to safeguard the solvency of the associate members by ensuring that each banking institution meets its payment obligations in order to prevent any negative impact on confidence in cooperative banks (Bundesverband der Deutschen Volksbanken und Raiffeisenbanken, *Statute of the Protection Scheme*, § 1). In that sense it exceeds traditional deposit insurance schemes.

Yearly contributions, constituting the guarantee fund, are charged to the credit cooperatives upon a (credit) classification system which is intended to enable early identification and correction of critical situations. Member banks with a good credit rating are rewarded with reduced contributions while banks with poorer ratings, showing a significantly higher probability of failure according to the classification result, are motivated through differentiated surcharges to improve their credit rating (Bundesverband der Deutschen Volksbanken und Raiffeisenbanken Banken 2003: 4). In addition to capital contributions, member banks are also obliged to guarantee collectively for the obligations of the protection scheme; these guarantees form the so called guarantee volume (Bundesverband der Deutschen Volksbanken und Raiffeisenbanken, *Statute of the Protection Scheme*).

7.2.2 The entrepreneurship level: the Finanzverbund

As mentioned, local credit banks (Raiffeisenbanken and Volksbanken) form the first entrepreneurship level of the cooperative banking sector. In their business activity, local institutions profit from the broad range of *Allfinanz* products and services provided by the central cooperative banks, namely the Deutsche Zentral-Genossenschaftsbank (DZ-Bank) and the (regional) Westdeutsche Genossenschafts-Zentralbank (WGZ-Bank), and their parent product companies (second level institutions).[11] In fact, the DZ-Bank act as leading central bank for more than four fifths of the Raiffeisenbanken and Volksbanken excluding the credit cooperatives of the Länder Rheinland and Westfalen served by WGZ-Bank. The share capital of the central institutions is directly or indirectly controlled by the local cooperative banks.

First and second level cooperative institutions form the so called Finanzverbund, a financial network not constituting a banking group from the legal point of view.[12] DZ-Bank itself is the resulting institution of the progressive merger of previous regional and supra-regional central banks; the process may in future involve also the WGZ-Bank in order to remove possible operational overlaps and cost duplications, leading to a unique central institution (*Genossenschaftsbanken, Ehre wem Ehre gebührt* 2004: 1034). DZ-Bank acts as: 1) central bank in the sense of supporting and serving the local cooperative banks; 2) holding institution controlling and coordinating the parent product companies which are again functional to the service needs of the Raiffeisenbanken and Volksbanken; 3) commercial bank being an important player in the German wholesale banking market also acting as interface between the cooperative network and the (international) capital markets (DZ-Bank, *DZ-Bank – Zusammen geht mehr* 2006: 6).

Over the years, the DZ-Bank and its participated financial companies have achieved leading market positions in relevant business areas as in the securities settlement, payment system, leasing, asset management, consumer credit and home building and loan (see endnote 11). Their success was also due to the consolidation process of the central institutions forced by the *Verband*, which was consistent with the above-decribed strengthening strategy. The clear separation between central production and local distribution momentum of banking products and services, especially of asset broker type, is intended to segment the market by strengthening the market presence of the local credit institutions so as to help them to serve the market efficiently and to fully exploit their distribution power by meeting specific clients' needs through the wide product offer of the Finanzverbund without having to produce the whole range of the products themselves (Krüger 2002: 10–12).

Relationship management lies in the responsibility of the local bank, which is eventually supported by the central product specialists. At the same time, primary banks outsource other business services, like data processing, to cooperative service companies generally serving regional or supra-regional areas. This job division should help local banks to lever variable revenues and reduce fixed costs which still have a high incidence on their profit and loss account putting many primary banks under strain (Bundesanstalt für Finanzdienstleistungsaufsicht 2003: 92). At the same time, the *Verband*-strategy aims to cut general administrative costs via mergers of local cooperative banks. Fixed cost reductions are estimated in the range of 20–5 per cent based upon national association's figures.[13] In turn, larger banks are also able to achieve better risk management control and sharpen compliance procedures which at present are critical management issues (Bundesanstalt für Finanzdienstl eistungsaufsicht 2005: 92).

In addition, the merger process should limit the competition and overlaps between primary institutions serving the same geographical area following the "one market – one bank" principle, providing – all other things been equal – higher revenues (Krüger 2002: 10-12). The merger process is depicted in Figure 7.1, which reports the number of cooperative credit banks from 1996 to 2005. Upon *Verband*'s expectations, the total number of primary banks should decline to 800 over the next years, pushing the average size measured by total assets up to 1 billion Euros (DG Bank 1999: 7).

Consistently with the legal and economic independence of cooperative banks at primary level, the Raiffeisenbanken and Volksbanken are free to make use of the product and service range of the central institutions. This provides a strong incentive to the DZ-Bank group to supply viable products at competitive market rates, otherwise facing competition from non-cooperative financial intermediaries.[14] DZ-Bank has constantly sought a potential captive cooperative market. Given the same economic conditions, local credit cooperatives would prefer the services of the Finanzverbund which would, in turn, strengthen the competitive capability of the central institutions to work efficiently by achieving adequate business volumes.

In this context, a key role is played by the pricing mechanisms governing the business relations between first- and second-level cooperatives – pursuing a correct alignment of interest – and by the DZ-Bank performance attribution via property rights held by the local cooperative banks. As far as the pricing mechanism is concerned, DZ-Bank has reviewed its policy over the last years, moving towards a clearer and more transparent price definition, in order to limit cross-subsidizing situations or tying policies. Generally speaking, the pricing policy follows a cost approach in the sense that each

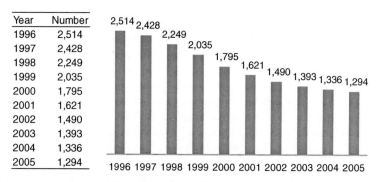

Year	Number
1996	2,514
1997	2,428
1998	2,249
1999	2,035
2000	1,795
2001	1,621
2002	1,490
2003	1,393
2004	1,336
2005	1,294

Figure 7.1   Number of cooperative primary banks
Source: Bundesanstalt für Finanzdienstleistungs aufsicht, Annual Report, 2005.
Deutsche Bundesbank, Bankstellenstatistik, 2002, 2004, 2006.

product or service is invoiced separately; in addition prices decrease in parallel to higher business volumes also via bonus and commission retrocession, representing implicit performance attribution. Following asset management's market practices, fee retrocession is of particular relevance especially for investment services (Deutsche Zentral-Genossenschaftsbank 2006; 2–16).

In addition to the implementation of a more transparent pricing policy, the central bank has established joint consulting committees (called *Beiräte*) formed by representatives of the local Raiffeisenbanken and Volksbanken as well as of the DZ-Bank (Deutsche Zentral-Genossenschaftsbank 2006: 2–16). This was in order to steadily adapt the product and service range to the needs of the primary banks, for each business division. The central institutions seem to have historically been able to adequately serve the cooperative sector by capturing large shares of the business volumes generated by local banks. WGZ-Bank estimates the amount of captive business volume (*Verbundquote*) to 90 per cent (WGZ-Bank 2006). At the same time, the DZ-banking group paid commissions and bonuses to the local cooperative banks in excess of 1.5 billion euros (2004: 1.3 billion), which accounted for around 40 per cent of the primary banks' total net commission income (Deutsche Zentral-Genossenschaftsbank 2006: 2–16; DZ-Bank 2006: 6). This is a major indicator of the strong business relations within the Finanzverbund.

A second key role in providing incentives to primary banks for making use of the central institutions' product range is the governance structure of the central banks (and consequently of their parent companies). The capital of WGZ-Bank and DZ-Bank is directly or indirectly controlled by the local cooperative banks.[15] Through the holding of the capital of the central institutions of the sector, first level banks (which are at the same time clients) benefit from their business success. Nevertheless, due to the successive mergers of the previous regional central banks, there is no perfect alignment of positions between all credit cooperatives, in the sense that the conversion ratios of the mergers may have altered the relative participation proportion, by assigning to the cooperative banks of a certain region (for example of the major old central banks) an amount of shares of the DZ-Bank more than proportional to their relative weight in the cooperative banking system. This circumstance may be mitigated by adopting appropriate pricing mechanisms as previously described.

At the same time, by article of association, the national association (BVR) is entitled to appoint one member (usually the chairman) of the supervisory board of the DZ-Bank (Deutsche Zentral-Genossenschaftsbank 2001: § 11).

This enables a strong interlink between the associative and entrepreneurship level of the cooperative sector and facilitates the implementation of the *Verband*'s strategies; it also helps in mitigating possible frictions among shareholders, on the one side, and between local banks and the board of directors of the central bank itself, on the other side.

Overall, considering the strong interlink business and financial interests, the German cooperative sector may be viewed as a banking group from the economic point of view. The capability of the Finanzverbund to act as a decentralized but coordinated banking entity is also testified by the publication of consolidated accounts since 2003.

As such, the Finanzverbund has recently (2005) been rated by major agencies recognizing that the sector has become increasingly integrated in recent years. Beside the individual ratings of the central banks and affiliated companies, the long-term and short-term ratings are applied to the roughly 1300 banks participating in the group (Fitch Ratings 2005); this also in consideration of the mutual support mechanism and protection scheme constituting strong peculiarities of the German cooperative banking system.

7.3 Concluding remarks

The German cooperative banking sector depicts an integrated system both at associative and entrepreneurship level. The cohesion degree has historically been favoured by the legal obligation of the Raiffeisenbanken and Volksbanken to be members of the regional associations in order to fulfill audit requirements. This imposition enabled a strong coordination and a strategic orientation of the sector at regional as well as at federal stage. In doing that, the *Verband* has been able to implement a valid job division between the first level cooperative banks and the central bank(s), largely separating the distribution and relationship management, which is responsibility of the local cooperative banks, and the production momentum, which is delegated to the central institutions and to their product companies. This organizational structure should help levering the variable revenue and lowering the fixed cost component of primary banks in order to strengthen their profitability. In parallel, the ongoing merger process at local bank level aiming to increase the average size of the cooperatives should reduce administrative costs and enhance bank management skills.

The key element in ensuring the success of that organization scheme is given by the fact that the local Raiffeisenbanken and Volksbanken – as independent entities – are free to make use of the products and services provided by the central institutions. This provides a strong incentive to the central banks to supply viable products at competitive market rates otherwise facing competition from non-cooperative financial intermediaries. Given the same economic conditions, local credit cooperatives will prefer the services of the *Finanzverbund* which, in turn, strengthen the competitive capability of the central institutions to work efficiently by achieving adequate business volumes. At the same time, proper pricing mechanisms of the services and products offered by the *Finanzverbund* and a correct allocation of the property rights of the central institutions among the cooperative banks are critical requirements to ensure exploitation of the (cooperative) captive market. This has historically proved to be the case. At present, beside legal considerations, the German cooperative sector may be viewed as an integrated banking group as testified by the consolidated financial statements and the rating attributions.

Notes

1. Excluding the cooperative mortgage banks (*genossenschatliche Realkreditinstitute*), the market share of the cooperative banking sector claims up to 13 per cent (2004 data [Bundesverband Deutscher Banken, *Markanteile der Bankengruppen*, 1996-2005). Please note that the German Bundesbank's statistics consider cooperative mortgage banks as part of the so called "mortgage banks", exhibited as a separate institutional aggregate (Deutsche Bundesbank, *Erläuterungen*, in Statistische Beihefte – Bankenstatistik).
2. The protection scheme, which is described in detail in the second section of the chapter, is not intended as a deposit insurance. Rather it is used as a safety net, aiming to safeguard the banking institution itself and not only the customers' deposits (see Bundesverband der Deutschen Volksbanken und Raiffeisenbanken 2006: § 1).
3. Sparda-Banken (12 entities), PSD-Banken (15) and Kirchenbanken (11) are credit cooperatives as well (DG Bank 1998: 6). They were established as credit unions of specific categories of workers (like for example railway employees) or institutions (like churches). Due to their limited number, they are not going to be considered separately.
4. At the end of 2004 of the total 1336 existing credit cooperatives, 46 per cent carried the denomination of Volksbanken, 40 per cent the indication of Raiffeisenbanken and 14 per cent the joint denomination of Raiffeisen-Volksbank. The author's calculation is based on BVR-figures (2005).
5. The last amendment of *Gesetz betreffend die Erwerbs- und Wirtschaftsgenosse nschaften* of 19 April 2006 was made necessary by the introduction of the European Cooperative Society (ECS). It modifies the minimum number of members requested for establishing a cooperative, and reduces the minimum number of directors and simplifies auditing requirements for small unions (see *Gesetz über das Kreditwesen* 1961).

6. Cooperative banks are entitled to insert a given percentage of the additional capital contributions to which members are obliged (*Haftsummen*) in the tier II capital calculation. This special regulation reflects the legal peculiarities of cooperative institutions see *Gesetz über das Kreditesen* 1961: § 10).

7. The geographic area of the *Regionalverbände* does not correspond to the one of the *Länder* due to historic reasons and repeated mergers. At the same time, the Sparda-Banken and PSD-Banken have their associations.

8. Audit reports do not have to be transmitted to the Federal Financial Supervisory Authority (BAFIN). However, BAFIN may request cooperative banks to submit the audit reports on their annual financial statements; that is, for troubled banks. In addition, BAFIN regularly orders general audits with a uniformly defined auditing task at cooperative banks. In 2005, together with the pre-audit reports, the number of reports submitted totaled more than 2,500 (Bundesanstalt für Finanzdienstleistungsaufsicht 2005: 92).

9. Please note that there have been cases of Volksbanken and Raiffeisenbanken refusing national membership but legally obliged to maintain regional association. Consequently these banks could not make use of the credit cooperatives' logo but were entitled to carry the denomination of *Volksbank* or *Raiffeisenbank*.

10. In accordance to the 2004 amendment of the audit regulation (*Bilanzrec htsreformgesetz* – BilReG), cooperative associations have to separate their audit activities from their remaining operations (see [Jessen 2005: 45; Esser, Hillebrand and Wlater 2006: 26–58).

11. Product companies operate in specific business fields like asset management, payment systems, consumer credit, leasing, and insurance. They include Bausparkasse Schwäbisch Hall, Union Asset Management Holding, R+V Versicherung, Deutsche Genossenschafts-Hypothekenbank, VR-Leasing, Norisbank, Münchener Hypothekenbank, Dwp-Bank (participated), and Transaktionsinstitut (participated). The majority of them is organized as joint-stock companies (Bundesverband der Deutschen Banken 2003; 3).

12. Even if incorporated in the form of joint-stock corporations, the central institutions (DZ-Bank, WGZ-Bank) and their parent companies are considered as part of the cooperative sector due to their shareholders' structure and captive business volumes.

13. Savings in administrative costs have been estimated in 30 per cent for a cooperative bank having a balance sheet total of over 500 million euros compared to a bank with 250 million total assets (DG Bank 2000: 17).

14. The DZ-Bank articles of association obliges the bank to serve reliably the cooperative banks (Deutsche Zentral-Genossenschaftsbank 2001).

15. Shares are often held through regional holding companies embracing the participation rights of the Raiffeisenkassen and Volksbanken of the various geographical areas. Each holding company originally controlled the regional central bank of the correspondent area. Following the merger process, the local holding companies obtained shares of the new entity originated by mergers in exchange of the participation rights shares held in the previously controlled regional central bank participating in the process.

References

Ashhoff G., Henningsen E. (2005) *Das deutsche Genossenschaftswesen. Entwicklung, Struktur, wirtschaftliches Potential*, Fritz Knapp Verlag, Frankfurt Am Main.

Backenköhler R. (2002) *Der moderne Genossenschaftsverband – Neue Wege für Dienstleistungen und Prüfung*, Newsletter des Instituts für Genossenschaftswesen der Universität Münster, no. 2.

Bundesanstalt für Finanzdienstleistungsaufsicht (2005), *Annual Report*.

Bundesverband der Deutschen Volksbanken und Raiffeisenbanken (1999) *Bündelung der Kräfte: Ein Verbund – eine Strategie*, Band 1,2.

Bundesverband der Deutschen Volksbanken und Raiffeisenbanken Banken (2003, 2004, 2005), *Consolidated Annual Accounts of the Cooperative Financial Services Network*.

Bundesverband der Deutschen Volksbanken und Raiffeisenbanken Banken (2003) *Consolidated Accounts of the German Cooperative Banking Sector*.

Bundesverband der Deutschen Volksbanken und Raiffeisenbanken (2006) *Statute of the Protection Scheme*.

Bundesverband Deutscher Banken (1996–2005) *Ertragslage bei den einzelnen Bankengruppen*.

Bundesverband Deutscher Banken (1996–2005) *Markanteile der Bankengruppen*.

Deutsche Bundesbank (2002, 2004, 2006) *Bankenstellenstatistik*.

Deutsche Bundesbank (April 2003, 2005, 2006) *Monthly Report*.

Deutsche Bundesbank (2005) *The Performance of German Credit Institutions in 2004*, Monthly Report, September, pp. 15–43.

Deutsche Bundesbank (2006) "Erläuterungen," *Statistische Beihefte – Bankenstatistik*.

Deutsche Zentral-Genossenschaftsbank (2006) *Jahresbericht 2006*.

Deutsche Zentral-Genossenschaftsbank (2001) *Satzung*, last amendment 2005.

DG Bank (1998) *The German Cooperatives. Presentation*.

DG Bank (1999) *Die deutschen Genossenschaften. Statistik*.

DG Bank (1999) *Die deutschen Genossenschaftsbanken. Statistik*.

DG Bank (2000) *Die deutschen Genossenschaftsbanken 1999, Bericht*.

DZ-Bank (2006) *DZ-Bank - Zusammen geht mehr*.

Esser I., Hillebrand, K.P., Wlater, K.F. (2006) *Unabhängigkeit der genossenschaftlichen Prüfungsverbände*, Zeitschrift für das gesamte Genossenschaftswesen, Band 56.

Fitch Ratings (2005) *Genossenschaftlicher Finanzverbund. Genossenschaftsbanken, Ehre wem Ehre gebührt*, Zeitschrift für das gesamte Kreditwesen, 19/2004.

Genossenschaftsverband Frankfurt (2006) *Kompetenzzentrum für Unternehmens führung*, Jahrbuch.

Gesetz betreffend die Erwerbs- und Wirtschaftsgenossenschaften (1889), New edition, Bek. v. 19.8.1994, last amendment 19.4.2006.

Gesetz über das Kreditwesen (1961) New Edition, Bek. v. 9. 9.1998, last amendment Art. 4a G v. 22. 9.2005.

Handwörterbuch des Genossenschaftswesens (1980) *Genossenschaftsverbände in der Bundesrepublik Deutschland*.

Jessen U. (2005) *Regelungen zur Unabhängigkeit der genossenschaftlichen Prüfungsverbände nach dem Bilanzrechtsreformgesetz*, Zeitschrift für das gesamte Genossenschaftswesen, Band 55.

Kramer J.W. (2006) *Co-operative Development and Corporate Governance Structures in German Cooperatives – Problems and Perspectives*, Paper presented at the XIV International Economic History Congress, Helsinki.

Krüger M. (2002) *Gestaltung der Zukunft kommt voran*, Bankinformation und Genossenschaftsforum, no.6.

Krüger M. (2004), *Neue Ära*, Bankinformation und Genossenschaftsforum, 12.

Lang J., Weidmüller, L. (2005) *Genossenschaftsgesetz. Mit Erläuterungen zum Umwandlungsgesetz. Kommentar*, Gruyter.

WGZ-Bank (2006) *Jahresbericht 2005*.

8
The Cooperative Credit System in Italy

Roberto Di Salvo and Juan Sergio Lopez

8.1 The Italian scenario

The pace of Italian GDP growth has showed a modest performance in the period from 2001 to 2006 reaching an average of 0.9 against an average of 1.8 in EU15. If the longer period of 1996-2006 is considered, the Italian economic performance improves to an average of 1.4, which remains lower than the EU 15 average of 2.3. While the Italian economy does not seem to be able to sort out the problems that slow down its growth, the Italian banking system has undergone deep changes since the turn of the twentieth century. Once dominated by the public sector, the Italian banking system is today almost completely privatized and counts, among its ranks, some of the major European banking groups. Still, the size of the banking industry has not reached the same dimension of the major European countries (see Figure 8.1).

Moreover, the average size (in term of assets) of the Italian banks is still modest compared to the other large European markets (see Figure 8.2).

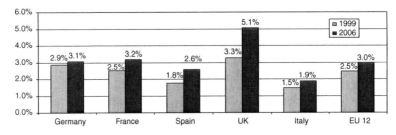

Figure 8.1 Banking sector: ratio of total asset to GDP
Source: ECB data published in "EU Banking Structures" 2008.

Nevertheless, the concentration of the market has increased sharply: taking into account the mergers carried out at the beginning of 2007, the first five banking groups add up to 61 per cent of the banking assets. Therefore the structure of the market emerging from the consolidation process is composed by three segment: few very large banks that account for 60 per cent of the assets; a couple of dozen medium banks that cover another 20 per cent of the market and around 500 small local banks (mainly cooperative banks) that account for the last 20 per cent.

The consolidation process has not hindered competition thanks to the sustained growth of branches. Total branches rose from 24,530 in 1996 to 32,338 in 2006. Therefore the average number of banks presents in provinces and municipalities has increased considerably.

Another important aspect is the increasing opening to the international markets: at the end of 2006, 26 Italian banking groups turned out to be significantly active on foreign markets. (The share of their foreign assets were more than 26 per cent.) At the same time, the presence of foreign banks in Italy accounted for more than 18 per cent of the total assets.

The privatization and consolidation process has led to an overall better performance of the banking industry in terms of profit and efficiency. The average ROE increased from a mere 2 per cent during 1995-97 to almost 12 per cent in 2006. Costs have been reduced, acting in particular on the labour force costs. (Total employees decreased 3 per cent from 1996 to 2006.) The increased profitability is due also to the diversification of income sources: the contribution of services to the intermediation margin has increased from 28.5 per cent in 1996 to 53 per cent in 2006. Finally, the credit quality has considerably improved due to the upgrade of the risk management techniques.

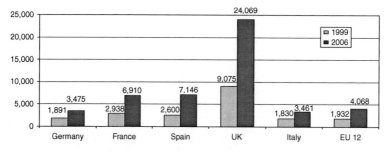

Figure 8.2 Banking sector: average dimension (total assets/number of banks)
Source: ECB data published in "EU Banking Structures" 2008.

Summing up: in the last decade the Italian banking industry underwent a considerable change of its structure and performance, improving efficiency and opening to the international markets. During this process observers and analysts raised the concern about the survival of local and cooperative banks. However, the recent history has shown that local cooperative banks not only survived but gained market shares at the expenses of large banks. The history and the evolution of credit cooperative banks, that will be next outlined, may give some explanation to this success.

8.2 Origins and rationale of credit cooperatives

Credit cooperatives were born in Italy at the end of the nineteenth century as a result of a combination of the critical conditions of the economy in rural areas and the action of a German priest, F. W. Raiffeisen who was dedicated to the promotion of new forms of financial support for peasants, small farmers and craftsmen. Indeed, usury and cyclical problems in the agriculture sector all over Europe and in Italy brought the need for basic financial services to a wide class of rural population. F.W. Raiffeisen first started his job in German speaking countries but his action was soon replicated in Italy and in other European countries (as for example, The Netherlands, France, Finland) through the network of the Catholic Church which often played and important role in the promotion of the Italian *Casse rurali*.[1]

As a consequence of a long period of growth, the movement of *Casse rurali* strengthened its position in large areas of the North-east and gradually in almost all Italian regions. At the beginning of the Fascism the *Casse rurali* were playing an important financial and social role in most rural areas, which often was considered as a political problem for the Regime. Thus, the action against the Church, followed by the crisis of the 1930s, implied a significant reduction of the number and business activity of *Casse rurali*. Nevertheless, when relationships between the Fascism and the Church were eased, a banking act was issued in 1937 (TUCRA) giving a specific regulatory framework for this type of bank, which turned out to be a significant recognition of its role within the Italian banking system.

Within the new framework, the *Casse rurali* have experienced a new long period of growth, coupled with the economic boom of the 1950s and 1960s. Gradually but constantly, market shares have been increasing together with the number of branches and the establishment of new *Casse rurali*. Even though Banca d'Italia was rather careful in allowing bank branching, basically for stability purposes, the policy in favour of a wider network of small rural cooperative banks was due to the need for extending basic financial services in non urban areas, under well determined restrictions stated by TUCRA.[2]

The institutional model underlying the regulation was based on the combination of several cooperative and mutual requirements which endowed the principles of self-help and economic democracy, aiming at the fulfilment of benefits for members and local communities. The "one-head-one-vote" and "open door" principles were basically ensuring the economic democracy, while strict limitations to profit distribution coupled the need for strengthening capitalization with the non-profit values of the cooperative. Furthermore, restrictions on business areas, membership and operations with non-members clearly depicted the model of the local cooperative and mutual bank in Italy.

8.3 A new wave of growth at the beginning of the new era

The constant growth of business activity and a strong capitalization process have brought the *Casse rurali* to be a small but not negligible part of the Italian banking system at the end of the 1980s. Then, when the liberalization and European integration process started to exert its influence on the structure and performance of the Italian financial system, policy makers, academics and scholars were often worried about the future of small local banks since deregulation and market integration were expected to increase competition and foster the search for scale economies.

Nevertheless, the liberalization of bank branching in 1990 was the starting point of a streamlining process for Casse rurali which brought about a significant increase of size, through either branching or merging with one another. Although scale economies in banking have always been considered a controversial issue, some degree of scale inefficiency was probably affecting the Casse rurali and might have been an important driver for concentration and branching.[3] Thus, the number of banks decreased significantly over the 1990s (from 693 in 1992 to 438 in 2006), while the branch network almost doubled, and staff also increased.[4]

The reasons prompting BCCs to embark on mergers and acquisitions were manifold: first, the drive to adopt a policy of external growth aimed at economies of scale, enabling the institution to enter new markets or defend its local base of operations (strategic-territorial motivations); second, the possibility of diversifying banks' activities with the associated

Table 8.1   M&A involving cooperative banks

Years	Number of M&A	Numbers of banks involved
1992	13	29
1993	25	50
1994	24	49
1995	20	41
1996	21	43
1997	8	17
1998	15	33
1999	22	52
2000	21	53
2001	28	58
2002	17	34
2003	13	26
2004	8	16
2005	3	6
2006	2	4

Source: Bank of Italy data.

benefits in terms of risk control and income growth (strategic-operational motivations); third, the hope of achieving a sounder balance-sheet situation in the face of operational imbalances (rescue motivations). The mix of motivations can vary considerably, depending on the operational position (in balance or not) and the role (active or passive) of the banks involved.

Most of the mergers involving BCCs were motivated by the drive to become more competitive in order to expand their capacity to reach new territories and new clients. In the same period, the impact of market integration and competition turned out to be less severe than expected, due to structural and natural segmentations of markets and different degrees of information asymmetries and market imperfections across countries, regions and segments. In this context, local and social rooting gave an important information advantage to the Casse Rurali. These were the strategic factors which allowed small, local, mutual credit institutions to be viable in a more dynamic and competitive environment. Technology and outsourcing also played a relevant role since innovation in IT eased small banks to have access to better technology and scale economies were exploited through the centralization of functions and services within the network of *Casse rurali*.[5]

Thus, a new model of cooperative credit was taking place within a wider network open to the market, while the old, small, stand-alone, no branched *cassa rurale* was phased out. As a consequence, the need for a revision of regulation was more and more evident. The adoption of the Second Banking Directive in Italy in 1993 was then a good chance to update or eliminate specific provisions concerned with *Casse rurali* and embrace these banks within the same banking regulatory framework complying with the "level playing field" principle of the Directive. Therefore, Italian credit cooperatives were allowed to offer all financial services as listed in the Directive. At the same time, some previous restrictions on membership (80 per cent of members were required to be farmers or craftsmen) were phased out by deep changes in the economy and then eliminated, allowing any resident in the area to be eligible member of the local credit cooperative. Coherently, the Casse rurali were re-named as Banche di credito cooperativo. So they lost their rural vocation by law and acquired a most comprehensive and up-to-date local and mutual banking endowment.

The new banking law and the ensuing by-laws regulation, released by the Bank of Italy, introduced a set of rules that define the present institutional framework of the BCCs. In particular the main aspects are:

- the opportunity of becoming members is open to whatever professional condition people may have, abolishing the former rule requiring 80 per cent of members to be farmers and artisans;
- a minimum number of 200 member and a two-million-euro initial capital is required for establishing a Banca di Credito Cooperativo;
- business has to be carried out "mainly" with members (application of the principle of mutual support); more than 50 per cent of risk weighted assets are to be related to members;
- each member may own more than one share, but the overall nominal value of the shares owned may not exceed 50,000 euro. In spite of the number of owned shares, each member has one vote in the general meeting (the one man – one vote principle);
- BCCs are obliged to allocate at least 70 per cent of the annual net profit to the statutory reserve which is in turn, not subject to distribution. An additional 3 per cent of the net profit shall be paid into a special mutual aid fund for the promotion and development of co-operation, especially in Southern Italy, thus contributing to the redistribution of resources in economically non-homogeneous areas of the Country;
- BCCs must operate in specific local areas, investing money where they obtain their deposits in order to contribute directly to the growth of the local economy; to this end 95 per cent of loans have to be granted to clients living or having business in the area where the BCC operates.

8.3 Recent trends

During the 1990s and the first years of the third millennium, the BCCs have significantly strengthened their market position and strongly enhanced the network organization in order to exploit scale economies and benefit from synergies. As shown in Figure 8.3, BCCs have experienced a significantly higher growth of loans than the rest of the banking system. As a result, across the period, the BCCs' market share has steadily increased.

The nation-wide share in the deposit market has risen up to nearly 9 per cent, while the share in terms of loans went up to 6.5 per cent. Indeed, markets shares in many areas of the country are more than 20 per cent. The increase of lending activity has been substantial over the past 5 or 6 years, attenuating only recently. At the same time the number of branches have been constantly increasing (from 2,093 in 1992 to 3,758 in 2006) representing today more than 11 per cent of the total branches of the banking system. The characteristic of this large network is that the outlets are distributed in almost every province of the country and mainly in small municipalities and rural areas.

Figure 8.4 shows clearly that the increasing lending by cooperative banks benefited mainly small and micro enterprises. Indeed, BCCs have increased loans to enterprises three times more than the other banks, while the performance has been only a bit more dynamic in the households sector (+20 per cent).

This increasing specialization of BCCs in the traditional interest-income generating business is mirrored in their income statement: almost no diversification of income sources has taken place in the past

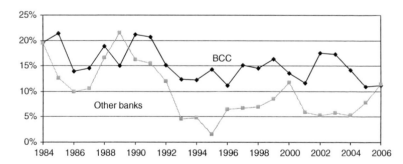

Figure 8.3   Loans rate of growth – BCC and other banks
Source: Bank of Italy data.

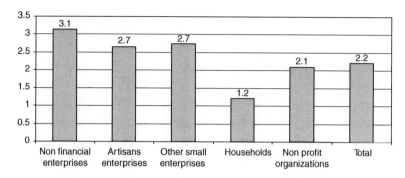

Figure 8.4 Loans growth by sector (1999–2006) – ratio between BCC and other banks
Source: Bank of Italy data.

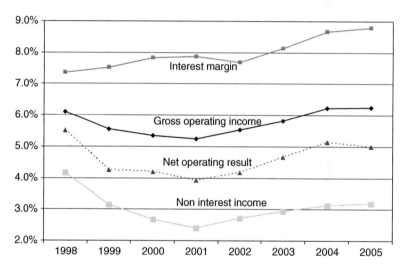

Figure 8.5 Income produced by BCCs as share of the total banking system
Source: Bank of Italy data.

years and, actually, an ever larger share of the total interest margin produced by the banking sector is due to the BCCs (see Figure 8.5) while the share of non interest income is still quite marginal.

Important improvements have been registered in the cost efficiency of BCCs. The ratio of total cost to total assets (see Figure 8.6) shows that the gap between the banking system and the cooperative banks has

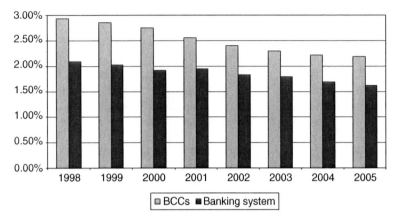

Figure 8.6 Ratio of total cost to total assets
Source: Bank of Italy data.

been partially filled, even though the characteristics of their business activity (relationship banking, proximity to customers trough a large network of branches, involvement in local development projects, and so forth) makes it almost impossible for them to reach the same level of unit costs. Finally, in spite of the rapid increase of loans, the regulatory capital ratio of the BCCs is still very high (on average around 16 per cent even though there are ample deviations among them) and the percentage of bad loans has remained lower than the average of the banking system.

The fast growth enjoyed by the BCCs is believed to be fostered, at least partially, by the streamlining process of major Italian banking groups which is still in course and might have shifted the business focus of many large banks from retail markets and small firm segments to large corporate finance and wholesale activities. Thus, BCCs might have benefited from strategy diversification and internationalization of large banking groups by having focused on retail credit and deposit markets, including the small and very small firm segment of the Italian economy. Nevertheless, the specialization of BCCs in the domestic retail market may bring about the risk of being crowded out by new forms and trends of competition – as for example, the growth in consumer credit and new attention to cottage industries from many players – while the low level of international business is leaving small and medium corporate BCC customers virtually without any kind of assistance abroad.[6]

Important changes have occurred also on the liability side of BCCs. In particular, the share of bonds in the liabilities has increased constantly replacing short term deposits. This process has reduced the mismatch between the asset and liability side produced by the rapid growth of long term loans. Table 8.2 shows the main figure of the BCCs in the period 2002-07.

8.4 Further developments

Reorganization of Information Technology services has been substantial (for example the reduction of different software platform used by the BCCs from more than 40 to a few), while outsourcing strategies have been also implemented with respect to back office activities. The regional federations and other local structures have increased their role in supporting BCCs as far as instrumental and auxiliary services are concerned. The second tier banking organization (ICCREA Group) has also been restructured in order to improve and extend the quality and scope of financial services to the local banks (payment systems, securities transactions, structured finance, specialized lending operations). Nevertheless, scale economies and synergies within the network may be further enhanced by stronger inter-cooperation between the ICCREA Group and the two second tier *Casse Centrali* operating in the independent Provinces of Trento and Bolzano, serving the local credit cooperatives.[7] Relevant benefits from further cooperation between the second tier structures are expected to arise in the field of international operations, back office services, and payment systems.

Within this compound environment, the BCCs and small local banks in general are challenged by the new strong wave of financial regulation, which has been promoted either by the world-wide financial market integration or by the European integration process. The burden of regulatory requirements even in a prudential control-based perspective is becoming more and more heavy for small-sized institutions. The introduction of the new international accounting standards, followed by the Basel 2 and MiFID implementation, may affect competitiveness of viable small credit institutions since organization requirements cannot easily be respected. Moreover, application of rules and principles may not be compatible with the nature of a small local bank; indeed, it must be taken into account that both new accounting standards and Basel 2 prudential requirements have been designed and developed to be applied to large financial institutions worldwide, for which the international business dimension and scope was prevalent and required

Table 8.2 Italian Credit Cooperative banks – main data

BCC	Local Banks	Banking Outlets	Members	Clients	Staff	Total Assets (billion)	Deposits (billion)	Of which Bonds (billion)	Loans (billion)	Market Share (deposit)	Market Share (loans)
2002	461	3,206	648,140	4,000,000	24,420	95.842	76.34	22.660	57.10	7.50	5.40
2006	438	3,758	822,893	5,000,000	27,835	136.941	111.08	39.568	94.31	8.40	6.60
2007	440	3,922	878,000	5,250,000	29,800	150.300	121.00	46.521	105.60	8.70	6.70

Source: own calculation on Bank of Italy data.

a strong policy in favour of customer protection, market discipline and prudential control.

Although small local banks do not directly access capital markets and are scarcely subject to market discipline, they had to cope with the introduction of IAS as the Italian Authorities called for a principle of integrity for the banking supervisory function, extending the new accounting standards to all banks, indifferently if quoted or not. In practice, the adoption of IAS within the BCCs has turned out to be rather complex, with a relevant opportunity cost which cannot be offset by the advantages of an easier and cheaper access to capital markets.[8]

Furthermore, Basel 2 sets forth one more challenge to BCCs and small sized banks, even though it is shared with the rest of the European banking system, including the local and cooperative banks. It is well known how the long consultation process has given the opportunity to adapt the new principles and criteria to the features of continental economy (importance of small and medium enterprises) and specificities of the European banking systems. Some important changes to the first draft of the New Capital Accord have actually reduced the expected negative impact of new prudential provisions on credit availability for small firms and capital requirements of small sized banks, which would be required to adopt the Standardized Approach for capital ratio computation.[9] Nevertheless, the complexity of the new prudential regulatory framework is extremely higher than the previous prudential rule, simply based on the eight-weighted-percentage of minimum capital requirement. Complexity and some degree of flexibility in choosing approaches and criteria, especially in the field of risk mitigation, bring about relevant organizational and professional efforts to be made by small banks. Many technical adjustments are also required in order to apply the new rules correctly to small sized institutions.

The BCC system is actively part of this process as the implementation of Basel 2 necessarily required a "systemic approach" in order to find the right balance between regulatory compliance and feasibility. Therefore, a significant effort has been aimed at framing the new regulation within the operational and organizational setting of the BCCs, with the final purpose of reducing the implementation cost for the single bank. On the one hand, common criteria and methodologies have been developed for an efficient and compliant computation of the new minimum capital requirement (First Pillar). On the other hand, the proportionality principle has generally been invoked with respect to the application of the prudential supervisory process (Second Pillar), since the complexity of methods and instruments to be realized for bank risk control and capital adequacy assessment must be calibrated according to the size of the bank and its organization and business model.

Finally, the strategic pattern of the BCCs as a system (or network) of independent banks has given further enhancement through the extension of its internal safety net. The experience of the two already existing guarantee funds within the BCC system has been very positive in terms of the banks' stability and reputation, since no BCC failure has ever occurred over the past decades while bank crises have always been solved by using internal resources only.[10]

Nowadays, the Basel 2 Directive gives the opportunity to recognize, under specified conditions, an institutional protection scheme within any banking network, by allowing zero-weighting for infra-network exposures. Even though the regulatory acknowledgment is limited to the application of a different risk class and weight within the Standardized Approach, the importance of such a provision may be considered as a formal recognition of the BCC network itself. Moreover, the compliance of the new protection scheme with well defined requirements gives also a different perspective to the network organization, which is expected to be rationalized as far as the risk control and governance are concerned.

8.5 Conclusions

The Italian banking industry has undergone a considerable change of its structure and performance, improving efficiency and opening to the international markets. The concern about the survival of local and cooperative banks has turned out to be insignificant, since their market shares have increased at the expense of large banks. Moreover, the BCC institutional and legal model has confirmed its viability in the new framework arising from Basel 2 and other regulations, enabling Italian credit cooperatives to face the market challenge also in future.

Nevertheless, the fast growth performed by the BCCs may have been fostered to some extent by the streamlining process of major Italian banking groups, which is not concluded yet, and may have shifted the business focus of many large banks from retail markets and small firm segments to large corporate finance and wholesale activities. Thus, BCCs may have benefited from focusing on retail credit and deposit markets, including the small and very small firm segment of the Italian economy. Moreover, the specialization of BCCs in the domestic retail market may bring about the risk of being crowded out by new forms and trends of competition (growth in consumer credit, a new attention to cottage industries from many players), while the low level of international business is leaving medium-sized corporate customers with poor assistance abroad.

In this context, the network strategy seems to be the only viable answer to the new challenges. Outsourcing has to be fostered and implemented according to cost efficiency criteria. The federation system has to increase its role in supporting BCCs as far as instrumental and auxiliary services are concerned. The second tier banking organization needs to improve and extend the quality and scope of financial services to the local banks (payment systems, securities transactions, structured finance, specialized lending operations). The scale economies and synergies within the network may be further enhanced by stronger inter-cooperation between the ICCREA Group and the two second tier *Casse Centrali* operating in the independent Provinces of Trento and Bolzano, serving the local credit cooperatives. Relevant benefits from further cooperation between the second tier structures are expected to arise in the field of international operations, back office services, and payment systems. Finally, the strategic pattern of the BCCs as a network of independent banks may be significantly enhanced through the extension of its internal safety net, which will enable small and local cooperative banks to be actively and fully part of the financial system.

Notes

1. See P. Cafaro (2000) and A. Fazio (1987) for a wide historical analysis of the *Casse rurali* movement.
2. See Bernasconi e Cartechini (2006) for an overview of the regulatory framework of *Casse rurali*.
3. The expected impact of deregulation on the Italian *Casse rurali* has extensively been analysed in Di Salvo (1996).
4. For a wide perspective of the concentration process among the *Casse rurali*, see Di Salvo *et al.* (1998).
5. See Carretta (2006) for an insight into outsourcing strategies in banking and in the BCC system.
6. Main trends and structural conditions of international business of BCCs are reported in a survey recently carried out by Federcasse.
7. Indeed, the *Cassa Centrale* operating in Trento has recently extended its geographical scope by developing second tier banking business in some other provinces of the North-east of the Country. On the one hand, an increased competition between the second tier banks of the network may imply more pressure in seeking more efficiency; on the other hand, it may also bring about some dispersion of resources and a reduction of external competitive capacity.
8. The extension of IAS to non-listed banks has been limited in Europe to Italy and few other small Countries.

9. See the Quantitative Impact Studies carried out by the Basel Committee, and, for BCCs, the analysis carried out by Lopez (2004).
10. The Deposit Guarantee Fund (FGD) was established in 1997 among BCCs according to the EC Directive on deposit insurance. The Bond Holders Guarantee Fund (FGO) was established in 2004 on a voluntary basis in order to extend protection to bonds issued by BCCs.

References

Bernasconi, F. Cartechini, M. (2006) *L'evoluzione del credito cooperativo italiano: norme e regole, attività e controlli.* Cooperazione di Credito, Rome, April, 192–3.

Cafaro, P. (2001) *La solidarietà efficiente. Storie prospettive del credito cooperativo in Italia.* Editori Laterza, Roma-Bari.

Carretta, A. (2005) *Politiche di outsourcing del credito cooperativo,* Cooperazione di Credito, Rome, July, 189–90.

Di Salvo, R. (1995) "Deregulation and scale economies in banking. The case of Italian casse rurali," Research Monograph, no. 1, IEF, University of North Wales, Bangor.

Fazio, A. (1987) "The rural and artisans banks: market shares and prospect," *Economic Bulletin,* no. 5, Banca d'Italia, October.

Lopez, J. S. (2003) *Il Nuovo Accordo di Basilea: una simulazione dell'impatto del calcolo del coefficiente di capitale sulle banche di credito cooperativo,* Cooperazione di Credito, Rome, July, 181.

9
The Credit Cooperative System in Finland[1]

Roberto Di Salvo, Juan Sergio Lopez and Igino Schraffl

9.1 A general view of cooperation

9.1.1 History and general characteristics

The cooperative movement developed in rural areas at the end of the nineteenth century to ease access to credit by the poorest segments of the population. The founding of a national confederation in 1899 (Pellervo-Suera) gave way to the evolution of the Finnish cooperative system: two years later, the confederation contributed to the approval of the first law on cooperatives, which was substantially amended in 1954 and subsequently modified in 1981 and in 2001. The first law was simply a literal translation of the German law on cooperatives; it was significantly supported by Hans Gebhard, whose ideas were similar to those of Friedrich Wilhem Raiffeisen. Gebhard became the pioneer of the Finnish cooperation: thanks to his action, a central institution for the development of credit cooperatives (Okobank) was established in 1902. From a legal point of view, cooperative banks were launched as Public Limited Companies to ensure they could face the administrative practices of the credit sector, notwithstanding their little experience.

At first, the Russian Governor of Finland opposed to the authorization of credit activity; the next year the Zar gave authorization conditioned to the exclusion of cooperative banks involved in "subversive" activity. The State's share in "Okobank" (including a considerable annual subsidy and a loan) was not compatible with the banking regulations, therefore the Bank had to submit to the norms of a Limited Liability Company. The cooperative movement was the main responsible for the Finnish *Risorgimento* and contributed to the National Independence from the colonial Russian rule. This really ethnic nationalistic spirit is still alive in people's mind and it contributes greatly to the organizational bond and the economic success of the cooperative movement. After the Russian independence (1917), cooperation, supported by the State, expanded so much that it became the main factor of the country's economic and social growth.

At present, the Finnish cooperative system includes, in addition to the Pellervo system, a consumer cooperative and an association of Swedish cooperatives (Finlands Svenska Andelsforbund), which separated from Pellervo respectively in 1916 and 1919. All together, they sum up two million members, out of about five million people in the country.

9.1.2 The main sectors of the Pellervo system

After World War II, mostly in the 1960s, there was a huge increase in the number of cooperative members in Finland as in central Europe. Simultaneously, a concentration process took place which often brought about the extension of a cooperative's area of activities to an entire province. In general, there are no regional federations due to the relatively small population and limited economic activity in many areas of the Country. In fact, the 16 regional offices act more as branches of the central institute than as real federations. On a national level, credit cooperatives are associated to a central institute – OKOBANK, while the other cooperative sector depends on Pellervo-Suera's head office. Pellervo-Suera thus acts as a sectorial national federation and an inter-sectorial confederation. In the last years, the trend has been different both across sectors and between local and regional cooperatives. The regional cooperatives seem to be at an advantage. In wholesaling the cooperative's market share is about 35 per cent of the whole sector; in retailing the percentage is 26–30 per cent and in the food sector about 33 per cent. The credit cooperatives have also significantly increased their share to 34 per cent of the total banking and financial activities.

The cooperation does its best in the agro industry sector where market share is about 90 per cent. This system is made up of:

- about 90 dairy product cooperatives headed by the Valio organization of 40,000 members and over 9,000 employees. Their activity has extended to other food items (jam, fish, mushrooms and fruit juice);
- 8 existing slaughterhouses and their marketing organization (TLK, Finnish farmer meat association) and a service company totaling 90,000 members and almost 9,000 employees;
- The cooperative organization MUNAKUNTA that gathers more than 4,000 egg producers (eggs are one of the Finnish's main foods);

- The central commercial wood making organization, METSALITTO, counting 135,000 members and one of the countries chief exporters. It owns paper, furniture and wood factories;
- The HAKKIJA cooperative provides farmers with machinery, goods and consultancy and recently it entered the construction and car industry as well as producing and exporting machinery to the food industry;
- The S Group is the largest Finnish company of the sector with 60 local and regional wholesale cooperatives that manage about 350 department stores and about 1,500 supermarkets, hotels and restaurants (the latter by the service company SOK). This group, counting 500,000 members, gives jobs to 24,000 people;
- 236 credit cooperatives with 600,000 members, 700 counters and 6,500 employees, operate on the national territory offering bank services;
- 130 insurance companies (Finnish law doesn't legally consider them cooperatives) and a reassurance loan company totaling 300,000 members. To further professional training and study activities the PELLERVO INSTITUTE OY was merged with the trade organization of the MTIC farmers.

In 1990, cooperative organizations with the participation of the two cooperative federations created the Finnish Cooperative Development Center (FCC), with a cooperative legal status. The purpose of this new institute was to support cooperative projects aimed at creating cooperations in the Third World and assisting, coordinating, informing and training them. The Pellervo Group represents nearly 10 per cent of the Gross National Product.

9.1.3 The role and functions of the National Confederation

Pellervo-Suera, with its over 500 affiliated cooperatives, represents the group leader in various important sectors. Despite the relatively small organizational structure, Pellervo-Suera provides to its members consultancy services, cost assistance, commercial premises, the assurance of a united group image and political representation. The main services provided to members are: information and publications, market research and consumer studies, legal services, professional training.

Although primary cooperatives have grown larger and more efficient, they have outsourced more activities to central institutions in order to maximize scale economies. Thus, strategies are mainly focused on strengthening central bodies and the network organization rather than fostering growth and size increase of the cooperatives at the first tier of the system.

9.2 The credit cooperation

9.2.1 General characteristics

The Finnish cooperative banks are called Osusspankkien (cooperative banks): their organizational system is bipolar and asymmetrical, as it has two entrepreneurial levels and three membership levels. Regarding the membership level, the local entities are under a national federation, named Ossuspankkikeskus Osk (Central cooperative of the cooperative banks – Group OP Bank) headquartered in Helsinki. Instead, the entrepreneurial level is led by the central bank Osusspankkien Keskuspankki (central bank of cooperative banks OKOBANK).

All primary credit cooperatives belong to the OP Group, even if it is not legally required to adhere to a federation of superior level (national or regional). They voluntarily submit to all the policies decided by the national federation and the central institute, which have a controlling and strategic role.

In the period 1960–80, the Finnish cooperative banks grew dramatically placing their sector among the best in Europe as far as computerization, highly qualified personnel, and sophisticated payment systems. At the beginning of the 1990s, an economic crisis hit Finland (due to the deteriorated trade with Russia) and the banking sector. The OP group kept its market share at one third and in 1994 it incorporated a considerable share of the Savings Bank of Finland. A great number of savings banks transferred their accounts to Group OP. Presently, the OP Group is the leading Finnish bank group and it represents the major retail-banking operator. Its clients are mainly households and small and medium enterprises and, to a lower extent, institutional clients, very active in international trade.

9.2.2 Sources of regulations

The change in Finnish legislation regarding cooperation presents some peculiarities due to the political situation. The general law applied to cooperatives in 1902 was derived from a German model; its specific credit regulations were inadequate. It was only in 1954 when the credit cooperation was granted an organic legislation. This law, which has been revised several times, still regulates the organization and company structure of credit cooperatives and dictates the rules for banks in general and credit cooperative institutes in particular. A unified banking act was issued in 1969 (law no. 542, 28/8/1969) at a time in which the economic growth of the country and the boom of the credit cooperatives was apparently coming to an end. However, this law associated the credit cooperatives to the other bank categories and deepened the role of the national federation and the central banking institute. The establishment of the central institute occurred before that of the local entities; therefore, there had already been a strong integration within the system which went by existing rules and existing statutes. A certain vagueness of the text is justified by the judicial autonomy of all the group. Its purpose was more of a formal than a practical law but it served the purpose of giving legal certainty to credit cooperatives. Credit cooperatives were considered "cooperative banks," especially on an operative level. Subsequently the legislator favoured the cooperative sector by allowing the cooperatives to follow the universal bank model. This permitted them to issue financial instruments (in particular new types of investment) able to reinforce capitalization and yielding some fiscal breaks such as tax free 2 years reduced rate deposits. The legislative concern was to identify cooperatives banks as credit agencies, since the general cooperative law stated "cooperative do cooperative activities:" art.1 says "Cooperative banks are cooperative companies that do bank activities, they can receive deposits from the public just like banks do." Changes in the law (law no. 1504 of 2001) did not drastically change the 1969 law, but they integrated the provisions coming from European regulations which Finland accepted before fully being part of the EU. To set up a cooperative bank, it is necessary to obtain the authorization by the finance Ministry and Controlling Authority, together with the central Fund guaranteeing bank cooperative deposits (a private law body).

As far as the members are considered, aside from the group members that go by the legal regulation of an ordinary company (OKO and others), the established cooperatives (primary units and national federation) are submitted to the general cooperative law dated 28/5/1954 an update of the 1901 version. Although similar to the German model, it allows membership to promote their service initiatives. The flexibility of the law allows the cooperatives to meet the needs of the market. The internal statutes give the members freedom of negotiation disciplining almost entirely the single companies. While the law offers subsidy, it also gives great room to internal regulation.

9.2.3 Organizational structure and governance

9.2.3.1 First-level cooperatives

As previously stated, the local credit cooperative came into being after the creation of the national credit Institute. Andelskassan Malax in 1902 was the first, even though Liedon Pita au Osuuskassa was the first to be recorded on the commercial register in 1903. After spreading extensively, in 1930 there were 1,416 local cooperatives. However, most of them were extremely small and, with the increase of the activities, the smallness of credit cooperatives became a growing problem. The only solution was to join these small cooperatives into bigger ones. As a result, presently there are 236 local cooperatives (at the end of March 2006), distributed all over the territory and operate in a non – competitive regime based on a sort of gentlemen's agreement.

The local cooperatives have independent decision power; however they operate according to strategies and common commercial policy the Group decides and also follow the indications they receive from the national Federation which offers them assistance. The central Institute has its own banking activities dealing with customers outside the local entities areas. The banking activity performed in the Grand Helsinki territory is carried out by the Helsinki OP Bank PLC, exclusively belonging to the National Federation. The remainder of the national territory is divided into 16 areas supervised by a branch of the national Federation of cooperative type. On a managerial and legal level, first level credit institutes are independent cooperatives principally active in retail banking with customers such as farmers, private entities, wood working companies, SMEs and local institutes. Members come from these groups. The elective committees and their role present no important difference from the central European credit cooperatives, because their regulations are those internationally accepted. No particular limits are imposed on the activities as long as they remain within the banking activities. Industrial, insurance, transport and real estate activities are not contemplated. However, statutes can impose more restrictive limitations.

9.2.3.2 The National Federation

The National Federation was established in 1928 as Osuuskassojen Kekuslitto (Central Union of the deposit and loan banks, OKI), now known as Ossuspankkikeskus Osk. Being the OP group representative institution, it is responsible to the Authority. It does not only provide services to the entire credit cooperative system as requested spontaneously by the regional associations. The Federation has a representative, assistance, training and supervisory role; it is supported by 16 regional offices (two are Swedish) promoting the cooperative system and easing vertical cooperation. The product and service sector is responsible for the development of innovative items, for the reduction of costs, promotion and growth of the group. The sales network is guided by the clients' relation sector which must develop competitive and adequate procedures for each local market. The centralized support division supervises the service and product quality, checks if prices are competitive and if the Group offer is homogeneous so as to avoid internal competition. ICT Services are responsible for the computer technology and telecommunications division. The control Sector of the Group takes care of the implementation and monitoring of the strategy. In 1969 (art. 63), it became necessary to establish an "Inspectorate" whose activity is guided and controlled by the supervisory committee (art. 4). It functions as an internal checking instrument for all cooperative movements including credit cooperatives. Its activity is merely complementary and instrumental but not a substitution of the supervision of the financial revision Authority (Rahoitustarkastus Finansispektiorem). Practically speaking, the above service is divided into 16 areas each having a regional revision, and each four areas have an extra one. The revision regards not only the Accounting of single local banks, but also technical assistance. They offer logistic consultancy and branch-opening procedural advice; they take important board decisions, give investment and activity suggestions. Every year, two thirds of the local firms are checked. According to the law (art. 11, 1959) the Inspectorate must receive updated information on modified statutes and important decisions made by the elective board, administrative matters, credit issued, warrantees (art. 48), balance sheets and meeting topics (art. 17). The central Federation has also a central school for training, where half of the training courses are held. The effort is great because each employee participates in a week seminar once a year.

Being responsible of the board, the Federation acts as OP Group leader; the central banking Institute is therefore formally one of its affiliates. Several special institutes are directly linked to OKOBANK, while many similar institutes are linked to the Federation namely: OP LIFE ASSURANCE COMPANY LTD, a life insurance company; OP FUND MANAGEMENT CO., a fund investment management company; OP BANK MORTGAGE BANK PLC, a mortgage bank (financing is obtained through the insuance of bonds); OP KOTIPANKKI OY, specialized in unsecured credit; D Finanssidata Oy, specialized in IT services.

9.2.3.3 The Central Banking Institute

As previously mentioned, the Central Banking Institute – OKOBANK – was established in Helsinki in 1902 by the State with the name OSSUSKASSOJEN KESKUSLAINARAHASTO OSAKEYHTIO; that is, central lending FUND for limited liability cooperative credit associations. The State's shareholding later became less significant as a result of the constant increase in the company's capital. Thus the State turned to

OKOBANK for grants and loans to the agricultural industry. In 1970, all limitations to the cooperative banks' activities were legally removed and the Institute was transformed into a commercial bank with the name OKOBANK. In 1975 the Institute began international financial operations. In 1987 the Institute launched mutual fund investment activities and in 1989 it was quoted at Stock Exchange. In June 2006, the Board of management decided to change the Institute's name to OKO PANKKI OY (OKO BANK P/C in English). At present, OKOBANK is legally a Public Limited Company, with over 60,000 shareholders, and it is the Group's supporting institution. At the same time, it carries out banking business on its own like a "universal" commercial bank. In 2006 the institute's Supervisory Board was replaced by the ten-member Board of Directors, representing a clearing committee, a risk management committee and a (management) review committee.

The Institute is also a leading bank of OKOBANK consolidated, which is comprised of: POHJOLA GROUP PLC (a non-life insurance co.), OPSTOCK LTD, A INSURANCE LTD, OKO ASSET MANAGEMENT LTD, EUROOPPALAINEN INSURANCE COMPANY LTD, POHJOLA PROPERTY MANAGEMENT LTD, OKO VENTURE CAPITAL LTD, SEESAM INSURANCE COMPANY LTD (a Baltic Republic based on insurance company, foreign offices and OPSTOCK LTD). Due to its legal status, OKOBANK is subject to the FINNISH COMPANIES ACT, recommendation of corporate governance and regulations pertaining to the financial and insurance divisions.

The local affiliated banks account for the majority of the fund raising by means of deposits, mainly certificates of deposit which have replaced fixed-term deposits remunerated at market price. The Institute also contributes to the fund raising, with its own deposits, such as capital market and international transactions. As a result of their present strategic orientation, the main areas the bank focuses on are credit and investment services and non-life insurance sector, especially at the corporate level that seems requiring a greater asset management.

In the private retail banking and SMEs segment, the Institute's performance is better than its competitors' one because of a higher capacity of dealing with opaque information. In the non-life insurance sector the Institute aims at reaching first place on a national level. In 2005, the ROE was 12 per cent, in 2006 13 per cent, by 2008 18 per cent; the solvency ratio at 8 per cent (7 per cent in 2006), the capital adequacy at 14 per cent, the profits dividends at 50 per cent (equal to 2006). The bank assets increased with the acquisition of POHJOLA in 2005. The last increase in capital occurred in 2006 by issuing shares totaling over

1.5 million euros. OKOBANK'S organizational chart presents two main departments: investment and bank services and non-life insurances. Its clients can receive the following services: financial and liquidity management, payment services (international), loans and bonds, leasing, factoring and investments (capital risks) OPSTOCK LTD, asset management and bond intermediation.

An important sector is represented by the institutional clients to whom the following services are offered: custody, distance, intermediation, international trade, payments, liquidity, management, investments, intermediation of bonds and accounting, billing, company credit cards, employee pension funds, risk guarantee. The local entities of the OP Group are obviously offered all services connected to liquidity management, financing and investments at the least cost.

9.2.3.4 The guarantee fund

The guarantee fund has been important since the beginning. In 1932 a national Fund for guarantee deposits was established; the credit cooperative obtained exemption from taxation on amounts deposited in this fund (1943). The compliance of the guarantee deposit FUND is regulated by the credit law which obliges the Department of Finance to certify the cooperative banks compliance in order to authorize their activities. The 1969 legislation had already assured the credit cooperative an adequate management and solvency security margin. The obligation to adhere to the FUND is not to be considered a disclaimer of their legal and managerial autonomy of the individual companies of the Group, because the law only formalized a self-disciplined primary norm which was already deeply rooted in reality. It's normal for a voluntary system of integration to possess a service system (network) apt to avoid failure. To avoid failure it is mandatory to check for the availability of resources that can foresee the innate risks of a hasty operation. The rules of the Fund regulations should be viewed as the Group's indirect legal and institutional acknowledgement. The Fund aids companies in temporary trouble by conceding interest-free loans or low-interest loans or even concessions without security. The contributions determined on the bars of the needs of the FUND, varies from a minimum to a maximum percentage of the total profits. According to article 62, at least a third of the FUND's resources must be deposited in the issuing bank or invested in government securities.

9.2.4 The Group's Activities

In order to correctly evaluate the credit activity of the Group, some characteristics of the country must be considered. Firstly, the political influence: the population still remembers the struggle for their national independence from Russia and communist threat later. The strong political Commitment of the cooperatives allowed for an extraordinary social cohesion within the cooperative movement in particular. This cohesion eliminates all obstacles that could occur in the vertical structuring of the Group.

The country's economy structurally changed from agricultural to industrial and then to tertiary sector. As a result of these changes, although the Group still kept privileged position in agricultural financing, it had to adapt to the needs of the rapidly changing market, mainly by way of mergers and measures of rationalization (optimization of the sales network and channels, and computerization of the internal structure). However, the competition is not mainly concentrated on the practical conditions, but rather on the quality of consultancy to customers. As a result, the Group must invest in a huge training effort and an efficient management of products and services which are more sophisticated and detailed. Great success came in 1970s, when they began to offer the so-called banking contracts, whereby cooperative firms could provide consultancy and assistance to corporate clients and receive credit necessary for projects and investments quickly and easily.

A further forceful push towards the optimization of profits derived from a well-sorted credit policy including a vast selection of options. In this case, as well, the risk management quality is fundamental in developing instruments and methods for a sophisticated evaluation of the clients guarantee. The Group made a costly investment in innovative technology during the 1980s. In the field of office automation the OP Group has been in the forefront in Europe since the 1960s. The majority of the transactions occur in real time thanks to the direct link up to Helsinki OKOBANK'S data processing center. So, since the 1980s any interface affecting proper communication has been eliminated and presently the compatibility is practically perfect. Efforts in the training sector have been costly too. Based on the concept that every employee must be "a banker on his own," each worker must hold great responsibilities counterbalanced by incentives and rapid career advancement. In the training process the worry is to avoid excessive personnel bureaucratization or technocracy, innate in banking, and to encourage a cooperative spirit instead.

The Group maintains the best market share in the private sector. In fact, mortgage loans rose greatly in the 1990s and so did consumer loans, mostly issued to University students; the "golden card" are the most popular credit cards in the country. The corporate market continues to advance steadily, especially short-term loans and commercial papers, but traditional services such as discounted bills and credit lines are not as requested as before. Foreign currency loans are very popular now among Finnish firms. In the agricultural sector, which is traditionally linked to the credit cooperatives, financing is directed mainly to the farming and fur companies. The financial intermediation, carried out by special institutes of the group, gained importance. Financial and property consultancy and mortgage loan funds are equally important. As far as capital markets are concerned, the group relies on offices situated in the main financial centers around the world.

The group has a good ranking in the field of risk-management, and it occupies the best ranking in reference to outstanding payments. In 1999, the new system SAS RISK MANAGEMENT was completed in cooperation with the German based SAS software house. The instrument, characterized by a greater flexibility than the old system, permits sophisticated simulations based on statistical models and stress-test. The instrument shows five risk levels, each corresponding to a series of measures to obtain recovery. In 2005 the Basel II project was planned and the results obtained up to now are truly satisfying.

In conclusion, despite the strong competition coming from the other banking categories, prospects for the future are positive as the group's potential market has room for growth because saturation has not been reached. In particular, the cooperative banks are not as worried as the competitors about the optimization of branches. Recently, the group acquired banks in difficulty, with little cost sacrifices and no reduction in human resources.

Note

1. The authors wish to thank Mrs Kyllikki Pankakoski of OKO Bank for her kindness and willingness in providing information and documents about the system.

References

Act on Cooperative Banks and other Credit Institutions in the Form of a Cooperative, no. 1504/2001, English translation, www.finlex.fi/en/, accessed January–July 2008.
Act on Credit Institutions, no. 1607/1993, English translation, www.finlex.fi/en/, accessed January–July 2008.
Cooperatives Act, no. 1488/2001, English translation, www.finlex.fi/en/, accessed January–July 2008.

Finnish Banks Financial Statements (2006), English translation, www.finlex.fi/en/, accessed January–July 2008.

Köppä, T. (1994) "Cooperation after the Welfare State: cooperative paths and highways in Finland in the 1990's," in Berliner Hefte zum Genossenschaftswesen, *Co-operation after the welfare state – Co-operative "paths" and "highways" in Finland in the 1990s,* Berlin: Inst. fuer Genossenschaftswesen.

Laurinkari, J., Laakonen, V. (1995) *Uudistuva osuustoiminta,* Helsinki: Helsingin Yliopisto, Helsinki.

OKO Bank (2003) *Annual Report 2002,* Helsinki.

Pättiniemi, P. (1998) "Social Enterprises in the European Countries – Chapter IV Finland," in Carlo Borzaga and Alceste Santuari, Alceste (a cura di), *Social Enterprise and new Employment in Europe,* Trento.

http://www.pellervo.fi/p-seura/pellervoseura.htm, website of the Confederation of Finnish Cooperatives, accessed January–July 2008.

http://rata.bof.fi/eng/about_us/etusivu.htm, website of the Finnish Financial Authority, accessed January–July 2008.

http://rahoitustarkastus.fi/eng/about_us/supervised entities and notifications, website of the Finnish Financial Authority, accessed January–July 2008.

Vilhonen, E. (2006) *Risk Management and Control,* Helsinki: OP Bank Group Central Cooperative.

Part II
The Cooperative Banking in the New EU Countries

10
Cooperative Banking in the Ten Newly Admitted EU Member Countries in 2004

Matteo Cotugno

10.1 Introduction

The economic and financial systems of the ten newly-admitted EU member countries have undergone sweeping changes over the last twenty years. In particular, those Countries may be grouped into two homogeneous clusters. The first one comprises the countries that remained under the influence of the Soviet Union until the end of the 1980s and that had in force – to a varying extent – a system of planned economy; that is, the Czech Republic, Estonia, Latvia, Lithuania, Hungary, Poland, Slovakia and Slovenia. The second one comprises those under the Anglo-American influence, where an economy based on free trade and private property was already operational; these are Malta and Cyprus.[1] In the first group, the passage from a planned economy to a market economy had initially led to a considerable economic growth attained within an inadequate regulatory context, in particular with reference to the laws concerning the conmixtion between bank and industry and the control over assumed risks. As a rule, the direct consequence of such a situation had been the surfacing of deep economic-financial crises that brought about a thorough reassessment of the national regulatory setup. On the other hand, the countries belonging to the second group suffered no transition problem, as the economic and financial system had developed after World War II according to the rules of the market, making the evolution of such countries fully assimilable to that of the continental context (Caviglia, Krause and Thimann 2003).

The financial system in general, and the banking system in particular, have crucially influenced the revival of the economy, undergoing far-reaching transformations through the passage from a system marked by state monopolism to a market system based on free competition.

The system of cooperative credit within the ten newly-admitted EU member countries has played a decisive role in a few instances (that is, in Cyprus), while in other countries this role has been fully marginal (that is, Malta, Slovakia and Latvia). In particular, in the countries connected with the former Soviet area, the cooperative credit system did not always succeed in coexisting with the monopolist banking system, and this was often the cause of deep supply gaps that were only bridged further to the fall of Communism. On the other hand, in the pro-European countries, Cyprus stands out for its strong cooperative credit system and Malta for the absolute lack of cooperative-type systems.

10.2 Overview of the economic systems in the ten newly–admitted EU member countries

Based on estimates of the International Monetary Fund, it may be noted that the clustering referred to in the introduction is definitely confirmed by an analysis of the variation in the gross domestic product. Cyprus and Malta qualify as "mature" economies, with development rates approximating those reported in the European area (with the exception of Malta which, in 2003 and 2004, reported negative growth rates).

Notwithstanding a considerable lack of homogeneity, the economies of the remaining eight countries have witnessed especially high growth rates, distant from those reported by the countries in the euro area. The Baltic Republics (Estonia, Lithuania and Latvia) have shown a

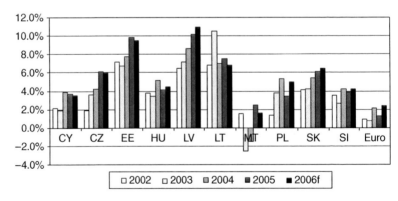

Figure 10.1 GDP real growth
Source: IMF data (2006).

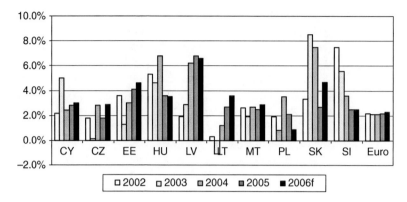

Figure 10.2 Inflation
Source: IMF data (2006).

definite consistency in their trend, due also to the historical events they have shared, given that, during the observation period, they reported mean yearly growth rates ranging around eight percent (8.2 per cent in Estonia, 7.7 per cent in Lithuania and 8.7 per cent in Latvia, respectively). Instead, other countries – such as Slovakia and the Czech Republic – reported on average a lower level of growth, with mean rates ranging between four and six percent. Finally, other countries reported intermediate levels of growth with rates that, in any event, were typically higher that the mean rate reported in the euro area.

There is less certainty as to the inflation trend, since there is evidence of a considerable stability of the datum in the euro area (being calculated as mean value of 12 observations) with respect to the other countries. The cluster previously made in respect of Cyprus and Malta is somehow confirmed, at least in terms of variability of the indicator. In recent years, the countries that had experienced an alarming inflation level (Slovakia and Slovenia) have implemented restrictive policies that are progressively reducing price rises and causing them to approximate the values reported in the euro area.

10.3 Overview of the financial and banking systems in the ten newly–admitted EU member countries

The grouping of the ten newly-admitted EU member countries into two clusters, as specified above, may be proposed once again with reference to the level of development of their financial and banking systems.

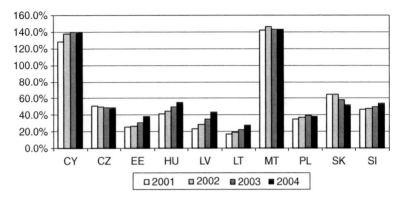

Figure 10.3   Deposit money banks assets/GDP
Source: World Bank-FinStructure data.

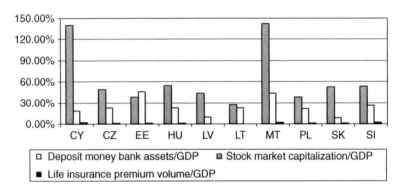

Figure 10.4   Financial intermediation in the ten newly admitted EU member countries (2004)
Source: World Bank-FinStructure data.

In particular, the indicators relative to the degree of development of a financial system show that Cyprus and Malta have a deposit money banks assets to GDP ratio that is significantly higher than that of the other eight countries. The same difference comes up again using other ratios that are representative of the degree of development of a financial system (for instance, stock market capitalization to GDP and Life insurance premium volume to GDP). Moving the analysis from the level of the indicator to its variability, the division into pro-American countries and pro-Soviet countries may be roughly confirmed. For instance, with reference to Estonia, Hungary, Lithuania and Latvia, the deposits to GDP ratio points to a significantly positive trend. Conversely, different countries such as Cyprus, the Czech Republic and Malta point instead to a situation of stationariness over time.

An analysis of the proposed indicators clearly points to a predominance of the banking system (with the exception of Estonia) to the detriment of direct intermediation channels and other typologies of intermediaries.

Concentrating the analysis exclusively on the banking system of the ten newly-admitted EU member countries, it may be noted that, over the last four years, some economies have experienced a system concentration process (Cyprus, the Czech Republic, Hungary and Slovenia) that in two cases (Cyprus and Slovenia) was accompanied by a decrease in the number of branches. On the other hand, Estonia, Poland, Slovakia and Lithuania have experienced an increase in the number of both banks and branches. Finally, countries such as Latvia and Malta have reported a substantial stationariness in the number of banks, with a significant increase in the number of branches.

In dimension-related terms, all the countries under consideration have reported even quite sizable increases in total assets that, at times, were accompanied by processes leading to significant cuts in the number of sectoral workers. For instance, the Czech Republic has experienced on average a 10.2 per cent increase in bank assets, in the face of a 2.5 per cent yearly decrease in the number of workers. Even Poland reported a

Table 10.1   Features of the banking system (number of credit institutions and branches)

Country	Number of credit institution				Number of branches			
	2002	2003	2004	2005	2002	2003	2004	2005
Cyprus	408	408	403	391	993	983	977	951
Czech Republic	84	77	70	56	1,722	1,670	1,785	1,825
Estonia	7	7	9	11	198	197	203	230
Hungary	227	222	221	215	2,992	3,003	2,987	3,122
Latvia	23	23	23	23	567	581	583	586
Lithuania	68	71	74	78	119	723	758	822
Malta	14	16	16	18	99	104	99	109
Poland	666	660	658	739	4,302	4,394	5,003	5,078
Slovakia	20	21	21	23	1,020	1,057	1,113	1,142
Slovenia	50	33	24	25	721	720	706	693

Source: ECB (2006).

Table 10.2 Features of the banking system (number of employees and total assets)

Country	Number of employees of credit institutions				Total assets (EUR millions)			
	2002	2003	2004	2005	2002	2003	2004	2005
Cyprus	10,613	10,480	10,617	10,799	40,943	41,890	46,540	60,366
Czech Republic	40,534	39,658	38,666	37,943	79,232	78,004	86,525	104,950
Estonia	3,934	4,280	4,455	5,029	5,221	6,314	8,537	11,830
Hungary	35,045	35,725	35,558	37,335	43,564	54,769	64,970	74,653
Latvia	8,267	8,903	9,655	10,477	7,250	8,482	11,167	15,570
Lithuania	8,420	7,557	7,266	7,637	5,010	6,425	8,509	13,099
Malta	3,459	3,401	3,353	3,383	16,273	17,803	20,589	27,195
Poland	161,814	154,569	150,037	152,923	116,044	103,659	131,904	152,086
Slovakia	18,452	18,350	18,261	19,850	23,748	23,751	29,041	36,399
Slovenia	11,855	11,816	11,602	11,726	19,995	21,541	24,462	30,049

Source: ECB (2006).

very similar trend (a +10.6 per cent increase in assets, and a mean –1.8 per cent decrease in the number of workers).

10.4 Overview of the cooperative credit system in the ten newly admitted EU member countries

The cooperative credit system in the former Soviet countries has been re-established further to the fall of Communism or, in a few cases, has coexisted with the state-owned mono-bank. For instance, Lithuania has a Credit Union network grouped under the Association of Lithuanian Credit Unions that works in the cooperative credit sector; the Dezelna Banka Slovenije dd. is a cooperative bank that works in Slovenia; the same applies to the Eesti Innovatsioonipank in Estonia or to the Coop Banka a.s in the Czech Republic. On the other hand, no form of cooperative credit may be found in Malta, Slovakia and Latvia. The most highly developed system in the ten newly-admitted EU member countries are, in order of relevance, the Cypriot system (*Cooperative Central Bank*) with a 30.06 per cent credit market share, the Polish cooperative system (The National Union of Cooperative Banks, Krajowy Zwiazek Banków Spóldzielczych) with an 8.83 per cent share, and the Hungarian system (Bank of Hungarian Savings Cooperatives Ltd, Magyar Takarékszövetkezeti Bank Részvénytársaság) with a 5 per cent share. In view of the above, the rest of this paper will focus exclusively on the systems relative to these three countries.

10.4.1 The Cooperative Central Bank Ltd in Cyprus

Cooperative-type organizations are at present the pillars of the Cypriot economy. Just to mention a significant datum, out of nearly 700,000 inhabitants of the State of Cyprus, almost 500,000 are members of cooperative societies connected with the sectors of credit, consumer credit, marketing and trading services (CCB 2006). Furthermore, as previously pointed out, the cooperative credit system covers nearly one third of the entire Cypriot banking sector (CCB 2006). The reason for such a success is mostly imputable to economic and legislative factors. With reference to the former, a deeply rooted agricultural-type economy and widespread phenomena of usury have turned into a fertile ground for the proliferation of cooperative-type organizations in every sector of the economy. On the other hand, with reference to the legislative-type factors, it should be stressed that the regulations governing credit cooperation in Cyprus date back to 1914 (Law no. 13 for Cooperative Credit Societies) and, in addition to giving legal certainty to the movement under consideration, have furthered its development and diffusion (CSSDA 2004).

The first cooperative credit bank, the Lefkoniko Communal Bank, was established in 1909 with the explicit aim of providing fair credit conditions to the agricultural world and, in so doing, reducing the phenomenon of usury that particularly vexed the poorest class. In 1914, the positive experience of the Lefkoniko Communal Bank caused the lawmakers to create a regulatory framework for cooperative-type societies that gave rise to the proper context for a balanced development of cooperatives in the credit sector. The nonparticipation of Cyprus in World War I had positive effects on the economy, thanks to a considerable increase in the demand for agricultural products from the countries involved in the war. In the face of a considerable expansion of the country's productive capacity, the return of peace in Europe caused Cyprus to plunge into a severe crisis. The setting up of the Cooperative Movement aimed at stemming the rampant poverty and the likely return of the scourge of usury, while giving impetus to the economy and developing the cooperative approach in five strategic sectors of the economy: credit, consumer, trading of agricultural products, processing and services. In 1923, after the positive experience gained in the credit sector, a law was passed to regulate the cooperative system in respect of other economic sectors (CSSDA 2004).

The Cooperative Credit Societies lacked the complex managerial setup required to allow granting medium- and long-term loans. In 1925, with a view to covering the medium-term financial needs of the agricultural world, this led to the setting up of the Agricultural Bank, a bank belonging to the Cooperative Movement specialized in medium-term loans, so as to smooth the progress of the agricultural world towards investments and modernization. Besides, the Department of Cooperative Development was established soon afterwards with a view to promoting the development of the cooperative model in all the economic sectors. These were the times that witnessed also the setting up of the Cooperative Central Bank Ltd (CCB) that, up to the present, represents the heart of the Cypriot cooperative credit model. The CCB's aim was to make the entire Cooperative Movement financially independent by providing credit exclusively to the cooperative credit societies, regardless of the economic sector in which they operated.

The cooperative societies join the Cooperative Movement in a voluntary manner in pursuance of the Cooperative Societies Laws and Rule. Given the central role played by the cooperative-type societies, the Cooperative Credit Societies and the Cooperative Savings Banks have not been assimilated to actual banks as they are considered standard mutual-aid and no-profit cooperative societies, just like consumer and services cooperatives. This is the reason why, for a number of years, the Cooperative Credit Societies have not been subjected to the supervision of the Central Bank of Cyprus and have not been under the obligation to comply with reserve and authorization requirements for the opening of new branches.

The Cooperative Societies' Supervision and Development Authority is entrusted with the supervision of the cooperatives and is required to make regular inspections, to monitor the management trend, and to take part in meetings, as well as to ensure the production of the audit report by the Audit Service of Cooperative Societies. The latter authority, set up in keeping with the Cooperative Societies Laws and Rule, is responsible for auditing all the cooperative societies and the costs of its services, consisting in an annual commission, are shared by the various cooperatives. It is chaired by five members appointed by the Council of Ministers, two of which are proposed by the Pancyprian Cooperative Confederation which, as specified below, is a third-tier cooperative.

Three cooperation tiers (not only with reference to the credit sector) are clearly identifiable in the Cypriot cooperation system. The first tier is represented by the Cooperative Credit Societies or the Cooperative Savings Banks, whose members share the mutual-aid purposes of the cooperative and work within the same territorial framework. The Cooperative Credit Society has set itself the goal of providing loans to its members under particularly favorable terms through deposits and payment of membership fees. The lack of any profit-making purpose, the "one member one vote" principle, and the strong link with the territory and the agricultural world are the characteristics that bring together the Cooperative Credit Societies. The second tier of the cooperative organization is represented by confederations, where at least a member is a first-tier cooperative (EACB 2007).

While the cooperatives belonging to the first tier are mostly connected with small-sized local realities, the cooperatives of the second tier are organizations that are active on a broader territorial framework. Finally, there is a third cooperation tier, represented by a federation that comprises at least a second-tier confederation. The third cooperation tier operates on a national scale with a view to coordinating the cooperative movement of the reference sector and promoting it at an international level. In case of the consumers' cooperatives, the Pancyprian Cooperative Federation represents the organization at a national level.

The Cooperative Central Bank Ltd (CCB) it a third-tier cooperative in the credit sector that was established in 1937 under the Cooperative Societies Laws and Rule with the specific purpose of providing financial and credit services to cooperative societies involved in the agricultural field. Membership in the CCB is restricted to societies registered under the Cooperative Societies Laws and Rules. Its current membership consists of 428 Credit Societies and Savings Banks, 365 of which are operational while 63 are not operational due to the Turkish occupation, and 62 non-credit Cooperative Societies, totaling 490 societies (CCB 2006).

The official accession of Cyprus to the European Union represents an important event for the economic life of the Country and a fundamental stimulus for the fulfillment of the obligations under the "Treaty of Accession" for the entry into force of the euro starting from January 1, 2008. The Strategic Action Plan for the Introduction of the euro, launched by the Cypriot Council of Ministers towards the end of 2004, laid the foundations for the adjustment of the legislative system required to do away with any inconsistency with the European directives. In particular, even the laws that govern the banking sector, including also cooperative banks, have witnessed important modifications through the amendment of the Central Bank of Cyprus Laws of 2002 and 2003.

In relation to the final agreement signed by the Cypriot Negotiating Team for the accession to Europe, the entire credit sector, with special regard to the cooperation sector, needed to be harmonized with the European directives (European Directive 2000/12/EC, recast Directive 2006/48/EC). In particular, the Credit Societies and Savings Banks were required to choose, on or before 2007, whether to affiliate with the Cooperative Central Bank Ltd or to continue their activity in an autonomous manner. In the first case, the supervision obligations would have been fulfilled at a consolidated level by the Cooperative Central Bank while, in the second case, it would be up to the individual banks to comply with the European supervisory regulations as laid down in the Capital Adequacy Directive (CAD). Besides, in pursuance of the European Directive 94/19/EC, all the credit cooperatives were required to join the Deposit Guarantee Scheme for Cooperative Credit Institutions. In 2004, a sweeping reform of the law on the Central Bank of Cyprus of 2002 to 2003 introduced the requirement for individual Credit Societies and Savings Banks to maintain a compulsory minimum reserve with the Central Bank of Cyprus, while the supervisory authority was entrusted to the central institute rather than to the Department of Cooperative Development (Cyprus Laws of 2002 and 2003).

To-date, the major cooperative credit organization in Cyprus is the Cooperative Central Bank, which represents the cooperative societies' bank and, in the form of national network, the only third-tier cooperative in the credit sector. Alongside the Cooperative Central Bank, there are a number of Credit Societies and Savings Banks that developed for the most part in small-sized local realities and that, working on their own or in small second-tier confederations, do not fall within the national network.

From an organizational point of view, the CCB is built around three departments: banking department, department of trading activities, and department of insurance services. Each one of them looks after specific business areas. In 1962, the Agriculture Bank was incorporated by the CCB, channeling into it even the medium- and long-term credit sector. Based on the regulations in force, all the cooperative companies are required to deposit their financial surpluses with the CCB that, through its banking division, provides also medium- and long-term financing and loans (CSSDA 2004).

The corporate governance of the Cooperative Central Bank Ltd provides for the presence of various bodies: the General Meeting of the bank passed the budget and appoints the members of the Board of Directors. The latter comprises a representative of all the cooperative credit societies that are CCB shareholders and, based on the "one member one vote" principle, elects the seven members of the Board that hold office for three years. In its turn, the Board elects the General Manager that, being the top-ranking manager of the Cooperative Central Bank Ltd, is vested with all the powers set out in the Law and the Bank's By-Laws (CCB 2006).

Seeing to a detailed analysis of the performance of the Cypriot banks, the ROE decomposition permits to single out the managerial areas that have contributed the most to the formation of the return on equity.[2] In particular, the performance of the Cypriot banking system in terms of return on equity (ROE) reports a trend on the increase that, starting from a negative value in 2003, has reached 11.05 per cent in 2006 with a leverage level (Total Assets/Equity) witnessing a considerable contraction.

With reference to the characteristic management, it may be noted that:

- the CCB constantly reports a lower Interest Margin on Total Assets ratio than the rest of the banking system (a condition that is fully ascribable to the Interest Margin dynamics, given that the assets growth rate of the banking sector has been much higher that the figure reported by the CCB (the average growth of the banking sector was +22.6 per cent with respect to an 8.77 per cent growth of the CCB);

- the incidence of the income components resulting from services, defined by the Intermediation Margin on Interest Margin ratio, always with the exception of 2006, is constantly lower for the CCB with respect to the banking system.

Insofar as it concerns the incidence of operational costs (measured by the Operational Result on Intermediation Margin ratio), throughout the years the CCB has reported a definitely higher level than the banking system. In this case, the characteristically high level of capitalization of the cooperative banks with respect to the banking system (ascribable to the appropriation of profits) is belied, even if to a limited extent. In any event, it should be stressed that, owing to the heavy losses reported by the CCB in the past years, the corporate reserves have been fully annulled and, for various years, the loss has been carried forward. Indeed, in confirmation of this fact, it may be noted that the leverage level in recent years has been constantly on the decrease and it is quite likely that a good managerial performance will lead to an alignment with the banking system.

It may be assumed that the legally binding centralization of services on behalf of Credit Societies and Savings Banks, as well as the liberalization of a few sectors of the economy that had been previously organized through monopolistic arrangements, will lead to positive results also in the forthcoming years.

10.4.2 The system of cooperative credit in Poland

The cooperative credit system in Poland has very ancient origins since it dates back to 1861, the year of establishment in the city of Poznan of the Towarzystwo Pozyczkowe dla Przemyslowców Miasta Poznania,

Table 10.3   ROE analysis relative to the Cypriot banking system

Year	NeR/GrR	GrR/OpR	IM/TA	Int/IM	OpR/IntM	TA/E	ROE
2003	165.66%	456.90%	2.25%	134.82%	−0.96%	17.21	−3.80%
2004	70.95%	89.24%	2.45%	131.45%	13.54%	18.33	5.06%
2005	78.38%	110.48%	2.25%	130.24%	20.82%	17.77	9.38%
2006	83.13%	111.41%	2.07%	128.54%	38.69%	11.60	11.05%

Source: BankScope data, Bureau van Dijk Electronic Publishing.

Table 10.4 ROE analysis relative to the Cooperative Central Bank

Year	NeR/GrR	GrR/OpR	IM/TA	Int/IM	OpR/IntM	TA/E	ROE
2003	93.33%	101.12%	0.73%	124.30%	66.92%	−304.27	−175.00%
2004	93.28%	87.50%	1.09%	122.44%	71.20%	186.27	144.16%
2005	95.49%	100.00%	0.87%	124.26%	78.70%	56.95	46.52%
2006	95.35%	100.00%	0.80%	130.20%	66.49%	44.53	29.43%

Source: BankScope data, Bureau van Dijk Electronic Publishing.
Legend:
IM   = Interest Margin
IntM = Intermediation Margin
OpR   = Operational Result
GrR   = Gross Result
NeR   = Net Result
E   = Equity
TA   = Total Assets

the first Polish cooperative credit bank. The provision of loans on fair terms to its members with a view to countering the phenomenon of usury, and a deep rootedness in the agricultural context were the peculiar features of this institution. Unfortunately, the history of Poland was full of conflicts and occupations: Prussia at first, and then Germany and Russia. Indeed, during World War II, the 1600 cooperatives that had been created up to that time were dissolved throughout the territory occupied by the Soviet army. On the other hand, the cooperatives set up in the territory occupied by the Germans kept on working and spreading, under the supervision of the German Department of Bank Inspection (Laszkiewicz 2005).

After the second world war, the Polish cooperative system, though scaled down, was still operational over the national territory, working through the municipal cooperatives, the credit cooperatives and the workers' credit cooperatives. The establishment of the Soviet regime did not bring the cooperative experience to an end since, even though the whole banking system had been monopolized, the cooperative banks kept on existing, albeit required under the law to join the Bank Gospodarki Żywnościowej (BGZ), a state cooperative bank. The BGZ was their central organizational and financial entity, and with regard to cooperative banks, it carried responsibilities vested to cooperative central unions, in accordance with the Act on the Cooperative Law – and at the same time held powers of banking supervision (NPB 2001).

In January 1989, the Polish Parliament passed two Acts related to banking – the Banking Act and the Act on the National Bank of

Poland (NBP). These provisions aimed at a thorough reconstruction of the Polish banking system, starting from the separation of powers in the matter of monetary policy and those relative to credit (two-tier structure). The establishment of 9 regional banks and nearly 400,000 branches of the NBP marked the beginning of a gradual privatization of the banking system.

The passage from planned to market economy was characterized by a period of severe economic and financial crisis that caused innumerable bank failures. When, in January 1990, the Act on Changes in the Organization and Operation of the Cooperative Movement became effective, even the cooperative credit system started acquiring the typical features of the market economies, notwithstanding innumerable difficulties.[3] In particular, with the coming into effect of the law referred to above, all the cooperative credit banks were entitled either to maintain their affiliation with the BGZ or to affiliate with one of the newly-established regional cooperative credit banks. From 1991 to 1993, the cooperative banks established three affiliating banks: these were Gospodarczy Bank Wielkopolski SA in Poznan (GBW SA), Bank Unii Gospodarczej SA in Warsaw (BUG SA) and Gospodarczy Bank Poludniowo-Zachodni SA in Wroclaw (GBPZ SA). These three regional cooperative credit banks, in addition to six other commercial banks, turned into the hub of the Polish banking system until 1997. Subsequently, the BGZ became a joint-stock company. This ruled out the possibility of creating a three-tier structure based on a local level, a regional level and a national level.

In fact, the fragility of the financial system forced the lawmakers to require the setting up of regional structures in order to promote mechanisms of aid and guarantee, as well as to allow even small-sized cooperatives to enjoy advanced services in the data processing, legal and treasury management field. If, on the one hand, the introduction of the Act of Changes in the Organization and Operation of the Cooperative Movement had allowed a complete reorganization of the Polish cooperative system, on the other hand it had somehow held back its development, since it had provided for a system of mutual guarantees. In view of the above, the larger and financially sounder cooperatives were unwilling to accept the mutual aid mechanisms and the possibility of having to bear the operating liabilities and inefficiencies of smaller cooperative credit banks. A revival of the cooperative system unquestionably called for a law that might succeed in amalgamating the different cooperative banks and in toning down the excessive differences in terms of efficiency and financial soundness.

The entire cooperative credit sector was thoroughly reformed in 2001 further to the issue of the Act on the Operations of Cooperative Banks, Their Affiliation, and Affiliating Banks, subsequently amended in 2003. In addition to confirming the course previously outlined by the legislator with respect to the cooperative structure to be adopted (two-tier), the aforementioned Act laid down specific constraints in terms of operations. In particular, all the local cooperative banks with total equity below five million euro could only work within the province where they had their registered office and, at the most, in the administrative districts of operation of their branches. Besides, these banks were required to affiliate with one of the three existing cooperative banks, with full freedom to change the group of affiliation and to decide mergers and acquisitions with other local cooperative banks.

Given the want of a "third tier" cooperative that might take responsibility for protecting the interest of the entire cooperative credit system, the National Union of Cooperative Banks (Krajowy Zwiazek Banków Spóldzielczych, KZBS) was set up in 1991 with a view to:

1) representing the cooperative movement within institutional and government bodies at both a national and an international level;
2) monitoring and supporting the cooperative credit banks development process;
3) taking part in the making of laws and regulations that might affect the cooperative credit sector.

Thanks to the activity carried out in a cooperative effort with Media Consulting Travel-Probank, the Union of Cooperative Banks sees also to the organization of events and meetings related to the cooperative world and to the issue of a magazine designed to popularize the cooperative culture.

In 2002, the General Meeting of the National Union of Cooperative Banks resolved upon the setting up of the National Credit Fund Guarantee of Cooperative Banking in Warsaw, with a view to allowing the access to credit to small- and medium-sized agricultural companies. In particular, the National Credit Fund Guarantee is a financial intermediary that after analysis of credit risk of the applying enterprise grants its guarantee that may be used to obtain credit from a Cooperative bank. The applying enterprise pays a commission for this financial service to National Credit Fund Guarantee so can enhance the request for funding. The peculiarity of this guarantee system is that it belongs to the very

Cooperative banks that, in relation to their total assets, subscribe shares of the registered capital and pay a yearly fee to cover the fixed costs of the fund (Mazur 2004).

Nowadays, the cooperative credit system in Poland is organized on the basis of three regional banks, the Bank of the Polish Cooperative Movement (Bank Polskiej Spółdzielczości SA), the Banking Cooperative Group (Gospodarczy Bank Wielkopolski SA), and the Mazowiecki Regional Bank (Mazowiecki Bank Regionalny SA), which are joined by the cooperatives whose total equity is below five million euro. In Poland, there is also the Crakow Cooperative Bank that, having a capital in excess of five million euro, works outside the mechanisms of affiliation with regional banks and has a nation-wide territorial reference context.

The total number of Cooperative banks connected with the three affiliating banks has decreased to a considerable extent over time, in consequence of a progressive concentration of the sector, even though they maintained their market shares (see Table 10.5). On the other hand, while the sector of the commercial banks has reported a slight increase in number, it is progressively reducing its market share (measured in terms of Total Assets).

The corporate governance of each cooperative bank provides for the presence of a variety of bodies: the General Assembly of Representatives, the Supervisory Board and the Board of Directors. The General Assembly is entrusted with the appointment of the members of the Supervisory Board, and the approval of the strategic bank guidelines and the annual accounts. The Supervisory Board comprises at least five members that are required to be members of the cooperative. The Supervisory Board appoints the chairperson of the Board of Directors with the assent of the Banking Audit Commission. The Board of Directors comprises at least three members of the cooperative and is entrusted with the most important managerial tasks.

The largest cooperative network operating in Poland is the Bank Polskiej Spóldzielczości SA, which was set up in 2002 further to the merger of Gospodarczy Bank Południowo-Zachodni SA with five Polish banks: Bank Unii Gospodarczej SA, Lubelski Bank Regionalny SA, Małopolski Bank Regionalny SA, Rzeszowski Bank Regionalny SA, and Warmińsko-Mazurski Bank Regionalny SA. Among the shareholders of Bank BPS SA dominate cooperative banks that own together 87.3 per cent shares, including affiliated banks – 80 per cent. However, such foreign financial entities as DZ Bank AG or Credit Mutuel play also an important role amongst shareholders. The Bank Polskiej Spóldzielczości

Table 10.5 The Polish banking system

	2003		2004		2005		2006	
Commercial banks (number)	58		57		61		63	
Total assets (million of euro)	125,572.66	93.04%	137,717.38	92.79%	148,941.82	91.98%	171,926.57	91.51%
Co-operative Bank (number)	600		596		588		584	
Affiliating banks:	2,303.61	1.71%	2,786.26	1.88%	3,639.67	2.25%	4,337.88	2.31%
Total cooperative banks of which affiliated to:	7,086.87	5.25%	7,920.50	5.34%	9,355.53	5.78%	11,619.01	6.18%
Bank Polskiej Spódzielczoœci SA	3,996.22	2.96%	4,431.31	2.99%	5,226.29	3.23%	6,381.08	3.40%
Gospodarczy Bank Wielkopolski SA	1,950.76	1.45%	2,282.01	1.54%	2,690.81	1.66%	3,424.03	1.82%
Mazowiecki Bank Regionalny SA	912.83	0.68%	1,032.06	0.70%	1,224.03	0.76%	1,540.36	0.82%
Non affiliated	227.06	0.17%						
Total cooperative sector (million of euros)	9,390.48	6.96%	10,706.76	7.21%	12,995.20	8.02%	15,956.88	8.49%
Total assets of polish banking system	134,963.14	100.00%	148,424.14	100.00%	161,937.02	100.00%	187,883.45	100.00%

Source: NPB data (2007, 2006, 2005, 2004).

Table 10.6 ROE analysis relative to the Polish banking system

Year	NeR/GrR	GrR/OpR	IM/TA	Int/IM	OpR/IntM	TA/E	ROE
2003	52.08%	103.84%	3.07%	179.40%	16.09%	9.88	4.74%
2004	90.21%	102.10%	3.08%	177.17%	26.42%	10.25	13.59%
2005	83.32%	107.62%	3.16%	170.52%	32.13%	10.67	16.57%
2006	81.82%	106.65%	3.01%	170.51%	34.92%	11.52	18.00%

Source: NPB data (2007).

SA affiliates 351 cooperative banks, which constitute 60 per cent of the Polish cooperative banking sector (Bank Polskiej Spółdzielczości 2006).

With reference to the performance of the Polish banks, the recourse to the ROE decomposition permits to single out the factors that have contributed the most to the creation of the return on equity.[4] In particular, the performance of the Polish banking system in terms of return on equity (ROE) reports a trend on the increase, although attained under progressively increasing leverage conditions (Total Assets/Equity).

With reference to the characteristic management, it may be noted that:

• the Polish cooperative credit system constantly reports a higher Interest Margin on Total Assets ratio than the rest of the banking system;
• the incidence of the income components resulting from services, defined by the Intermediation Margin on Interest Margin ratio, proves systematically more limited in the cooperative credit system than in the rest of the banking system.

As far as the incidence of operational costs (measured by the Operational Result on Intermediation Margin ratio) is concerned, the cooperative credit system has reported a slightly higher level than the banking system. It needs to be stressed, though, that even in this case, the level of capitalization of the cooperative credit banks proves on average in line with the level reported by the banking system.

Taking into consideration the evolution of the trend of growth reported in the last few years and the positive influences on the economy resulting from the accession to the EU, it may be assumed that the Polish cooperative credit banks will continue their expansion phase, in all probability increasing the margin from services resulting from the extension of the range of increasingly more complex and high-value added products.

Table 10.7 ROE analysis relative to the Polish cooperative banking system

	NeR/GrR	GrR/OpR	IM/TA	Int/IM	OpR/IntM	TA/E	ROE
2003	69.95%	98.92%	5.33%	153.81%	19.31%	9.80	10.73%
2004	81.97%	99.54%	5.54%	147.53%	24.95%	9.97	16.58%
2005	82.13%	100.03%	5.22%	139.93%	25.15%	10.29	15.53%
2006	80.37%	102.79%	4.28%	143.29%	23.89%	10.99	13.29%

Source: NPB data (2007).

10.4.3 The Bank of Hungarian savings cooperatives Ltd

Towards the end of the nineteenth century, the economic situation of the Hungarian agricultural sector was definitely critical: the widespread poverty and the difficulty in finding loans were the unifying factor of the agricultural world, often vexed by phenomena of usury that hindered its renewal and development. The first agricultural cooperative was set up in 1879 in order to counter this phenomenon and, indeed, with the specific aim of gathering savings from well-to-do families and providing credit at fair terms to the agricultural sector. The cooperative movement developed quickly, driven also by the German model inspired by F. W. Raiffeisen who, in 1885, was invited to the International Agrarian Conference in Budapest. After World War II, the cooperation in the credit sector came to a standstill since, besides dissolving all the cooperatives that had been established until then, the law of 1947 centralized all the credit intermediation operations in a single national bank, the National Bank of Hungary (NBH) (Ieda 1998).

Therefore, during the Soviet period, the NBH served both as the central bank and as a commercial bank. This condition gave rise to a twofold problem. Firstly, a financial system with this type of organization lacked an efficient mechanism of allocation of resources, since the state-owned enterprises were the main beneficiaries of the investment financing provided by the mono-bank. Secondly, given the scarce pervasiveness of the commercial network, considerable difficulties were met in finding financial resources. The full-blown crisis of 1956 caused the Soviet government to review the preceding policy guidelines in respect of the centralization of the credit activity, seeing to the introduction of two provisions. In particular, notwithstanding a few operations-related constraints,[5] it became once again possible to set up savings cooperatives (*Takarékszövetkezetek*). The year 1959 marked the establishment of the OTP National Savings Bank, a commercial bank that was to operate exclusively in the retail-banking sector and to guarantee the commercial coverage of the entire Hungarian territory.

The passage from planned to market economy in 1986 caused the banking system to move towards a progressive liberalization. At first, the activities that were under the NBH (central bank and commercial bank) were finally separated through the creation of two banks. One had the typical functions of a central bank, while the other served as a commercial bank that, through two divisions, was responsible for the provision of credit to industrial and agricultural enterprises. Later on, the first three commercial banks (Hungarian Credit Bank Ltd, MHB; National Commercial and Credit Bank Ltd, K&H; and Credit and Development Bank of Budapest Ltd, BB) were authorized to carry on the credit intermediation activity (Estrin, Hare and Suranyi 1992), marking in such a way the end of the monopoly of the banking sector.

The bank and enterprise conmixtion that had been inherited from the monopolistic Soviet regime and a regulatory framework that was not yet appropriate were among the major causes of the financial and economic crisis experienced in those years. In particular, the competitive inefficiencies of the industrial system were soon shifted on the banks, giving rise to generalized conditions of insolvency, chain bankruptcies, monetary crises accompanied by the devaluation of the national currency, and two-digit growth rates of domestic prices.

It was in those years that the government tried to stem the financial collapse by passing the Banking Act of 1991 and introducing two projects, the so-called "bank-consolidation" and "credit-consolidation" projects (1993-94), under the terms of which the state bailed out the most important commercial banks: banks were able to swap enterprise debts for Government bonds and to write off approximately half of the bad credits. Besides, in 1992, the need to give the Savings Cooperatives a modern legal framework, caused the government to pass the Law on Cooperatives, Law I, subsequently supplemented by Law CXLI of 2000 that, *inter alia*, provided for the explicit authorization of the Hungarian Financial Supervisory Authority and the Country Court of Registry to carry out the credit intermediation activity. At the same time, the privatization of the banking system was accompanied by an increased competition thanks to the entry into the market of international competitors either as subscribers of venture capital or through the opening of new foreign branches.

The end of the period of transition and the return to conditions of economic stability supported the proliferation of cooperative-type organizations that, until 1989, had been represented by a single association.

The significant expansion of the cooperation phenomenon and the need to protect the specific interests of each individual sector (credit, consumption, labor) led to the setting up of three associations specialized by segment typology.

In particular, the 260 Savings Cooperatives that existed at that time established the National Federation of Saving Cooperatives (OTZ) which was to coordinate a series of common initiatives, to centralize the marketing policy, to standardize the catalogue of financial products and services and, finally, to create a protection and guarantee scheme for all the member cooperatives, with a view to making the Hungarian cooperative credit system sounder.

In fact, before long, by signing the Integration Agreement, the Savings Cooperatives set up the National Fund for the Institutional Protection of Savings Cooperatives (OTIVA), a protection scheme to be entered into on a voluntary basis according to the Law on Financial Institutions. The objectives of this National Fund included the control of member cooperatives; the development of the integration as well as the prevention and/or the management of crises (Toth 2004).

The signing of the Integration Agreement represented the fundamental preamble for the establishment of the central bank of the savings cooperatives; that is, the Bank of Hungarian Savings Cooperatives Ltd (Magyar Takarékszövetkezeti Bank Részvénytársaság) whose registered capital is subscribed in full by the Savings Cooperatives. During the banking consolidation phase (1993), the state became the only owner of the bank and, in 1997, saw to its subsequent liberalization through the assignment to DZ Bank AG of a 71 per cent capital share. The remaining assets were held by the Savings Cooperatives (26 per cent) and Allianz Hungària Ltd (5 per cent). In 2004, based on agreements entered into with DZ Bank AG, the Savings Cooperatives became once again the reference shareholders of the Bank of Hungarian Savings Cooperatives Ltd, with over 64 per cent of the subscribed capital.

Nowadays, the Bank of Hungarian Savings Cooperatives Ltd (hereafter referred to as Takarèkbank) is the central bank of 150 savings cooperatives that work in the Hungarian territory. In its capacity as central bank, it manages the treasury of all the affiliated banks and the international payments services, and sees to the arrangement of complex products that will be subsequently sold by the individual savings cooperative. Through its control over specialized companies, Takarèkbank offers the centralization of all the data processing services (through Takinfo and Orient+). The other centralized activities relate to specialized products, including project financing, factoring (Banküzlet) and asset management (managed by the Takarék Fund Zrt.). Finally, Allianz Hungària Ltd is

Table 10.8   ROE analysis relative to the Hungarian banking system

Year	NeR/GrR	GrR/OpR	IM/TA	Int/IM	OpR/IntM	TA/E	ROE
2003	82.09%	105.38%	7.46%	106.29%	54.91%	7.33	27.63%
2004	82.49%	85.82%	8.40%	104.43%	54.73%	8.18	27.80%
2005	81.30%	94.04%	9.21%	106.38%	44.77%	7.38	24.76%
2006	75.98%	90.76%	9.45%	106.50%	38.35%	7.96	21.18%

Source: BankScope data, Bureau van Dijk Electronic Publishing.

responsible for the production of products related to the social security and insurance division (Takarèkbank 2006).

The saving cooperatives have a market share close to 5 per cent (having regard to collected deposits) and 6.4 per cent in terms of total assets, representing the reference point for the agricultural economy. They are organized into 1600 branches and cover the entire Hungarian territory. The cooperative group ranks sixth in order of importance, with total assets amounting to three billion euro. Thanks to the outsourcing of advanced services to the Bank of Hungarian Savings Cooperatives Ltd, it succeeds in recovering efficiency and offering a full range of services at favorable conditions to its customers.

The analysis of how the return on equity (ROE) is formed allows noting that, with reference to the Hungarian Bank of Savings Cooperatives, the level reached by the indicator in the last four years has been considerably lower than that of the rest of the banking sector. Such a datum must also be interpreted taking into account the fact that the leverage level (TA/E) of the Hungarian Bank of Savings Cooperatives has been considerably higher than that of the rest of the banking sector. Using the ROE decomposition, with reference to the characteristic management, it may be noted that:

- the Hungarian Bank of Savings Cooperatives reports a considerably lower Interest Margin on Total Assets ratio than the banking system. This datum must also be interpreted taking into account the fact that the total assets growth reported by the Hungarian Bank of Savings Cooperatives in the last four years is considerably higher than the figure reported by the rest of the banking system;
- the incidence of the income component resulting from services, defined by the Intermediation Margin on Interest Margin ratio, always with the exception of 2006, is constantly higher for the Hungarian Bank of Savings Cooperatives with respect to the rest of the banking system.

Table 10.9 ROE analysis relative to the Hungarian Bank of Savings Cooperatives

Year	NeR/GrR	GrR/OpR	IM/TA	Int/IM	OpR/IntM	TA/E	ROE
2003	79.72%	44.14%	1.47%	165.56%	52.42%	23.44	10.53%
2004	84.77%	36.92%	0.77%	207.24%	82.81%	27.84	11.57%
2005	75.57%	33.19%	1.14%	157.93%	81.32%	33.53	12.35%
2006	77.53%	32.52%	0.64%	216.59%	122.48%	30.83	13.24%

Source: BankScope data, Bureau van Dijk Electronic Publishing.

In regards to the incidence of the operational costs (measured by the Operational Result on Intermediation Margin ratio), the level reported throughout the observation period by the Hungarian Bank of Savings Cooperatives is definitely higher than that of the banking system. Indirectly, this should point to levels of operational efficiency of the cooperative system that are definitely lower than those of the rest of the banking sector.

10.5 Conclusion

The analysis of the economic-financial systems of the ten newly-admitted EU member countries allows grouping them into two clusters. The first one, comprising the States of Malta and Cyprus, denotes an economy that has reached a stage of maturity and a financial system that is highly developed and fully assimilable to that of the European countries. On the other hand, the countries falling within the second group are brought together by the fact that they have been under the Soviet regime for almost 50 years and that they report high rates of growth of the economy and a level of development of the financial system that is significantly lower than that of the European countries, even though witnessing a considerable increase.

In this economic context, this chapter has analyzed three of the most important cooperative systems: the cooperative systems of Cyprus, Poland and Hungary. With reference to Cyprus, the cooperative system stands out as a three-tiered organizational structure, governed by the Cooperative Societies Laws and Rule, which permeates all the sectors of the economy. The development of the cooperative credit system in Cyprus has caused it to reach a market share equal to one third of the entire banking sector. Organized as a third-tier network, the Cooperative Central bank Ltd is the largest cooperative bank working in Cyprus, with nearly 490 affiliated companies. The affiliated banks are subject to the supervision of the Central Cooperative Bank that, in its turn, is subject to the supervision of the central institute. Besides being responsible for the production of sophisticated financial services and products, the Central Cooperative Bank manages the treasury of all the cooperative banks and societies.

The cooperative credit system in Poland has very ancient origins, but the Soviet regime prevented its development until 1989. After a transition period (1989-91) characterized by severe economic and financial crises, the entire banking sector has been thoroughly reformed and denationalized through the setting up of nine regional banks. The cooperative credit sector is currently regulated by the Act on the Operations of Cooperative Banks, Their Affiliation, and Affiliating Banks, which makes it mandatory for a local bank lacking a minimum capital of five million euro to affiliate with a cooperative group. At present, there are in Poland three cooperative groups and a cooperative credit bank (the Crakow Cooperative Bank) that, exceeding the legal limit, does not belong to any network. With a market share in excess of 8 per cent, the credit cooperative system in Poland represents an important reality of the Country that is bound to witness further developments after the privatization of many sectors of the economy.

Even the Hungarian cooperative system has very ancient origins and experienced vicissitudes similar to those of the Polish system. After the dissolution of the cooperatives in 1947, a minimum cooperative-type credit intermediation activity was restored in 1956. The actual revival occurred with the fall of Communism in 1989 and the privatization of the banking system. With nearly 150 Savings Cooperatives and a 6 per cent share of the market, the Hungarian cooperative network plays on a central bank (the Hungarian Bank of Savings Cooperatives) that sees to the production of advanced financial products, international payment services and the supervision over the individual banks.

Notes

1. The names of the ten newly admitted EU member countries have been shortened as follows: Czech Republic, CZ; Estonia, EE; Cyprus, CY; Latvia, LV; Lithuania, LT; Hungary, HU; Malta, MT; Poland, PL; Slovenia, SI; Slovakia, SK.
2. The same approach is used in the case of Rabobank in this volume.

3. Suffice it to consider that from 1993 up to now, 131 cooperative credit banks have gone bankrupt and 48 have been wound up (Cf., NBP 2001).
4. The same approach is used in the case of Rabobank in this volume.
5. The savings cooperatives could only collect deposits, intermediate housing loans and grant consumer credits (purchasing consumer goods) (see Toth 2004).

References

Bank Polskiej Spółdzielczości SA (2006) Annual Report, Warsaw, Available from: http://www.bankbps.pl/upload/annual_report_cca210a138.pdf, [Accessed 31 July 2009]

Caviglia G., Krause G., Thimann C. (2003) Key features of the financial sector in EU accession countries, European Central Bank, Frankfurt, Available from: www.ecb.int [Accessed 7 July 2007].

Co-operative Central Bank Ltd (2006) Annual Report and Financial Statements, December, Nicosia, Available from: http://www.centralbank.gov.cy, [Accessed 7 July 2007].

Co-operative societies' supervision and development authority (CSSDA) (2004) "The co-operative movement in Cyprus," December, Nicosia, Available from: www.moi.gov.cy/pio, [Accessed 7 July 2007].

EACB (2007), "Member organization," Available from: www.eurocoopbanks.org, [Accessed 10 July 2007].

Estrin S., Hare P, Suranyi, M. (1992) "Banking in transition: development and current problem in Hungary," Discussion paper, n. 68, Centre for Economic Performance. London, London School of Economics and Political Science.

European Central Bank (2006) Opinion CON/2006/42, August, Frankfurt, Available from www.ecb.int, [Accessed 7 July 2007].

European Central Banking (ECB) (2006) EU Banking Structure, October, Frankfurt, Available from: www.ecb.int [Accessed 7 July 2007].

Gołajewska M., Wyczański P. (2002) "Stability and Structure of Financial Systems in CEC5," National Bank of Poland, Warsaw, Available from: http://www.bankbps.pl. [Accessed 7 July 2007].

Ieda O. (1998) "The rural cooperatives and members' liability from a historical perspective: the Hungarian case," Matsushita International Foundation, Available from: http://src-h.slav.hokudai.ac.jp/kaken/ieda2001/pdf/ieda.pdf, [Accessed 31 July 2009].

IMF (2006) Economic World Outlook, Statistical Appendix, April, Washington, Available from: imf.org, [Accessed 12 August 2007].

Mazur M. (2004) National credit guarantee fund of co-operative banks, ICBA, Seminar, Available from: www.ica.coop/icba, [Accessed 14 July 2007].

National Bank of Poland (NBP) (2007) Summary evaluation of the financial situation of Polish banks 2006, July, Warsaw, Available from: http://www.bankbps.pl, [Accessed 14 July 2007].

National Bank of Poland (NPB) (2001) "The polish banking system in the nineties," Working Paper, Warsaw, Available from: http://www.bankbps.pl, [Accessed 14 July 2007].

Toth K. (2004) The institutional protection fund of the hungarian Savings Co-operatives (OTIVA), ICBA, Seminar, Warsaw, Available from: www.ica. coop/icba, [Accessed 14 July 2007].

World Bank (2005) "Financial Structure and Economic Development Database, Excel™ spreadsheet," http://www.worldbank.org/research/projects/finstructure/database.htm, [Accessed 14 July 2007].

11
Credit Cooperatives in Romania

Candida Bussoli

11.1 Introduction

Romania is the most important country in the Danube-Balkans region in terms of surface area, population, and strategic location between the Balkan peninsula and Eastern Europe. Having an open economy, it presents itself as an emerging market on the European scene.

As it is evident in data from the Romanian Institute of Statistics, the main macroeconomic indicators give the country a dynamic image: the gross domestic product showed a positive trend, traceable to the services sector, which moved beyond the 50 per cent marks in terms of its

Box 11.1 General information

Currency: The new Leu
Surface area: 237,500 km$_2$
Population: 22,303,552 (2006)
Capital: Bucharest, 2,013,911 inhabitants
Demographic growth: – 0.12% (2006)
Life expectancy: men 68.14, women 75.34 (2006)
GDP: $183.6 billion (2005)
% GDP by sector: 10.1%, 35%, 54.9% (primary, secondary, tertiary) (2004)
Economic growth: 4.5% (2005)
Foreign debt: $35.68 billion (2005)
Inflation rate: 9% (2005)
Unemployment: 5.9% (2005)

Import volume: $38.15 billion (2005) **Export volume**: $27.72 billion (2005) **Historical and political information**: Independence from Turkey on 9 May 1877. Communist dictatorship of N. Ceausescu from 1965 to 1989. Proclaimed a republic on 30 December 1947. Form of government: semi-presidential.

Source: Centre of Services and Documentation for International Economic Cooperation: INFORMEST.

percentage weight in the GDP; also the industrial sector confirmed its role as one of the driving forces of economic growth; the dynamics of final domestic consumption, and especially the figures for private consumption, register an elevated growth rate; the rate of unemployment, which had already fallen below 10 per cent in 2001, reached 5.3 per cent of the total active civil population in the first half of 2006; the inflation rate followed a similar downward trend, falling from 45 per cent in 2000 to 6 per cent in 2006.

Since the collapse of the Communist regime in the 1990s, Romania has achieved noteworthy macroeconomic stabilization, with significant repercussions on its production activities and financial system. One of the key components of the abandonment of centralized economic planning was the process of privatization that affected all sectors, favouring the full liberalization of the market and resulting in a decisive change in direction from the nationalization of industrial enterprises, banks, transportation systems and mining operations initiated following the end of the Second World War.

Romania's entry in the orbit of the satellite countries of the Soviet Union had dragged the country into a state of grave inefficiency, absence of competitiveness and advanced obsolescence of skills and plants. It also rendered the financial system completely subservient to the decisions of the central government: the banks held extremely reduced decision-making powers in terms of the making loans, and the services they offered were limited in scope and very simple. The granting of credit depended on production decisions taken centrally and not on the merit of the company to be granted the financing.[1]

The transformation of the Romanian economy into a market economy occurred after a certain delay in contrast to other Easter European countries. This was because of the strong isolationism established at the behest of Ceausescu, a condition that attenuated the influence of the thoroughgoing changes caused by the Perestroika in the Soviet Union. It was only after the collapse of the regime, the introduction of a democratic system, the presence of a parliament and plurality of parties that the country was able to proceed with a full liberalization of the market.

The path followed was plagued by widespread corruption, making necessary regulatory initiatives of prevention and repression. Time was needed for the recovery of the Romanian economy due to the difficulties posed by the fragility of the financial system. Romania's particularly reduced level of financial development resulted in a limited use of bank funds, especially in rural zones, where the population is highly reluctant to use banking services, having little confidence in financial institutions in general.[2]

The circumstances described above made clear the urgent need for system-reforming laws. A series of measures were introduced from 1991 onward, with repercussions on both the securities and credit markets. The Securities and Stock Exchange Act was approved in 1994, providing the legal reference framework for the regulation of capital markets. The reform of the banking system had begun earlier with the first legislative initiatives dating back to 1991, together with the restructuring of the Banca Naţională a României (National Bank of Romania) (BNR).

The present chapter analyses cooperative credit in Romania. The first section reviews the principal phases in the evolution of the Romanian banking system. The second section focuses on the historical development and activities of credit cooperatives, and intermediaries which can draw on a wide amount of coverage in terms of the distribution of their branches,[3] even in rural areas; the last section is set aside for some brief concluding considerations.

11.2 The Romanian banking system

Banks hold a dominant position within the Romanian financial system, as compared to other institutions whose positions on the market are relatively limited (see Table 11.1). This is because during the early years of its transformation into a market economy, the flow stabilization and restructuring of the real economy impeded the diversification of financial institutions.

The first steps in the restructuring of the Romanian banking system were taken at the end of 1990, with the reorganization of the Banca Naţională a României (National Bank of Romania), which

Table 11.1   The Romanian financial system in 2002–05

Financial intermediation institution	Share in GDP			
	2002	2003	2004	2005
Credit institutions (1)	31.19	30.76	36.59	44.76
Insurance companies (2)	1.51	1.78	1.90	2.21
Investment companies (3)	0.09	0.09	0.21	0.17
Financial investment companies (4)	1.45	1.45	1.29	1.76
Leasing companies (5)	1.48	1.81	2.97	3.63
Other institutions specialized in lending	0.41	0.4	0.65	0.93
Total	36.13	36.29	43.61	53.46

(1) Net assets of credit institutions, including CREDITCOOP
(2) The value of assets according to centralized balance sheets
(3) Assets of investment funds, including the funds administered by IMC (Investment Management Companies), which are not NUUCITS members
(4) Net assets of Financial Investment Companies (FICs)
(5) Financed net assets

was subsequently provided with a new statute, under the Law No. 312/2004 on the Statute of the National Bank of Romania, or *Legea privind Statutul Bancii Nationale a Romaniei*. The primary role of the BNR is to ensure the stability of the national currency. It thus holds the exclusive prerogative for managing monetary, currency and credit policy, as well as payments; it is also responsible for overseeing banking activities.[4]

The BNR is led by a *Consiliu de administratie* (Board of Directors) with nine members. The Board is appointed by the Parliament for a five-year term of office, with the possibility of renewal. Operating within the Board is an Executive Committee consisting of the Governor, the *Prim-Viceguvernator* (Senior Deputy Governor) and two *Viceguvernatori* (Deputy Governors).[5] In terms of its functions, the BNR pursues monetary policy with the standard instruments of refinancing banking institutes and setting minimum reserves of liquidity. Currency policy is implemented by issuing regulations to support the domestic currency, setting exchange rates and preserving and managing reserves in foreign currency.[6] As for its oversight functions, the BNR is responsible for issuing authorizations for the performance of banking activities and for the ongoing control of the legitimacy of the operations carried out by banks, through inspections, evaluations and the examination of documents, as well as the levying of penalties.

The legislative framework governing banking activities consists primarily of the following measures:

- Law no. 83/97 on the privatization of merchant banks, or *Legea pentru privatizarea societăilor comerciale bancare la care statul este acţionar* (Law on the Privatization of banks in which the State is a Shareholder);[7]
- Ordinance no. 99/2006 on credit institutions and the upgrading of capital, or *Ordonanţa privind instituţiile de credit şi adecvarea capitalului*;
- The regulations on the insolvency of credit institutes, or *Ordonanţa Guvernului nr. 10 din 22 ianuarie 2004 privind falimentul instituţiilor de credit*, approved, completed and modified under Law no. 278/2004.
- Government Ordinance no. 39/1996 on the organization and operation of the Credit Guarantee Fund of the banking system, or *Ordonanţa Guvernului no. 39/1996, privind organizarea şi funcţionarea Fondului de Garantare a Creditelor din Sistemul Bancar.*

The first of these measures was particularly important, seeing that it authorized the reorganization of the state units into commercial enterprises: this inevitable transformation was carried out gradually by the Romanian banking system, which, in the wake of the collapse of the Communist regime, was seeking to adjust the legal format of the banks to a market economy by turning them into joint-stock companies, whose capital continued to be publicly owned, splitting off the commercial activities formerly engaged in by the BNR and, most importantly, dealing with a situation characterized, in terms of investments, by an enormous mass of uncollectible receivables and, as far as organizational matters were concerned, by a drastic lack of skills and know-how. The resulting structure of the Romanian banking system was a two-part arrangement: on the one hand, the National Bank of Romania, serving as the issuing institute, and, on the other, the commercial banks, engaged in offering banking services. Gradually, alongside the banks still controlled by the State, there come into being banks funded with private capital.

Today the Romanian credit system is open to banking institutes established in the form of joint-stock companies, with capital held entirely or predominantly by the public sector, or with private capital in which the majority stockholder is either foreign or Romanian. As shown by Table 11.2, which covers BNR figures for various years, there are currently more private than public banks: from the 17 privately-held banks in operation at the end of 1995, the number has risen to 38 by the end of 2005. Analyzing the statistics in greater depth, we see that the strongest trend regards the banks controlled by foreign countries; in contrast, the banks controlled by Romanian capital show a downward trend. The noteworthy presence of foreign capital in the Romanian banking system facilitates access to outside funds, making the management of credit risk more efficient while maintaining a favourable impact on the stability of the system as a whole.

The banks carry out their activities in compliance with the principles of prudent management and in accordance with the law on banking activities, which expressly stipulates that a bank's statute must clearly indicate its organizational model, specifying the tasks assigned to its internal structures (see Iordan *et al.* 2005). The considerations referred to above, being tied to the stability and propriety of the intermediaries, point to the problem of the quality of credit and efficient allocation of resources, issues whose weight was widely felt by the Romanian financial system during its transformation into a market economy. An initial, readily discernible sign of the difficulties addressed, which is to a certain extent still present, regards the breakdown of the timing of the loans: as a rule, they are short-term, demonstrating the instability of the economic framework, which prevents expansion of the timeframe. In response to this undeniable difficulty, there has been a gradual improvement in the quality of loans: the coefficient of debtor solvency

Table 11.2   Banks and bank branches in Romania

	1990	1995	2000	2005
COMM. BANKS				
Banks with capital totally or primarily state-held	5	7	4	2
Banks with capital totally or primarily held by private parties	2	17	29	38*
– of which banks whose capital is totally or primarily in Romanian hands	2	9	8	8
– of which banks whose capital is primarily in foreign hands	–	8	21	30
Total	7	24	33	40
Foreign bank branches	5	7	8	6

* including CREDITCOOP.

has risen together with the level of assets of business enterprises with a resulting decline in the credit-risk ratio (see BNR statistical publications and Annual Report). The most recent figures present a high level of credit quality: maintenance of high-quality credit portfolio with low level of overdue and disputed credits (0.27 per cent of total credits) and low level of credits classified as doubtful or losses (2.6 per cent of total credits); substantial share of investments in highly-liquid assets (38.8 per cent); high liquidity of banking system (only 81 per cent of deposits from customers represent credits to customers) (see BNR *Romanian Banking System* June 2006).

The system would thus appear to be oriented towards a virtuous cycle of dynamic expansion and development, thanks in large part to a heightening of the competitive pressures, a circumstance accentuated by the entry of foreign operators: the more efficient allocation of resources manages to offset the greater risk brought about by the expansion of the real rate of growth of the loans (see Montesano 2002); the range of services offered is continually growing, in terms of both quality and quantity; the credits to operators with problems of solvency present a downward trend. The considerations referred to above would make it appear that the process towards a full market economy is definitively underway (see Coletti *et al.* 2003).

The level of concentration of the system, measured in terms of the percentage weight of the assets of the five leading banks out of the assets of all banks, appears moderate (Table 11.3), though higher than that of the countries of the euro area. The downward trend in the level of concentration and the increase in the portion of the bank market whose majority holdings are in the hands of foreigners orient the system towards higher levels of competitiveness.

One of the distinguishing features of the Romanian banking system is its high level of profitability which, combined with an adequate level of capitalization, ensures noteworthy protection against possible shocks.

Table 11.3 The banking sector concentration (top five commercial banks)

	Dec 2002	Dec 2003	Dec 2004	Dec 2005	Mar 2006
Assets	62.8	63.9	59.2	58.8	57.8
Loans	56.2	57.1	55.7	61.2	60.5
Securities	74.2	75.4	61.5	60.1	63.0
Deposits	63.0	64.9	59.5	57.0	56.2

Source: BNR (2006), *Financial Stability Report*.

In 2005 the profitability indexes, expressed in terms of ROE and ROA, remained at high levels, registering 15.4 per cent and 1.9 per cent respectively.[8] This situation, which is also a characterist of the past, has worsened before too long, on the basis of the following factors: the downward trend of the margin of interest compressed by the growing competitiveness of the system; the intention of the banks operating in the retail sector to undertake increasingly large investments for the development of a network of relations with the local territory with the objective of promoting customer loyalty; the costs to be sustained for the implementation of the Basil II agreement. The profitability indexes differ significantly, depending on the size of the bank: profitability is high in the case of the larger-size banks, which play a leading role in the system, preserving its capacity to absorb potential shocks; in the case of small banks, the level of profitability is lower, and this has a direct impact on their capacity for growth.

11.3 Credit cooperatives in Romania

11.3.1 Historical development

The first credit cooperatives came into being in the second half of the nineteenth century. They were based on the German systems of Raiffeisen and Schulze-Delizch. During 1870-80, credit and economic firms (*societati de credit si economie*) appeared and spread in almost all of the country's main cities and towns. By the *fin-de-siècle*, the ever increasing spread of "people's village banks" (*banci populare satesti*) signalled the consolidation of the cooperative movement in Romania.[9] Ever since, credit cooperatives in Romania have experienced periods of alternating fortune. They have been highly influenced by historical, economic, social and political circumstances. It was not until 1990, in the wake of the events tied to the collapse of the Communist regime, that development proved constant as it benefited from the changed political and economic scenario more oriented in the direction of liberalization and the market.

Cooperative activities are governed by Legislative Decree no. 67 of 1990, which is designed to regulate the activities of consumer and credit cooperatives on the bass of the principles stipulated and formalized by the International Cooperative Alliance. During this period, credit cooperatives carried out a range of different activities, but their financial operations were for members only. This law was reformed by Law no. 109 of 1996, the legal groundwork for cooperative credit activities. This all-encompassing act restored to the credit cooperatives their title of "people's banks" (*banci populare*) while clarifying and reinforcing the legislative framework in the sector.

Box 11.2 The evolution of cooperative credit in Romania

1851 – The first people's bank is founded in Ardeal, in the territory of Bistriţa.

1855 – An association of savings, credit and mutual assistance entitled "Înfrăţirea" is founded in Brăila

1860 – Ion Ionescu de a Brad founds a people's bank and a scholastic savings house in the village of Brad in the Roman district.

1867 – Visarion Roman lays the groundwork for the "Savings and Loan Company" of Răşinari, in the Sibiu district, the first credit cooperative as well as the first Romanian financial institution of Ardeal.

1870 – P. S. Aurelian founds the "Economia" Savings and Loan Company in Bucharest (based on the Schluze-Delizsch model).

1871–1881 – Savings and loan companies are established in almost all the countries, cities and some villages.

1886 – C. Dobrescu Argeş founds the "Frăţia" People's Bank in Domneşti and the "Economatul" consumer company in Retevoieşti, in the Arges district.

1887 – The Romanian Commercial Code is drawn up, including "provisions of cooperative enterprises" stimulating the establishment of cooperative type firms.

1891–1902 – Numerous cooperative credit companies are established, also referred to as rural people's banks.

1898–1902 – Spiru C. Hareţ, regarded as the founder of the people's banks, makes an admirable effort to establish the cooperative movement in rural areas, marking the consolidation of the cooperative movement in Romania.

1903 – The Law on People's Banks and Central Houses is passed, with subsequent modifications extending the sector to include all categories of cooperative organizations.

1917 – The Central House of Cooperation and Lending of Assets to Farmers is founded.

1929 – The Law on the Organization of Cooperative Activities is passed, undergoing numerous modifications, up through the year 1939.

1938 – The INCOOP, the National Institute of Cooperation is founded.

1954 – Under Decree no. 445 of 10 December the Bank of Agriculture is founded.

1970 – The law on the organization and operation of consumer cooperatives is issued.

1990 – On 8 February Legislative Decree no. 67 is issued on the organization and operation of consumer and credit cooperatives.

1996 – The Romanian Parliament approves law no. 109 on the organization and operation of consumer cooperatives and credit cooperatives.

2000 – The Romanian Government issues Emergency Ordinance no. 97 on cooperative credit organization.

2002 – The Romanian Parliament passes Law 200/2002 approving Government Emergency Ordinance no. 97/2000. On September the CREDITCOOP cooperative network receives its operating authorizations from the BNR and in October the Central House of CREDITCOOP becomes a member of the Deposit Guarantee Fund of the banking system.

2003 – The Central House of CREDITCOOP becomes a member of the Romanian Association of Bank and of the European Association of Cooperative Credit Banks.

2004 – The Romanian Parliament approves Law no. 122 modifying Government Emergency Ordinance no. 97/2000 of the organizational structure of cooperative credit enterprises.

Under Law 109/96, the system of credit cooperatives is structured on three organizational levels: a basic level, consisting of the largest number of credit cooperatives, which are grouped together; on the regional level, in "territorial homes," which, in turn, on the national level, are members of the "Home of Credit Cooperatives."

During 1997-98, independent people's banks came into vogue. Referring to themselves as "credit cooperatives" (*cooperative de credit*), they took advantage of the imperfections in the legislative system of the period. While they failed to respect the principles of cooperative entities in their operations, they avoided to comply with the standards regarding the minimum level of capitalization required for commercial banks.[10] This dangerous situation of anarchy led the government to take action, in the form of more stringent measures governing the scenario in order to interrupt the proliferation of institutions not operating within the framework of an authorized and regulated system. In 1998, a government ruling prohibited the establishment of new credit cooperatives; then, in July of 2000, Urgent Government Ordinance no. 97/2000 was issued on the organization structure of credit cooperatives and approved by the Romanian Parliament under Law no. 200/2002, which granted the BNR the power to control banking activities carried out within the framework of cooperative credit.[11]

In accordance with the new legislation, the credit cooperatives remained independent, apolitical and non-government associations of individuals who voluntarily grouped together for the primary purpose of carrying out banking activities to assist their members and to pursue objectives of an economic, social and cultural nature. Credit cooperatives are established by a variable number of members, and their capital varies, being subdivided into shares of equal value. Each cooperative, organized in its own territory of operations, must join a "central house" (*casa centrala*), established through the grouping together of individual units. The Central House has an area of operations that includes at least three territorial areas of operation of member cooperatives. The members' voting rights are based on the principle of "one person, one vote," though this rule is waived in the case of the Central House, whose member cooperatives vote in proportion to their respective numbers of members. The Central House carries out functions of regulation and supervision, coordinating the activities of the member cooperatives – having been granted powers of representation, control and supervision – and performing banking functions for the units of the network.[12] The Central House guarantees all the obligations of its member cooperatives, establishing a guarantee reserve for the purpose.[13]

As of 31 December 2003, the creditcoop network consisted of the "Central House," with 21 branches, plus 547 credit cooperatives. Until 31 May 2004 the credit cooperatives were required to establish a minimum system of 3 billion lei of their own funds: this led to an intensive process of concentration that resulted, as of 25 February 2004, in approval by the National Bank of Romania of merger requests presented by 504 credit coops,[14] in pursuit of the following objectives:

- achievement of the minimum threshold of three billion lei for the funds of an individual credit cooperative;

- assurance of improved conditions of development for the credit cooperative meeting the threshold;
- procurement of increased levels of efficiency through cost reductions;
- establishment of new methods for the supervision of the credit cooperatives purchased, which become working outlets (secondary offices) of the purchasing cooperatives;
- the creation of more advantageous investment conditions for the members of the cooperatives;
- facilitated control, on the part of the Central House, over the affiliates and the transfer of funds within the network.[15]

As of 31 December 2004, there was a network of credit cooperatives consisting of a Central House with 16 branches and 133 member cooperatives. At present, the branches number 19, while the number of member cooperatives has slightly fallen to 124.

11.3.2 The activities of the cooperatives

The activities of the member cooperative organizations of the network of the "Creditcoop" Central House are regulated, authorized and supervised by the BNR, as it is the case for the activities of other types of credit intermediaries. Within the limits of the authorization issued by the BNR, and in accordance with the regulation of the Creditcoop Central House, the member credit cooperatives of the creditcoop network can carry out the following operations:

- the collection of deposits from the members of the cooperatives, as well as from individuals or organizations that are domiciled or have their registered offices or carry out their activities in the territory of operation of the credit cooperative;
- the granting of loans, including mortgages, in accordance with the legal provisions on mortgage credit, to members of the cooperatives for real-estate investments;
- the granting of loans to small-scale businessmen, religious organizations, family associations or individuals who exercise regulated, self-employed professions and have their registered offices or carry out their activities in the territory of operations of the credit cooperatives;
- the administration of credits in the name and on the behalf of the State, with resources made available to members of the cooperatives, as well as small-scale businessmen, religious organizations, family associations or individuals who exercise regulated, self-employed

professions and have their registered offices or carry out their activities in the territory of operations of the credit cooperatives;
- the issue and management of instruments of payment and credit;
- Payments and reimbursements;
- Transfers of funds;
- Operations involving loans between cooperatives or with other banks;
- Operations involving the sale and purchase of foreign currency against the domestic currency, carried out at official rates with members of the cooperatives and with other individuals, small-scale businessmen, religious organizations, family associations or individuals who exercise regulated, self-employed professions and have their registered offices or carry out their activities in the territory of operations of the credit cooperatives.
- Mandated operations, in accordance with the rules issued by the BNR.

Within the limits of the authorizations grated by the BNR, the Creditcoop Central House performs the following activities:

- the collection of deposits;
- the granting of loans to individuals who are not members of the affiliated credit cooperatives, as well as to organizations that have their domicile, residence or registered office, or that perform their activities, in the area of territorial operations of the Central House;
- operations of factoring and the discounting of commercial notes;
- the granting of loans in the name and on the behalf of the State, from sums made available to the member credit cooperatives;
- operations on the inter-bank market;
- the issuing and management of instruments of credit and payment;
- payments and reimbursements;
- transfers of funds;
- issue of guarantees and undertaking of commitments;
- transactions on its own behalf or on the behalf of clients, in accordance with the rules currently in force and regarding: currencies; negotiable monetary instruments (checks, promissory notes, certificates of deposit); state securities; value securities issued by the authority in favour of local public administrations;
- consulting regarding the activities developed by the organizations of cooperative credit.

Over the years, the CREDITCOOP network of cooperative credit has registered continuous development: the banking products and services offered have been diversified, and the economic results obtained have grown from year to year. Looking at assets, the statistics show continuous growth, confirmed in recent years as well: total assets went from 331 million RON in 2004 to 443 million RON (approximately 125 million euro) in 2005.

Investments are essentially geared towards client lending operations (68.5 per cent) and company-treasury and inter-bank operations (20.7 per cent). The structure of the liabilities entered on the balance-sheet as of 31 December 2004 was as follows: operations with clients 60.5 per cent; own capital 26.3 per cent; company-treasury and inter-bank operations 12.4 per cent, other liabilities 0.8 per cent.[16] The credits portfolio presents an expensive trend lower than the growth of deposits on account of the high rates of earned interest: the interest rates on investments, based on the indications of the Central House, are set independently by the 124 Boards of Directors and fall within an interval of 14 per cent to 25 per cent; the level of the rates on deposits varies from a minimum of 0 per cent to 10 per cent.

Creditcoop shows extremely favourable performance in terms of income, despite the fact that its market share has been stagnant in recent years: the ROA has reached peaks of 3.6 per cent. According to data taken from the official website of the Creditcoop Central House and of the BNR, the net profits of Creditcoop for the year 2005 were 13.68 million RON (approximately four million euro), a figure higher than that of many commercial banks in Romania. Following the processing of liberalization and the opening-up to international relations, the credit cooperatives have established contacts with similar organizations in the countries of central and eastern Europe. In April of 2003 the Creditcoop Central House became a member of the European Association of Cooperative Banks, confirming the major process of development accomplished and the rich prospects for future growth.

There are numerous problems, however, with regard to the presence of credit cooperatives that have not obtained authorization to establish networks, because they are unable to satisfy the stringent requirements of the legislators. Of the ten networks of cooperative credit that grouped together to initiate the authorization procedure, only four have managed to reach the final phase of the authorization process, and three were not authorized, because they did not meet the prerequisites contemplated under Law 97/2000. Following completion of the appeal procedures, the rejected networks are to be liquidated.

Naturally, the resulting situation is characterized by a loss of jobs and the dismantlement of financial intermediaries, with the shares being returned to the members of the cooperatives and the deposits to the clients, and with noteworthy repercussions on credit operations underway in the zones in which these banks operate. Given the scenario, the legislative framework in force has been supplemented and measures have been issued permitting the reorganization of the unauthorized cooperatives, so that they can obtain authorization to operate.

In particular, the old law has been coordinated with the regulations of the EU, in order to eliminate the restrictions regarding the domicile of the members of the cooperatives and the nationality of the administrative officers and the directors of the central houses. In general terms, the new governing measure, Law 122/2004, stipulates that:

- the central house guarantees all the obligations of its member credit cooperatives in accordance with the rules it issues. To this end, the central house established a "mutual" reserve, allocating 5 per cent of the taxable income to this provision;
- Membership in a cooperative is open to any individual possessing full legal capacity, domicile or residence in the territorial area of operations of the credit cooperative, after he or she has signed or accepted the articles of foundation of the cooperative and under-written or paid in the minimum amount for a membership share, as stipulated in the articles of foundation;
- In order to aid each member of the cooperatives who requests a loan, a social fund shall be established with the amount to be set in the articles of foundation.

The measure in question was preceded by Laws nos. 7/2004 and 8/2004, designed to ensure a unified approach to the authorization of credit cooperatives while establishing for the cooperatives network operating prerequisites in line with sound and prudent banking practices.[17]

11.4 Conclusion

The system of credit cooperatives in Romania, despite its historic roots and long-term tradition, currently finds itself in an important phase of transition. The process of integration, initiated under Law 97/2000 and continued with Law 122/2004, is bringing about a complete reorganization of the sector: the reduction in the number of funded units has led to a natural selection of the best candidates, the most efficient operating mechanisms and the most skilled managerial personnel without causing a decrease in the number of members (approximately 750,000) or territorial coverage. The legislation has also had positive consequences in terms of the level of capitalization of the central houses,[18] a circumstance particularly favourable when it comes to improving the operating conditions of the system of cooperative credit, which is characterized by a marked gap between the average earned and paid interest rates, in addition to being weakened by investment conditions presenting a maximum duration of five years.

These circumstances can also be traced to the fact that 65 per cent of the credit cooperatives carry out their credit activities in rural areas and 35 per cent in urban areas.[19] This means that a large portion of their clientele comes from segments of society which show modest earnings, do not always possess an adequate financial and banking education and, in certain cases, lack even the most basic information on the system and on financial instruments. The scenario illustrated highlights the importance of the role of credit cooperatives in Romania. However, at the same time, it brings to the fore questions on their future and the capacity of the member cooperatives of the Central House to preserve adequate operating balances within a credit system subject to radical change.

Romania's entry in the European Union, the transformation to international accounting standards and the introduction of the new Basil Agreement constitute a new set of challenges that the system of cooperative credit must deal with, in light of the role it plays within the Romanian economic system. Credit cooperatives cover the entire national territory and can be found even in locations where there are no other types of banking institutions. The entire network is deeply rooted in the local territory: the majority of its employees live in the same cities and towns where they work, making it easier for them to know, both professionally and personally, their current and potential clients, thus favouring the establishment of solid relations of trust which, in turn, create favourable conditions for the formation of a more advanced financial culture and adequate economic development in rural zones (see Popescu 2004).

At this point, it is of critical importance that conditions of greater stability are promoted within the cooperative system, and that other networks are introduced. This is in order to interrupt the monopoly status which, for all intents and purposes, the Creditcoop network currently enjoys as the sole network authorized, at present, to carry out cooperative credit activities in Romania. Moreover, this is also part of an attempt to establish a higher level of competition in the sector in order to move in the direction of increasingly ambitious objectives of development and efficiency.

Notes

1. For that matter, business enterprises obtained financing at extremely low rates and had no interest in paying back the debts within the deadlines and at the amounts stipulated, seeing that subsequent loans did not depend on the past history of dealings with the credit system.
2. The percentage of companies in which any member holds a bank account is 9 per cent, and only 5 per cent posses a banking card (see Somesan 2006).
3. The 37 per cent of rural municipalities have a credit cooperative (see Eurobarometrul Rural 2003).
4. In accordance with the provisions of Law 312/04, the primary functions of the BNR are:

   • Definition and application of monetary and exchange policy;
   • Authorization, regulation and prudential supervision of credit institutions;
   • Promotion and control of the proper operation of payment systems, in order to ensure financial stability;
   • Issue of bills and coins as legal instruments of payment within Romanian territory;
   • Implementation of currency regulations and supervision of compliance with the same;
   • Administration of the Official Reserves of Romania.

5. The BNR enjoys a greater degree of independence than other state institutions. Members of the Board are appointed by Parliament, but the law indicates the sole circumstances under which they can be removed from their positions: motives of incompatibility that arise; guilty sentences that pass the final level of appeal; acts that damage the BNR.
6. Currency policy is a task that the BNR carries out by "issuing regulations regarding operations in gold and other foreign assets, for the purpose of supporting the domestic currency; setting the exchange rates for its own operations on the exchange market; authorising and monitoring those who carry out transactions on the currency market; setting a maximum limit for the possession or gold and foreign assets, both by organised entities and individuals; preserving and managing reserves in foreign currency" (see Montesano 2002: *Il sistema bancario rumeno*, OSSFI, p. 592).
7. Art. 2 of Law 83/97 stipulates that banks can be privatised under three different procedures: a) an increase in their share capital and an infusion of private capital, in cash, following a public offer or a private investment; b) the sale of shares by a State Owned Fund, for cash, to Romanian individuals or organized entities whose capital is entirely private, or to Romanian organized entities in which the majority of the capital is privately held; c) through a procedure that combines the two approaches illustrated above. The State Owned Fund can retain a portion of the capital and, on the strength of this holding, appoint a representative to the Board of Directors to defend the interests of the State.

8. In 2005 the banking industry ended the fiscal year with a profit for the sixth straight year. 63 per cent of the income was generated by operations with non-banking clients, 20 per cent by inter-bank operations and 17 per cent by operations in securities (see BNR *Financial Stability Report* 2006).

9. The main promoter of the movement was Spiru Haret, a sociologist, educator, mathematician and politician considered to be the founder of people's banks and credit cooperatives. He was the primary supporter of the expansion of the cooperative movements and the author of the first law on cooperatives.

10. Accounts of the period point to a situation in which illicit use of credit cooperatives manifested itself primarily in two ways: on the one hand, new depositors were attracted by offering them extremely high interest rates (20–30 per cent) that were never paid, nor were the amounts deposited ever returned to them; on the other hand, lines of credit for up to 200,000.00 euro were granted, but without any funds actually being supplied, except in the form of fictitious accounting entries.

11. "The fact that people's banks were not subject to any licensing or operating restrictions for many years led to the spread of dubious business practices and to a dramatic undercapitalization of these institutions. The crisis in the people's bank sector was brought clearly to light by the failure of Banca Populara Romana in June 2000. The collapse of the biggest people's bank ultimately forced the NBR to take measures to censure adequate supervision of such institutions, culminating, at the end of 2000, in a new legal framework for them. As a result, existing people's banks have to register with the NBR. Thereafter, they have two options: if they fulfil all the statutory requirements (i.e. capital adequacy), they can either continue to operate as commercial banks or join a network of at least 100 people's banks headed by a central institution" (see Gardò 2005).

12. This assumes that the numerical operations are carried out, but also that the funds are transferred exclusively to the branches.

13. Deposits made with member credit cooperatives of the CREDITCOOP network are guaranteed by the "Deposit Guarantee Fund of the Banking System," or FGDSB. In addition, the CREDITCOOP network has a fund of its own – the mutual guarantee reserve – established with the contributions of the member credit cooperatives.

14. Of 540 merger requests, 98 were for the making of purchases and 406 from parties being purchased.

15. Data taken from the official website of the Creditcoop Central House: www. creditcoop.ro. Dates of accessing this website were 2004, 2005, 2006.

16. Data taken from the official website of the Creditcoop Central House: www. creditcoop.ro. Dates of accessing this website were 2004, 2005, 2006.

17. In particular, Law no. 8/2004 introduced requirements regarding the minimum capital of cooperative credit organizations, with the goal of gradually reaching a minimum capital level of five million euro for the central house of a cooperative credit network and ten million euro for an entire network.

18. Up through May of 2004, a central house's capital and own funds had to be more than 15 billion lei; up through 29 June 2006, the minimum amount was set at 3.5 million euro and, after that date, the minimum capital had to be the equivalent of five million euro. The central house shall be required

to ensure that the minimum aggregate capital of the funds in its network is equal to the equivalent of seven million euro, up through 29 June 2006, and to ten million euro after that date.
19. The role of credit cooperatives could entail major opportunities for development in the sector of micro-credit (see Perret 2003).

References

Various Authors (2002) *Strengthening Cooperatives and Participative Enterprises in Eastern Europe*, Business Support Programme-Final Report, October.

Various Authors (2004) *La dimensione economico sociale dell'allargamento ad est* Dossier CISS, May.

BNR (various years) *Buoletin Lunar*.

BNR (various years) *Relazioni annuali*.

BNR (2006) *Romanian Banking System*, June.

BNR (2006) *Financial Stability Report*.

Brown, J.D., Earle, J.S., Lup D. (2004) *What makes small firms grow? Finance, human capital, technical Assistance, and the business environment in Romania*, IZA DP N. 1343, October.

Buscu S. (2005) *Cooperativele de credit, intre afaceri corecte inselatorii*, Curierul National, November.

Coletti, E., Colombo De Felice, G., Tirri V. (2003) *Structure and performance of central and eastern European banking sector*, Research Department Banca Intesa, July, Milano.

Commission of the European Communities (2004) *Regular report on Romania's progress towards accession*, October.

Djankov S. (1998) *Enterprise Isolation in Transition Economies: evidence from Romania*, April.

EBRD (2004) *Strategy for Romania*, November.

Eurobarometrul Rural (2003), *The Gallup Organization*, Romania.

Gardò S. (2005) *Banking markets in central and eastern Europe: Romania on a consolidation course*, Diebank, Austria.

IMF (2004) *Romania: selected issues and Statistical appendix*, Country report no. 4/220, July.

Iordan M., Iordache F., Chilian M. (2005) *Sistemul bancar românesc în perioada 1990–2003: restructurare în contextul integrării europene*, București: Institutul de Prognoză Economică.

Mauri, A., Baicu, C. G. (2002) *Storia della banca in Romania*, Working paper no. 18, July.

Montesano M. (2002) *Il sistema bancario rumeno*, OSSFI, year II.

Organisation for Economic Co-operation and Development (2002) *Entrepreneurship and enterprise development Romania*, Policy Review, March.

Perotti, E., Carare, O. (1996) *The evolution of bank credit quality in Transition theory and evidence from Romania*, CERT, October.

Perret G. (2003) *Report on the current state of microfinance in Romania and proposed work plan*, MSME Programme, May

Popescu, C. (2004) "Cooperativele de credit isi cauta un loc de piata bancara," *Adevarul Economic*, no.15, April.

Popescu C. (2004) "Exigente sporite pentru comperativele de credit," *Adevarul Economic*, no. 38, p. 24, September.

Somesan T. (2006) "Cooperativele de credit renasc din propria cenusa," *Saptamana Financiara*, no. 56, April.

Tudorache B. (2006) "Noua lege bancara nu va distruge Creditcoop," *Saptamana Financiara*, no. 68, July.

12
The Bulgarian Cooperative Banking System

Matteo Cotugno

12.1 Introduction

In June 2004, Bulgaria concluded its negotiations to join the European Union (EU). On April 25, 2005, it signed its Treaty of Accession to the EU, which became effective from January 1, 2007. The economic criteria laid down in the Maastricht Treaty (with the exception of inflation) have been nearly met, while further efforts are required to meet the political criteria (judicial system, crime, corruption, and so forth). (ICE 2006).

Over the last twenty years, the Bulgarian economy underwent sweeping reorganization processes leading to its passage from a system of centrally planned economy to a market economy. Even the banking sector has witnessed far-reaching structural changes, from its Soviet-style monopolistic model to privatization and, following the crisis of 1996–97, to the change in its organizational and regulatory setup (Vincelette 2001).

The cooperative credit system has played an important role in the Bulgarian economy, both before the second world war and during the Soviet period, when the financial intermediation function was monopolized by the State. At present, however, owing in particular to an inadequate regulatory setup, it has lost its leading role. The cooperative credit system in Bulgaria is built around a number of different realities. A few of them are the outcome of private initiative (Central Cooperative Bank), some are financed by government organizations (Agriculture Credit Cooperatives), and others are financed by non-governmental organizations (Nachala Cooperative) as micro-credit schemes in support of a few sectors of the Bulgarian economy.

This chapter is organized as follows. The initial part describes the peculiar characteristic of the Bulgarian economic system with reference to the major macroeconomic variables. The subsequent paragraph analyzes the characteristics of the Bulgarian banking system (concentration, development, and so forth), with a view to detecting the specificities of a system undergoing a considerable evolution after the collapse of the Soviet-type system. Then, the last part analyzes the organizational setup of the Bulgarian cooperative credit system, determining its characteristics based on the type of network taken into consideration.

12.2 The Bulgarian economic system

Until November 1989, the Bulgarian economy was molded on the Soviet system, with State control over all the economic sectors (including financial intermediation). The fall of Communism and the transition process has resulted in a remarkable economic recovery that, nonetheless, was not backed up by the required structural and legislative reforms. After the financial crisis of 1996–97, the progress made in recent years by the Bulgarian economy is definitely outstanding, so much so as to meet most of the parameters established by the Maastricht Treaty for accession to the EU. The GDP has grown in the last eight years at a 4.6 per cent mean rate, exceeding nearly systematically the level attained by the ten new EU member states. The growth of the domestic demand has represented the motive power of the Bulgarian

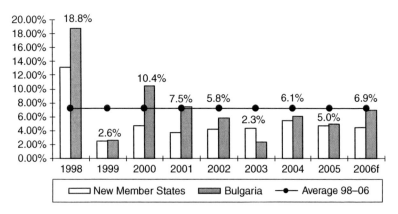

Figure 12.1   GDP real growth
Source: IMF data (2006), *World Economic Outlook* 2006.

economy, which has been paced down by restrictive economic policies in order to curb inflation (IMF 2006b).

In fact, the high inflation rate still gives rise to concerns: in the 1998–2006 period, it has increased on average by 7.3 per cent and is expected to get to nearly 5.5 per cent by 2006. Indeed, in recent years, the policy of the Bulgarian government is concentrating on this macro variable, which represents the last obstacle to its full accession to the EU. In particular, it has curbed government spending to a considerable extent, and the formulation of the monetary policy has been very restrictive after the significant credit boom in 2004 (IMF 2006b).

The progress made is confirmed by the improvement of the Country rating that, in August 2005, moved from BBB– to BBB (Fitch and Standard & Poor's). The vulnerabilities of the Country are on the decrease, but the latter still requires to speed up the pace of its reforms against corruption and to check the credit and government spending variables in order to curb inflation.

12.3 The financial and banking system

12.3.1 From the Soviet period to the 1996–97 crisis

The development of the Bulgarian financial and banking system has been affected by the Communist regime (1944–89), as it had been molded on the characteristic traits of the monopolistic model present in other Eastern European countries such as Poland, USSR, Czechoslovakia, Romania and East Germany. In that period, the banking system was made up by a single bank – the Bulgarska Narodna Banka (BNB: Bulgarian National Bank) – which operated in its dual capacity as a central and commercial bank through a territorial network of branches. Unlike other Soviet-type regimes, the Bulgarian banking system featured the variant of a second institution, which lacked the statute of a bank and that was responsible for gathering the Bulgarian household savings: the State Savings Bank (at present, DSK). In 1964, the Bulgarian government recognized the need to externalize the BNB regulation of international trade and this brought to the establishment of the Bulgarian Foreign Trade Bank (BFTB – at present, Bulbank), which was to deal with international banking operations (Koford and Tschoegl 2002).

The function of intermediation between savers and investors was internalized in the State-owned banking system since the assets gathered through the State Savings Bank were employed by the BNB in State-owned industrial enterprises in order to finance investments in capital assets and circulating capital. The risk management function was utterly inexistent in such a system, as the capital allocation was centralized and pertained to the State. Besides, such a banking system failed to allow the formation of those competences that, in addition to evaluating and managing risks, are indispensable to select deserving entrepreneurial initiatives and to discriminate prices based on riskiness. On the other hand, that banking system had given rise to exchange risk management competences, even if rudimentary (Bonin 2001).

The first signs of an opening of the banking system appeared in 1981, the year of establishment of Mineralbank, a bank specialized in providing credit to small and medium-sized enterprises of the mining sector. Actually, the major change in the organization of the banking system occurred with the end of the Soviet period in 1989, when the BNB lost its monopolist commercial bank role and confined its competences to monetary and currency policies.

In any event, the banking system had still to be built from scratch, as there were no institutions, no adequate legislative system, no banking culture and, besides, even the competences that are typical of those who have to allocate capitals with a view to creating shareholder value were missing. The initial steps taken in the time of transitional were the setting up of seven new sectoral banks in 1989, which took the place of a few BNB branches.[1] The year 1990 is seen as being representative of the maximum expansion of the Bulgarian banking system: by the end of the year, the latter comprised 70 banks, of which seven were sectoral banks, two were specialized banks (Bulgarian Foreign Trade Bank and State Savings Bank) and 59 were commercial banks.

In spite of its huge progress, the Bulgarian banking system was still fragile. There was no suitable regulatory setup in respect to the banking sector and the bankruptcy regulations. Most banks were owned by the State, and the level of overdue bills inherited from Soviet times in bank portfolios was huge in the face of the limited capitalization of a number of banks. In 1992, with a view to doing away with this drawback, the State established the Banking Consolidation Company (BCC) that was entrusted with the task of reducing the undercapitalization of State-owned banks (71 per cent in 1991) through the direct subscription of equity stakes in the banks and the merger of a number of banks (Vincelette 2001).

The first results were not late to come. In 1992, 22 state-owned were consolidated through the setting up of the United Bulgarian Bank. In 1993, 12 additional state-owned banks were consolidated in a single bank – the so-called Express Bank. The system was gradually consolidating and it got to the brink of the economic and financial crisis (1996–97) with 35 banks. Throughout the transition years, the most urgent reform had been put off: in terms of total assets, the State kept on having an extremely high equity stake in the banking system (84.8 per cent in October 1996) and there was a very close connection between banks and enterprises.

Many economic sectors were still monopolistic and under state control. In particular, the sectors of mechanics, chemistry, transport and telecommunications, and energy kept on benefiting from bank loans although lacking creditworthiness (Gomel 2002). Furthermore, the BNB was required under the law to make good the losses generated by the banks of the system, discouraging the risk management and credit selection activity. In no time, the economic crisis turned into a financial and monetary crisis. For two years in a row, the GDP had been utterly negative (–10.1 per cent in 1996, –7.0 per cent in 1997). At the same time, the devaluation of the Bulgarian Lev (BGN) had caused prices to increase in an exponential manner; the CPI was equal to +310.4 per cent in 1996 and to +578.6 per cent in 1997. Besides, the BGN had been devaluated to a considerable extent with respect to the dollar.[2]

The government took innumerable measures to come out of this deep crisis and, above all, passed a renewed prudential and supervisory legislation to regulate the banking system. In particular, the introduction of the Law on Banks on June 25, 1997, reformed to a considerable extent the prior regulations in force since 1992. It introduced the minimum capital adequacy requirement of 12 per cent of the total risk-weighed assets, limits to the concentration of assets, as well as rules for evaluating guarantees, classifying assets and calculating appropriated surplus. Besides, the accounting standards were modified and new rules in the matter of currency reserves were introduced. On the other hand, the International Monetary Fund established the Currency Board entrusted with the task of supervising public spending with a view to consolidating the national debt of the State.

12.3.2 The current situation

Nowadays, the Bulgarian financial system has been completely renewed and privileges the banking channel, rather than direct channels, as the means of intermediation of resources. Even non-banking financial intermediaries represent a small percentage with respect to banking intermediaries. In particular, the total banking assets on GDP has moved from 33.7 per cent in 1998 to 73.2 per cent in 2005. The stock-exchange market is witnessing a considerable expansion, particularly with respect to the last three-year period (in terms of GDP capitalization) moving from 7.82 per cent of the GDP in 2003 to 22.79 per cent in 2005 (see Figure 12.2).

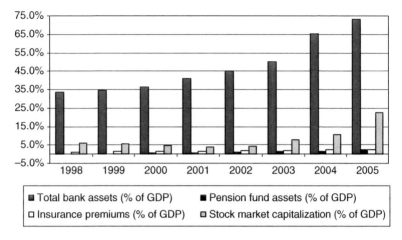

Figure 12.2   The structure of the Bulgarian financial system

Table 12.1   The structure of the Bulgarian banking system

Bulgarian banking system	2001	2002	2003	2004	2005	2006
Commercial bank	35	34	34	34	33	33
Cooperative bank under law on bank (1)	1	1	1	1	1	1
Cooperative bank under cooperative act (2)	43	43	43	43	44	44

(1) It is the Cooperative Central Bank, the only Bulgarian bank operating according to the Law on Banks.
(2) We are dealing with 33 Agriculture Credit Cooperatives, in addition to the regional offices of the Nachala Cooperative.

Further to the crisis of 1996–97, the number of banks in the Bulgarian system has somewhat stabilized, rarely exceeding a total of 35 (including the branches of foreign banks) (see Table 12.1).

This is not supposed to mean that the banking market is static. In fact, there are frequent M&A operations and corporate shake-ups that, with the passing of time, have modified the degree of concentration of the sector. In fact, the first four Bulgarian banks represented by the end of 1999 over 55 per cent of the total assets, a figure that dropped to 42 per cent in 2005 (Figure 12.3).

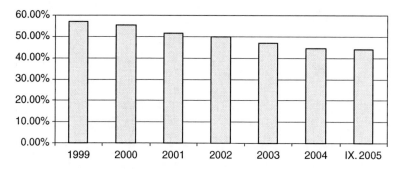

Figure 12.3   The total bank assets share of the first four banks
Source: BNB (2005).

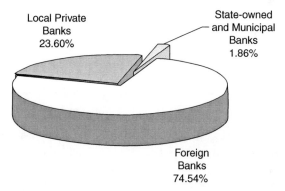

Figure 12.4   Control on bank assets and capital (2005)
Source: BNB (2005).

To-date, the privatization of the banking system may be deemed to have been completed. In fact, a mere 1.86 per cent of the total assets is State owned,[3] most of the system is in foreign hands (74.54 per cent) and a minor part is in the hands of national private entities (23.6 per cent) (see Figure 12.4).

Despite the restrictive policy imposed by the BNB to check the rise in prices, the amount of the loans granted by the banking system to both corporate and private customers is definitely on the increase. In particular, total loans have witnessed on the whole a 44 per cent average yearly growth. The most impressive increases are reported in the 'housing mortgage loans to individuals' sector, with yearly variation rates

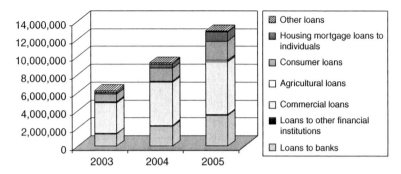

Figure 12.5   IMF loans granted to corporate and private customers (thousands of Euros)[4]
Source: BNB statistics (2005).

in excess of +120 per cent, in the 'loans to banks' sector (58 per cent average yearly rate) and 'commercial loans' (33 per cent average yearly rate) (see Figure 12.5).

12.4 The cooperative credit system in Bulgaria

The origins of the cooperative credit system in Bulgaria date back to the beginning of the twentieth century, through the intervention of farmers and small and medium-sized agricultural firms. The savings and credit cooperatives based on the Raffaisen approach represented an important link of the Bulgarian banking system until the end of World War II. The cooperative credit system kept on working in rural areas even during the Soviet era, particularly in order to make up for the wants of a highly centralized banking system based on a single central and commercial bank. Above all, the BNB branches were only present in major towns, leaving a considerable supply vacuum in those rural areas that were not served by financial intermediaries. The lack of competences, the perception of a high riskiness of the agricultural business, as well as a not at all clear definition of the legal framework with respect to the examination of guarantees, caused the utter failure of any initiative to re-launch the agricultural system that played on commercial banks (Popov 2003).

The first Bulgarian cooperative credit bank dates back to 1910, when the Bulgarska Zemedelska Banka saw to a spin-off of the cooperative-type banking activities to form the Bulgarska Centralna Kooperativna Banka (Bulgarian Central Cooperative Bank). In fact, the origins of the Bulgarian Central Cooperative Bank drew on the rural world and

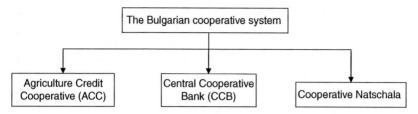

Figure 12.6   The Bulgarian cooperative system

date back to 1862, when a large number of autonomous rural credit associations decided its establishment to serve as a treasury for the local administrations and as a deposit and lending bank for local agricultural farms (Koford and Tschoegl 2002). The cooperative movement acquired greater local characteristics during the communist period, even though without referring to national associations or federations, given that the entire banking system was to remain under State control. At present, the cooperative movement is built around three different entities (see Figure 12.6):

- The Central Cooperative Bank (CCB);
- The Agriculture Credit Cooperatives (ACCs), which refer to a national federation (Federal Agriculture Credit Cooperatives: FACCs);
- The Nachala Cooperatives.

As previously pointed out, the main obstacle to an adequate growth of the system of cooperative credit in Bulgaria has been the want of an appropriate regulatory framework. In the face of the structured and modern banking rules and regulations worked out further to the 1996–97 crisis, the Bulgarian governments that followed one another – just as the BNB – failed to promote a development of the banking system other than in a commercial direction. In fact, the BNB's need to ensure the full governance of the monetary and credit policies has required, through the revision of the Cooperative Act, the prohibition for Cooperatives to take deposits from their customers.

Therefore, the bank regulations currently in force provide for a two-tiered banking system.

1. Banks can be established in compliance with the Law on Banks, subject to the prior authorization of the BNB and the district court

having jurisdiction. For all purposes, these are commercial banks but, should they so require, they can work according to the logics that are typical of the cooperative credit system. In such a case, they shall be subject to the BNB supervision and shall not benefit from any facility for the fact of having taken the cooperative form. Since the Law on Banks has been worked out for commercial banks, the intermediary subject to it that wants to work under a cooperative scheme is required to recreate in its statute the typical provisions of the cooperative model.

2. The banks established in compliance with the Cooperative Act have a legal framework, which already includes provisions for the cooperative model. However, at the same time, they are subject to considerable limitations, as they are not allowed to take deposits from their customers. Indeed, this limits their growth to the amount of their equity. In fact, Article 38 of the Cooperative Act passed in 1991 had laid down that "a cooperative shall be free to engage in savings and loan activities by virtue of a resolution of its General Meeting." The crisis in 1996–97 has led to a reformulation of this provisions, whereby "The cooperative may engage in depositary and crediting operations by resolution of the General Meeting and with the authorization of the Bulgarian National Bank and as provided for in a separate law." In fact, the text is connected with article 2 of the Law on Banks that lays down that "the provisions of this Law shall not apply to mutual aid funds of cooperatives extending loans only to their members on the account of contributions made by them and cooperative funds."

In other words, a cooperative bank cannot carry out a deposit-taking activity unless it is authorized to do so by the BNB and it is subject to the Law on Banks, thereby falling within the case referred to in paragraph 1 above. "Mutual aid credit cooperatives of private farmers, established as per the agricultural capital fund scheme in compliance with the agreements for utilization of the financial grant, concluded between the government of the Republic of Bulgaria and the Commission of the European Union" are not required to apply for the authorization, since article 17 of the final and transitional provisions of the Law on Banks explicitly provides for their exemption.

Despite the pressures put by the Cooperatives registered under the Cooperative Act on the Bulgarian Parliament and the BNB, the latter have not yet approved an ad hoc regulation for deposit and credit cooperatives, leaving the credit intermediation sector mainly in the hands of commercial banks and confining cooperative credit to a narrow market niche. It is to be hoped that the current regulatory setup be reconsidered to allow the Bulgarian cooperative credit system to acquire the same relevance it has in other EU Member States.

12.4.1 The Central Cooperative Bank

The Central Cooperative Bank was established in 1991 through the agency of the Central Cooperative Union (the national federation of Bulgarian Cooperatives), a few regional cooperative unions and nearly 1100 cooperative-type enterprises. Their objective was to succeed in unifying the financial resources of the Bulgarian cooperative system to allow its proper development (see Central Cooperative Bank, *Annual Report*). The Central Cooperative Bank is the only Bulgarian cooperative bank registered under the Law on Banks and, therefore, is subject to BNB supervision. Its organizational setup is fully similar to the structure of a commercial bank. In fact, there are no local or regional banks that take part in a federation or a central bank, but there are 39 branches that cover the national territory as well as 140 agencies abroad (see Central Cooperative Bank, Presentation, 2006).

Since March 1999, the CCB has been listed in the Bulgarian Stock Exchange and is currently controlled by the CCB Group Assets Management EAD, a company that, in its turn, is 100 per cent property of Chimimport JSC, a financial holding which has equity interests in the financial sector, as well as in such sectors as legal consulting services, trade of chemical products, rubber by-products and fertilizers and transport. The acquisition by Chimimport took place at the beginning of 2002, when the Bank Consolidation Company AD divested itself of 32.77 per cent of the CCB capital (see Central Cooperative Bank, *Annual Report*).

The CCB has a two-tier system of management, at the top of which there is the General Meeting of Shareholders. The Supervisory Board consists of three members that are elected directly by the General Meeting and is responsible for appointing the Management Board and the Procurator. The Management Board elects the Executive Directors with the approval of the Supervisory Board.

At present, the CCB represents a relatively small reality with respect to the rest of the Bulgarian banking system: its size, measurable in terms of percentage of total balance sheet assets out of the total assets of the banking system as a whole, is equal to 2.46 per cent. In terms of volume of loans granted, its market share is equal to 1.87 per cent – a percentage, which gets to 2.46 per centwith reference to deposits,

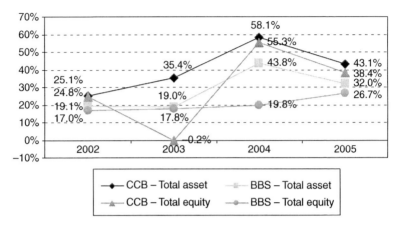

Figure 12.7 Total assets growth, equity growth (percentage variations with respect to the previous year)
Legend: CCB = Central Cooperative Bank; BBS = Bulgarian Banking System.
Source: Annual Central Cooperative Bank balance sheets and BNB statistics.

realized with 5313 customers/members, and about half a million customers (2004 data). The CCB works as a universal bank with a diversified portfolio of products and a partiality for the agricultural sector. In terms of growth of the total balance sheet assets, in recent years the CCB has systematically reported a higher rate of growth than the banking system.

In particular, in the 2002–05 period, the CCB has reported, on average, an annual rate of growth close to 42 per cent, as against the 28 per cent growth rate reported by the Bulgarian banking system (see Figure 12.7). The average equity growth rate has been in both cases lower than the assets growth rate (+29 per cent for the CCB and +20 per cent for the banking system), witnessing a management characterized by growing leverage levels (see Figure 12.7).

The fact of being a cooperative bank penalizes to some extent the CCB performance, measured in terms of return on equity (ROE). Notwithstanding a rather high ROE, given also the particularly low level of leverage of the Bulgarian banking system, its value is generally lower than the figure reported for the rest of the banking system (see Tables 12.2 and 12.3). The recourse to the ROE decomposition permits to detect the different managerial areas of ROE generation.[5] In particular, in recent years the performance of the Bulgarian banks in terms

Table 12.2   The Bulgarian banking system ROE decomposition (*)

Year	ROE	NeR/GrR	GrR/OpR	IM/TA	IntM/IM	OpR/IntM	TA/E
2001	19.30%	72.08%	108.3%	3.89%	1.81	47.60%	7.39
2002	13.77%	76.63%	104.3%	3.54%	1.83	35.35%	7.52
2003	16.65%	77.63%	108.3%	4.35%	1.54	39.02%	7.59
2004	15.89%	80.70%	105.7%	4.12%	1.49	33.31%	9.12
2005	16.52%	85.07%	103.4%	4.14%	1.46	32.71%	9.50

(*) The calculation is based on the entire Bulgarian banking system, including foreign branches.
Source: BNB data.

Table 12.3   Cooperative central bank ROE decomposition

Year	ROE	NeR/GrR	GrR/OpR	IM/TA	IntM/IM	OpR/IntM	TA/E
2001	10.81%	100.00%	97.66%	5.40%	1.92	15.37%	6.93
2002	22.92%	100.00%	96.93%	3.27%	1.78	58.61%	6.95
2003	11.42%	80.35%	113.60%	3.61%	1.28	28.67%	9.43
2004	10.39%	79.54%	111.14%	3.28%	1.13	32.92%	9.60
2005	8.55%	85.00%	101.51%	3.65%	1.05	26.04%	9.93

Source: Annual Report of the Central Cooperative Bank.

of ROE has been definitely satisfactory, despite the high capitalization level.

With reference to the characteristic management, it may be noted that:

• except for 2001, CCB has constantly reported an Interest Margin on Total Assets ratio that was lower than the figure reported by the rest of the banking system (an effect due in part to the high rate of growth of the CCB assets when compared to the banking system);
• always with the exception of 2001, the incidence of the nominal elements deriving from services, defined by the Intermediation Margin on Interest Margin ratio, has been constantly lower in the CCB than in the banking system.

In regards to the incidence of operating costs (measured by the Operational Result on Intermediation Margin ratio), every year – except for 2002 – the CCB reported a higher level than the banking system. In this case, the high level of capitalization, which seems to characterize cooperative banks with respect to the banking system (ascribable to the appropriated surplus) is belied, however limitedly. In fact, in the past three years, the Total Assets on Equity ratio in CCB proves higher than in the banking system.

12.4.2 The Agriculture Credit Cooperatives

In the early 1996, a few groups of agricultural enterprises established the Agriculture Credit Cooperatives (ACCs) working within the legal context of the Cooperative Act, with a view to granting credit to their members according to logics that were typical of the cooperative models. In the same year, the Ministry of Agriculture and the European Union[6] had launched a programme to sustain the Bulgarian agriculture, the so-called Agricultural Capital Fund Scheme (ACAS), appropriating a fund amounting to 14 million euro for initiatives in support of the agricultural world. In May 1996, 33 Agriculture Credit Cooperatives benefited of the funds put at their disposal by the Ministry and European Union and, after a short period required for recruiting and training staff, towards the end of 1996 the Cooperatives began to disburse the first loans to their members (Dimitre 2006).

The typical organization of each Cooperative consists in a variable number of members, generally included between 200 and 600. At present, the 33 Agriculture Credit Cooperatives have a membership close to 10,000, mostly farmers or persons connected with the agricultural world (Popov 2003). The ACC corporate governance comprises a general meeting, a management board and an audit board (see Figure 12.8. The general meeting includes all the members of the Cooperative and

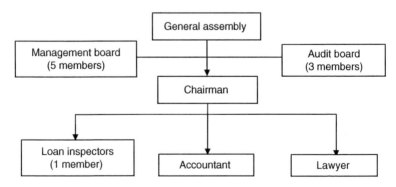

Figure 12.8　The agriculture cooperative credit management structure
Source: Dimitre (2006).

meets at least once a year to outline the strategic policies and adopt the yearly balance sheet and income statements. Besides, the general meeting elects the management board and the audit board. As laid down in article 21 of the Cooperative Act "each member shall be entitled to one vote which shall be cast personally, regardless of his share of the nominal capital." Instead, there is no mandatory provision to appropriate the accumulated year-end profits. In fact, it is only mandatory to appropriate 20 per cent of the profits made, while it is up to the general meeting to decide the allocation of the rest and, possibly, its distribution in the form of dividends (see Cooperative Act, article 35, 1996).

The organizational structure of each individual ACC also provides for the presence of a Chairman of the Agriculture Credit Cooperative; that is, the person responsible for the bank who acts as a liaison with the outside, chairman of the management board and coordinator of human resources. Generally, in each ACC there is at least a loan inspector who is responsible for credit operations, as well as an accountant and a lawyer who are responsible for keeping the branch accounting and for debt collection, respectively. In addition to coordinating the personnel working in each branch, the Chairman participates in the meetings of the national federation of the cooperative credit banks. In fact, each one of the 33 local cooperatives joins a national federation (Federal Agriculture Credit Cooperative – FACC), which represents the interests of the ACC with respect to national and local authorities. For the time being, it is

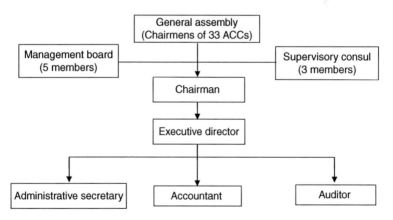

Figure 12.9 The FACC management structure
Source: Dimitre (2006).

a closed system that does not accept new members. The Federation is registered under the Act for Legal Persons with Non-Profit Activities, in keeping with the agreements entered into by the Bulgarian government and the EU (Popov 2003).

The highest body of the federation is its General Meeting, composed by the chairmen of the 33 ACCs. Each chairman is entitled to one vote in order to elect the Federation managing bodies, with special reference to the Management Board (comprising five members) and the Chairman of the Federation, as well an executive director of the Federation who is entrusted with day-to-day management tasks and the coordination of the unitary management of the 33 ACCs. Each ACC contributes to the Federation costs in relation to its assets.

The ACCs have total assets amounting to 25 million BGN, with an average value of assets for each individual Agricultural Credit Cooperatives amounting to 826 thousand BGN. There are nearly 12,000 cooperative members. The cooperatives were capitalized with a seven million euro grant from the EU PHARE programme and 4.5 million BGN from the Bulgarian government. In addition, they benefited from loans falling within bilateral agreements with a number of German cooperatives (Dimitre 2006). The prohibition to accept deposits from their customers represents a significant limit and holds back to a considerable extent the development of the ACCs in Bulgaria.

12.4.3 The Nachala Cooperatives

The Nachala Cooperative belongs to an international network called "Opportunity International," and is a non-governmental organization (NGO) which intends to create the conditions for development opportunities in poor areas, promoting micro-credit operations. The Nachala Cooperative has been set up in 1993 as a foundation and, after 18 months of inactivity due to the 1996–97 crisis, it has has resumed its activities through 11 regional offices (Popov 2003) under the Cooperative Act in 1999. Owing to the limits imposed by the legislation, the Nachala Cooperative has had recourse to the assistance of the United States Agency for International Development (USAID) that subscribed nearly 98 per cent of its equity. The remainder has been collected through the subscription of shares by its members and the appropriation of profits (Microfinanza Rating 2004).

The corporate governance of the Nachala Cooperative provides for the presence of a members' representative body – that is, the General Meeting – which meets once a year to adopt balance sheet and income statement, and resolves upon the fundamental strategic guidelines of the Cooperative. Every three years, the General Meeting elects the Board of Directors, the Chairman and the Control Council.

Nachala works with 57 staff members, 29 of which are loan officers. The top management comprises the Chairman, the Operational Director, the Human Resource Manager and the Chief Financial Officer (CFO). Another important element of the Cooperative organizational setup is represented by two Regional Directors under the direction of the Operational Manager. The Regional Directors coordinate the activity of the regional branches, dividing the sectors of operation into a Northern area and a Southern area of the Country. At present, Nachala features a good level of decentralization, with an excellent autonomy of the eleven regional branches. However, the disbursement of the loans is only made through the central office located in Sofia, while the loans that have been granted are repaid at a local level.

The financial structure of Nachala witnesses the consequences of a law on cooperatives that restrains the deposit-taking activity. By the end of 2004, 86 per cent of its resources were represented by equity, nearly 7 per cent by long-term liabilities and the rest by short-term liabilities (see Figure 12.10. Such a prospect limits to a considerable extent the development of the Cooperative that is unable to meet the growing demand for credit in Bulgaria (see Figure 12.11).

In 2004, the ROE and ROA were negative (–1.8 and –1.4 per cent respectively) and compounded by a structurally low level of efficiency. In recent years, the Nachala Cooperative has been considering the possibility of changing its legal status registering under the Law on Banks (Microfinanza Rating 2004).

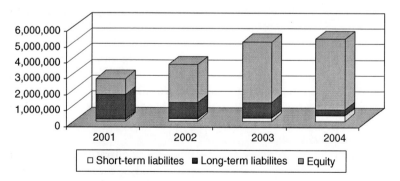

Figure 12.10 Liabilities and equity (US $)
Source: Microfinanza Rating (2004).

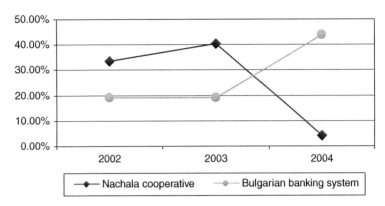

Figure 12.11 Total assets growth (percentage variations with respect to the previous year)
Source: Microfinanza Rating 2004 and BNB.

12.5 Conclusions

Until 1989, the banking system had been inspired by the typical logics of the planned-economy, with a centralization of the resources trading services and the presence of a single State-owned bank. The opening of the economic system to market logics has occurred quite swiftly but, being there no adequate legislative context, in 1996–97, problems inherent in the system led to a bank panic that, in its turn, led to an impressive financial crisis that caused a considerable depreciation of the national currency, strong inflationary tensions and a total reorganization of the financial system.

Considerable relevance has been attached to the cooperative credit system in the years prior to the Soviet-era and, to a lower extent, even during the Soviet times. Its current role has become less important, particularly on account of a legal context that is not too favourable. The main Bulgarian cooperative bank is the Central Cooperative Bank; that is, a single entity that manages branches throughout the territory. In short, it is not a federation of local banks, but a single national bank with branches like a commercial bank. In addition to the Central Cooperative Bank, another cooperative credit system has become operational: it refers to a national federation and comprises a number of Agriculture Credit Cooperatives. Its registration under the Cooperative Act implies that it is not allowed to take deposits from the public, and this limits to a considerable extent the expansion of the movement.

A second type of cooperative system is represented by the Nachala Cooperative that, being registered under the Cooperative Act, is affected by the same limitations as the Agriculture Credit Cooperatives.

A reformulation of the regulatory framework is a critical issue for the life of cooperative credit in Bulgaria although, so far, it has been avoided owing to the will to centralize the banking system on the exclusively commercial-type model.

Notes

1. The Agricultural and Cooperative Bank, the Biochemical Bank, the Construction Bank, the Economic Bank, the Electronics Bank, the Transportation Bank, and the Transport, Agricultural, and Building Equipment Bank, which was also known as Balkan Bank (see Koford and Tschoegl 2002).
2. By the end of 1995, 65 BGN were needed for a US Dollar. By the end of 1996, 178 BGN were needed for a USD and by the end of 1997, 1674 BGN were required for a USD (see BNB Statistics).
3. Only two non-private banks will be left. One is the Municipality Bank owned by the City of Sofia. The other is the state owned Business Promotion Bank, which is not allowed to take deposits from the population and was established to channel KfW funds to SMEs.
4. 1 Euro = 1.96 BGN, June 2006.
5. The same approach has been used in this volume in the case of the Rabobank.
6. The European Funds refer to the Poland/Hungary Assistance for Restructuring Economy (PHARE) Programme.

References

Bonin, J. P. (2001) "Financial intermediation in Southeast Europe: banking on the Balkans, Department of Economics," Wesleyan University, Working Paper.
Bulgarian National Bank (BNB) (2005) Commercial Banks in Bulgaria, Sofia, Available from: http://www.bnbank.org/bnb/home.nsf/vPages/Publications_BNB_Periodic_Banks_in_B_200512/$FILE/ETb-Dec2005K.pdf/ [Accessed 31 July 2009].
Bulgarian National Bank (BNB) (2006) Commercial Banks in Bulgaria, Sofia, Available from: http://www.bnbank.org/bnb/home.nsf/vPages/Publications_BNB_Periodic_Banks_in_B_200612/$FILE/ETb-Dec2006K.pdf/ [Accessed 31 July 2009].
Central Cooperative Bank (2006) Annual Report, Sofia, Available from: http://www.ccbank.bg/uf/other/documents/report2006_en.pdf [Accessed 31 July 2009].
Dimitre, N. N. (2006) "Possibilities of agricultural credit cooperatives for creating tenable small farming in Bulgarian rural areas," Contributed paper presented at the IAMO Forum 2006, June, Germany.
European Central Banking (ECB) (2005) EU Banking Structure, October, Frankfurt, Available from: http://www.ecb.int/pub/pdf/other/eubankingstructure102005en.pdf [Accessed 31 July 2009].

Gomel, G. (2002) "Banking and financial sector in transition countries and convergence towards European Integration," Available from: http://eaces.gelso.unitn.it/Eaces/work/Papers/Gomeleaces_080502-rev.pdf [Accessed 7 July 2007].

ICE (2005) Bulgaria, congiuntura economica 2005, Sezione per la promozione degli scambi dell'ambasciata d'Italia, Country Report, Rome, Available from: www.ice.it [Accessed 7 July 2007].

ICE (2006) Bulgaria. International Monetary Found, Rome Available from: www.ice.it [Accessed 7 July 2007].

ICE (2006a) World Economic Outlook 2006, Rome, Available from: www.ice.it [Accessed 7 July 2007].

ICE (2006b) IMF Country Report No. 06/131, April, Rome, Available from: www.ice.it [Accessed 7 July 2007].

Koford K., Tschoegl, A. E. (2002) "Foreign banks in Bulgaria, 1875–2002," Working Paper Series, Department of Economics College of Business & Economics University of Delaware, Working Paper no. 2002–06.

Microfinanza Rating (2004) "Nachala Cooperative – Bulgaria," December, Available from www.nachala.bg [Accessed 7 July 2007].

Popov, I. (2003) "The Cooperative System in Bulgaria," Report on the occasion of the IRU-Law Seminar, Berlin, November.

Vincelette, G. A. (2001) "Bulgarian Banking Sector Development, Post-1989," Southeast European Politics, vol. 2 (1), pp. 4–23.

13
Concluding Remarks

Vittorio Boscia, Alessandro Carretta and Paola Schwizer

The intense process of integration within the European Union countries and concomitant international trends have dramatically changed the structure, conduct and performance of the European financial and banking systems. Overall, each national banking system is theoretically more competitive, even if actually the retail segment of banking market still remains quite protected and represents in many respects the "last great barrier" towards the full integration of the European banking market. Nevertheless, the oligopoly of a wide number of retail banks will be gradually eroded under the pressure of competition and the less efficient banks will lose their power and share in the local markets.

These structural and competitive changes involve also cooperative banks. Their traditional features and competitive advantages might be threatened by the new competitive environment. In order to assess the main structural and competitive answers given by the European cooperative banking to this new scenario, this book has investigated the main features which characterize the cooperative banking of a wide sample of European countries, implementing a "country case-study" methodology. The first part of the book has dealt with the cooperative banking systems of countries which joined the European Union before the 2000; the second part has dealt with a group of newly European countries.

Overall, it has emerged that it is not possible to deal with the European banking system as a unified and single system. Indeed, among the European countries there are still large differences in the economy, society, history, culture, and so forth that have differently influenced the intensity and the modality of the diffusion of cooperative banking model across Europe. This notwithstanding cooperative movement has started from common features, theories, values, ideals, and principles.

Apart these general findings, the analyses have highlighted some other interesting insights. In particular, with reference to performance, the analyses have not shown stable differences among type of banks – cooperative banks vs. commercial banks – in terms of economic value-added and cost efficiency. This means that the vitality and the increasing market share of cooperative banks derives from qualitative factors which provide them competitive advantages and characteristic features like for example "mutuality."

Moreover, from the analysis of the several country case-studies, it has been possible to identify several cooperative banking models, in terms of homogeneous area, dimension (of membership, business and operational area) and common organizational structures. Firstly, it has been recognized two broad geographical homogeneous areas: the first area may be named as "Rhine area" and encompasses Germany, Netherland and Italy. The "Latin area," instead, is mainly formed by France. Other cooperative models instead have developed in other areas without distinctive features; that is, Spain and Portugal. In other European countries, the development of cooperative banks has delayed, despite the presence of a potential demand (that is, families, farmers and artisans, and small entrepreneurs). Probably, this has been due for several reasons: economical, for the relatively high cost of capital to establish the bank; legislative, for the lack of a specific regulation on cooperative; social, for the bad reputation of cooperation, considered often close to previous communist system.

Secondly, the analysis has highlighted other cooperative banking models classified in terms of dimension of memberships, of business and of operational area. The first cluster of cooperative banks is made up of large membership base, a wide business scope and an extensive operational area (the banque populair, volksbank, banca popolare model), mostly established in urban areas. Within this setting, most of distinctive advantages of cooperation seem to be lessened. The second cluster is formed by small, local cooperative banks with strong mutual features (the Raiffeisen model), originally developed in rural areas. They seem to retain most of the distinctive advantages of cooperation and of limited dimension. At a third cluster belong cooperative banks which share some core cooperative features of the two previous clusters (that is, small-sized banque populair): basically, they keep a local stance and are usually rooted in a well-defined community.

Finally, the third cooperative banking models resulted by the analyses regards the organizational structures established at central level. In many countries, indeed, cooperative banks have established common organizations (network, group or centralized entities and associations) to which outsource special services. Such entities may be qualified according to several factors. Functions: some of these entities have only political tasks, since they represent the interest of their participants; others have some operative functions, allowing their members to exploit scale economies and synergies from consolidation and coordination. Organizational structure: some central organizations are at "three-tiers," like in France (the three tiers are local, comprising cooperative banks and outlets, regional federations, and national federation); other organizations have a "two-tiers" form, like in Nederland, where the two tiers are at local and national. Each tier has its objectives and tasks.

To conclude, the review of the cooperative banking of the selected countries has not allowed to assess better performance for cooperative banks vs. commercial banks, nor to verify superior models of cooperative banking nor to identify European countries with better cooperative system. Thus, the differences across national cooperative systems demonstrate that European cooperative banking sector is still far to be a "single system." Nevertheless, in each country, it has been possible to assess that a restructuring process is started, according to its own characteristics and state of development. Thus, probably, under the pressure of the integration process and of competition, European cooperative banking will find common policies and in few years it will be possible to deal with it as a real "system."

Index